The
BIG
IDEA BOOK
For
New Business Owners

The BIG IDEA BOOK

For New Business Owners

Straight Talk From an Expert
on How to Get Your Business
Up and Running Easily

by Barbara Weltman

MACMILLAN SPECTRUM
A Division of Macmillan General Reference
A Simon and Schuster Macmillan Company
1633 Broadway, New York, NY 10019-6705

International Standard Book Number: 0-02-861560-3

Library of Congress Cataloging Card Number: 96-79497

99 98 97   9 8 7 6 5 4 3 2 1

Interpretation of the printing code: the rightmost number of the first series of numbers is the year of the book's printing; the rightmost number of the second series of numbers is the number of the book's printing. For example, a printing code of 97-1 shows that the first printing occurred in 1997.

Publisher: Theresa Murtha
Editor in Chief: Richard Staron
Production Editor: Beth Mayland
Designer: A&D Howell
Cover Design: George Berrian

Printed in the United States of America

This book is dedicated in loving memory to my father,
Leonard Obadiah, who embodied the entrepreneureal spirit.

Contents

Introduction

Do you have a great idea for a new business? Have you been laid off from a large company (or fear a layoff) and now want to go out on your own rather than try to re-enter "corporate America?" Are you tired of trying to climb the corporate ladder, and instead want to be your own boss? Have you started a business but can't seem to make it go? All you may need to succeed, besides determination and hard work, is a little help from the experts.

Since 1989, this country's economy has undergone a revolution. The emphasis on industrialization has decreased, while the push toward information increased. As a result, big businesses downsized, laying off millions of talented, hardworking employees. Small businesses increasingly became the focal point of the new economy. In fact, while big businesses continued to reduce their work force, very small businesses (those with four employees or less) created an impressive number of new, well-paying jobs—not only for those who started the businesses, but also for the workers they hired. The common belief that the jobs created by these small businesses were just minimum wage "hamburger flippers" or sales clerks is simply not borne out by the facts.

More impressively, small business creation has come not only from those laid-off from management positions at large corporations (who were predominantly white males), but from minorities and women. Small business ownership by women and minorities has more than doubled in recent years. There was a 40% increase in women-owned businesses between 1990 and 1995! (And an 80% increase between 1985 and 1995.) Today, about one-third of all U.S. businesses are owned by women, while the percentage of women-owned service businesses is now over 50%!

Self-employment is booming, with estimates of unincorporated businesses running from about 16 million to as high as 36 million. According to Internal Revenue Service statistics, while only 11% were self-employed a decade ago, more than 13% of the work force is self-employed today. Nearly half of those that are self-employed are age 45 or older, many coming off of years of employment (and experience) with big corporations. According to the American Association of Retired People (AARP), in 1993, 87.5% of managers over age 40 who were discharged from corporate America chose to become entrepreneurs rather than re-enter the job market.

In addition, an increasing number of those who retire from a job are joining the ranks of small business owners. In a recent *USA Today*/Gallup poll, 70% of baby boomers indicated that they planned to work after retirement. They plan to start second and even third careers!

Small business is not only found in office complexes and strip malls; it is increasingly located in spare bedrooms, garages and other spaces within the home. Yes, home offices for small business owners are booming—one new home-based business every ten seconds! In fact, one New York marketing firm claims that 38% of all U.S. households now have at least one person earning some money from home. While some of these are telecommuters employed by corporations, many of these people are running their own business. Most estimates put the number of home-based business owners at about 25 million, up from just 20 million in 1991. Their average income has been reported as high as $58,000, with 1.7 million earning six figure incomes or more!

In 1995, the White House held a conference on small business, with both President Clinton and Vice-President Gore in attendance. The purpose: To voice problems faced by small businesses and offer solutions that could ultimately be brought to Congress for redress. One of the key problem areas identified by the conference is access to capital. Small business owners have voiced their difficulty in both getting the necessary capital to start their businesses and in obtaining additional capital to grow their businesses. The conference made a number of suggestions on how to improve access to capital for small businesses. By and large, these suggestions were directed at the Small Business Administration's current policies and practices. For example, the SBA was encouraged to change its rules to facilitate financing home-based businesses. It was recommended that the SBA be elevated to permanent cabinet status. Also, the conference recommended that the Small Business Investment Corporation (SBIC) program be expanded, and that a new agency called Venture Capital Marketing Association (Vickie Mae), which would be similar to the Federal National Mortgage Association (Fannie Mae), be created to provide additional access to capital. Some of these recommendations have already been implemented.

Another problem area addressed by the conference was government regulation. All businesses, regardless of size, are currently subject to extensive regulatory restrictions (what businesses cannot do) and compliances (what businesses must do). Paperwork galore. This burden, however, falls more acutely on small businesses that, by their nature, lack the resources to deal with the regulations. According to one survey, small business owners spent about three business days each month complying with government regulations—taxes, payroll, employee rights and zoning to name a few. Many small businesses do not even know about all of the regulations (such as OSHA, EPA, Americans With Disabilities Act) to which they may be subject. Some may find themselves in trouble down the road. Small businesses must meet the cost of regulatory compliance whether or not they are making money. The conference suggestions for improvements in this area included, among other ideas, requiring a cost-risk benefit analysis for all federal regulations and creating simplified access to all federal information, resources and regulations. In March 1996, the Small Business Regulatory Enforcement Fairness Act of 1996 was signed into law. It requires plain language federal regulations, directs agencies to place an emphasis on compliance rather than punishment, establishes a small business advocacy review plane and provides an opportunity for judicial review of regulations affecting small business.

Another area of concern to small business is the tax burden. Several laws significantly benefit small business: an increased health insurance deduction for self-employed individuals, a higher dollar limit on expensing equipment, and reform of the rules for S corporations (corporations whose income is taxed directly to stockholders). Two changes have already been implemented: The IRS has raised the amount of expense for which a receipt is needed to claim a deduction for travel and entertainment from $25 to $75. The IRS has also made improvements in the area of worker classification (as employee or independent contractor).

Government seems to be committed to addressing issues faced by small business. It remains to be seen how quickly and meaningfully change will take place.

While the horizons for small business seem to be expanding, keep in mind that not all businesses succeed. About 40% fail within the first five years. Of course, this means that 60% succeed for at least five years. Home-based businesses do even better, with nearly 85% remaining open after three years. But before investing your time, energy and money in a business, ask yourself whether you have what it takes to succeed.

- **Do you have an entrepreneurial spirit?** Do you have the desire to be your own boss and the stomach to handle the risks of running your own business? Do you desire financial independence and creative freedom? Can you persist in the face of unfavorable odds and numerous setbacks?

- **Are you up to the task?** Are you physically fit enough to endure the long hours that start-ups typically entail? Are you emotionally mature enough to handle the ups and downs that visit most businesses? Do you have the skills in a myriad of areas—sales, personnel management, finance—to oversee your business? Can you make decisions, lead others and plan ahead? Are you smart enough to learn what you need to know?

- **Do you have the capital, or access to capital, to underwrite your venture?** Have you saved enough to see you through the startup phase of your business? Are you willing to risk it all if need be? Can your family or friends help you out financially? Will your credit enable you to get outside financing?

Another problem area for small business is cash flow—having sufficient funds to pay employees, suppliers and distributors while meeting debt servicing costs. Again, recognizing the problem will direct you toward finding solutions.

Thirty years ago, Napoleon Hill, author of "Think and Grow Rich," promised that under his "law of success" a person could achieve financial success by having a strong desire, faith, persistence and sufficient mental power to do so. Today, you need more than just a positive attitude to make it in a competitive business world. You need not only a wish to succeed, but also the knowledge of how to go about doing it. This book will provide you with some practical ideas for raising the money to start or expand a business, as well as ways to conserve your funds and stretch the dollars you have. Each idea will suggest inexpensive ways to accomplish certain tasks. Not every idea may be suitable for your type of business. For example, some ideas may apply only to manufacturing-type businesses, while yours is a service business. Pick and choose those ideas that can be readily adapted for use in your company. I hope that the suggestions in this book will serve to stimulate your creative power of thinking up new ways of cutting costs to help your business grow and succeed.

In using this book, be sure to note that addresses, telephone numbers, web sites and other information changes constantly and quickly. The information contained in this book was verified at the time of publication, but please recognize that you may find that some referrals are outdated. For your convenience, you can find all the telephone numbers and web sites noted throughout the book also listed in the appendixes.

I would like to acknowledge the invaluable help of the following in preparing this book: My husband, Malcolm Katt, who contributed to the research of this book; my friend Bruce Glickman, CPA, and my cousin Liana Toscanini who reviewed some material and made valuable suggestions; Elliott Eiss, editor of *J.K. Lasser's Your Income Tax,* who worked with me in a number of areas; and to my mentor, Sidney Kess, who gave me untold support throughout this project.

CHAPTER 1

Transforming an Idea into a Business

Having a great idea for a business is not enough. You need to develop the idea and see if it makes sense as the basis for a business. Do you have an idea for a product or service? You do not necessarily need to invent a "better mousetrap" in order to launch your venture. You simply must be able to clarify what you will be doing, and be sure that you will do it well.

In this Chapter, you will find ways to pick the best type of business for you. You will also find out how to ensure success and avoid problems by setting out a plan of attack.

IDEA 1: Take Your Personal Inventory

The ideal business is one that best utilizes your skills and experience and capitalizes on your interests. What are you good at doing? Do you have expertise in a certain field? Obviously, you stand the best chance of success with a business in which you have proficiency. Do you have a hobby that you would like to turn into a business? A strong love for something can go a long way in carrying you over the rough spots. No one knows your interests and strengths better than you do, so it is up to you to identify the product or service that would be the best basis for your business.

To determine whether you are suited to owning your own business and what that business should be, take a personal inventory of your talents and temperament. Be totally honest with yourself

1

in order to see if you can handle the challenges and stresses of running a business. This is not a scientific process; it is a way of helping you decide whether or not to go forward with your desire to be a business owner.

Personal Inventory Checklist for a Small Business Owner

Your Personal Traits	*Yes*	*No*	*Not Sure*
Do you want to be your own boss?	_____	_____	_____
Can you readily make decisions (e.g., financial, technical)?	_____	_____	_____
Can you take responsibility?	_____	_____	_____
Can you plan ahead?	_____	_____	_____
Are you organized?	_____	_____	_____
Are you a leader?	_____	_____	_____
Do you like competition?	_____	_____	_____
Are you a hard worker?	_____	_____	_____
Are you physically able to work long hours?	_____	_____	_____
Can you handle stress?	_____	_____	_____
Are you able to make financial sacrifices?	_____	_____	_____
Your Skills and Experience			
Do you have the know-how to run a business?	_____	_____	_____
Are you a fast learner?	_____	_____	_____
Have you ever run a business before?	_____	_____	_____
Have you ever been a supervisor or manager?	_____	_____	_____
Have you ever worked in the industry that you are thinking about entering?	_____	_____	_____
Do you have a higher education?	_____	_____	_____

Assuming that you have determined that you have what it takes to be a small business owner, now decide what that business should be. What type of business do you know? Wholesale, retail, manufacturing? What industry are you up on? You may want to be in computers, but if you've spent your career thus far in fast food, you may get in over your head.

IDEA 2: Hone Your Idea

Having an idea of what you want to do only goes so far. You must hone your idea and transform it into what you hope will be a viable business. Details are important!

It is not enough to simply be a "consultant" or "sales representative." You must narrow down the area or products you will be involved in. For example, say your background is in computer programming. Will your business provide programming services for other companies? Will you teach corporate employees or private individuals how to use various software programs? Will you create your own programs and market them to consumers? Find your niche.

Suppose you want to open a retail store. Will your store's concept work best in a large city or in a suburban mall? How much floor space will you need? What suppliers will you use? What kind of terms of sale will you offer to customers?

Narrowing down your business subject is only the first step in crystallizing your business idea. You must ask yourself some hard questions:

- *Is the concept practical?* You may, for example, have a wonderful idea for a product, but find that it is just too expensive to produce, making it impractical to sell.

- *Is there any need for your product or service?* If you come up with a new concept, are you sure the public will want it? It is advisable to do some market research in the early stages of formulating your business idea to assess demand. You may find that what you think is a great idea is simply not wanted by consumers or other users. If you find out at the start that you are barking up the wrong tree, you will certainly have saved yourself considerable time and expense. (Free and low-cost marketing sources are discussed in Chapter 4.)

- *If you are offering an existing product or service, how do you plan to fit within the market?* How will you compare with other companies in the market? Will you offer higher quality, better service? Just because you can do something well is not a guarantee of success when you are trying to break into an existing market. What will you have that other businesses in the market do not have? Again, some market research will inform you of the competition and perhaps show how you can carve out your share of the market. Unfortu- nately, you may just learn that the market is already saturated and that there is no place for you at this time unless you can create additional demand.

$$Extra Savings

You can do market research without spending a fortune. As a start, check U.S. Census information in your local library. Learn about demographics in your area (the number of people, age distribution, household income and how income is spent). Also, call trade associations which may provide free industry data. Do your own market surveys by developing a questionnaire and canvassing a local mall or industrial park to find your answers. Check out data that can be found on the Internet.

Preparatory work for starting a business is not a simple task. It can take many months of planning, research and investigation. Rushing ahead with a half-baked idea will probably result in a full-blown failure. Be prepared to spend many months (even up to a year) honing your idea. You greatly improve your chances of success by the degree to which you examine your business idea.

IDEA 3: Buy an Existing Business

Instead of starting from scratch, you may be able to use your talents most effectively by taking over an existing business. "Business opportunities" are routinely advertised in local papers and on the Internet. For example, the National Business Exchange allows you to view business descriptions for free; the cost of downloading a contact name and number is 95¢. You can find the National Business Exchange at http://www.directory.net/lexis-nexis/sba. There are also companies that will locate business opportunities for you. However, these companies may charge a substantial fee (several thousand dollars) that may be well beyond your means. A business opportunity may be right under your nose. You may even be working for a company that, with a little bit of planning, you can own! If the company you now work for is owned by one person who has no children or other family members interested in the business, the owner may put it up for sale when he/she wants to retire. If you already know the business, you will have a leg up in running it and may be able to negotiate for its purchase.

However, don't assume that buying an existing business guarantees success. This alternative has its own pitfalls. For example, an existing business may have created a bad credit history or an unfavorable reputation in the area of quality or service that a subsequent business owner has to deal with. Also, this alternative entails most of the same difficulties in starting a business from scratch. You still need the capital to acquire the business (although it is generally cheaper than starting up a new business) and you still need the know-how to run the business and make it grow.

In buying an existing business, there are several stages you need to go through before it is yours.

Investigation Stage

Let's assume that you find a business that would you consider buying. What should you look for? And what should you look out for? You'll want to check the following areas:

- *Income and expenses.* Look at the books and tax returns (you should insist on this) to see how income and expenses have been running for the past three years or so. This will give you some idea of where the business stands. Is it profitable? Can you make it more so? Be sure to run a credit check on the business to see if it is up-to-date on payments and has a good credit rating.

- *Contracts and leases.* Look at existing contracts with suppliers, dealers and customers. Also, check out current leases for office/plant space. Determine the extent of the business's present commitments.

- *Payroll.* Look at current staffing. Is it adequate? When the present owner leaves, how will this affect the running of the business? Are there existing benefit promises to personnel (health insurance, pension plans)? Do you plan to continue these benefits? Change these benefits? Are payroll taxes up to date?

Warning

If you buy an existing business, you can become personally liable for outstanding employment taxes.

You should also use the help of experts to review the material you have gathered; have an accountant review the books for you, and have an attorney look over the contracts and leases. Do not stint on professional assistance at this phase of your investigation. A few dollars saved may wind up costing you many more in the future.

In addition to reviewing the hard and cold facts of the books and tax returns, you should do some informal investigations of your own. Look around. Does the business look busy? Talk to employees, clients, suppliers and others to learn about how the business is really doing.

Negotiation Stage

Let's assume that you are generally satisfied with how the business looks and want to go forward with the purchase. You must negotiate for the price. This is not as simple a process as it may seem. You are dealing not only with a dollar amount, but also with how and when the purchase price will be paid. Does the owner insist on cash? Can the payments be made in installments over several years? An installment payment plan will avoid the need to raise outside capital beyond what is needed for a down payment. Instead, the owner finances the purchase for you. You will be paying the interest on the purchase price directly to the owner. Consider whether or not the projected income from the business be sufficient to pay the installments.

Will the owner continue to have some continuing interest in the business (as a shareholder or a consultant)? If the business is incorporated, are you going to buy the stock or the assets of the business? (Buyers generally prefer an asset purchase since they can choose only desirable clients and it does not saddle the buyers with the business's liabilities; sellers prefer a stock sale since it is simple to transact and shifts liabilities to the buyer.)

Even when the dollar amount and payment method have been worked out, the negotiation stage is not yet complete. Unless you are buying only stock in the business, you should be aware that both buyer and seller need to allocate the purchase price of a business among the assets of that business. This allocation will affect your future write-offs for depreciation and amortization. The allocation is made on IRS Form 8594 according to the fair market value of the assets. (The residual method—a special valuation method—must be used for valuing goodwill and going concern value.) The allocation of the purchase price to the business assets must be made in the following order:

1. Cash and items like cash

2. Marketable securities and similar items

3. Other tangible and intangible assets (except goodwill and going concern value)

4. Goodwill and going concern value

By using this allocation order, goodwill and going concern value receive a portion of the purchase price only if the total price exceeds the value of the other assets.

Example: A business has $1,000 cash and $9,000 equipment. The owner sells the business to another for $12,000. In this case, $2,000 ($12,000 – $10,000) can be allocated to goodwill or going concern value since the price paid for the business exceeds the value of the other assets.

Warning

You are bound by the allocation and cannot argue for different values to be assigned to various assets. This is true even though the IRS is *not* bound by the allocation and can challenge an asset's value.

As mentioned earlier, the allocation of the purchase price will affect the amount of depreciation and allocation that you will be able to claim with respect to various assets. In the past, certain intangibles could not be amortized (deducted according to a rate over a set period). However, a change in the law now permits intangibles acquired during the purchase of a business to be deducted over a 15-year period. These intangibles include goodwill, going concern value, work force in place, patents, copyrights, formulas, processes, designs, patterns, know-how, customer lists, licenses, covenants not to compete, and franchises, trademarks and tradenames.

A buyer and seller have some flexibility in the allocation process. For some assets, buyer and seller have adverse interests. For example, a buyer may want to allocate as much of the purchase price as possible to a covenant not to compete (an asset that falls within category 3). This allows the buyer to deduct the allocated amount in full. A seller may want a greater allocation to goodwill, rather than to a covenant not to compete. The reason: The seller can treat the gain allocated to goodwill as capital gain while the portion of the gain allocated to a covenant not to compete is ordinary income.

Assuming negotiations move forward, at some point you will be asked to sign a "letter of intent" which will obligate you to buy the business if all the terms can be worked out. The letter of intent is designed to weed out "tire kickers" from serious buyers.

Contract Stage

The final steps in buying an existing business involve a formal contract. This ensures that both parties get what they have negotiated for. The contract should be drafted, or at least reviewed, by an attorney. It should contain the following points:

- A description of what is being sold (the assets, assumption of contracts and liabilities for the buyer).

- The purchase price, and how it is to be paid (the terms/method of payment).

- Allocation of the price to the assets agreed upon by the parties (IRS Form 8594).

- Warranties by the seller (the accuracy of disclosed financial data given to the buyer, and undisclosed liabilities that may arise).

- Risk of loss pending closing (what falls on the buyer; what falls on the seller).

- Miscellaneous factors (e.g., covenants not to compete).

- Procedures for closing the sale (the time and place and other factors).

Final Stage

After the contract terms are settled and a date is set, you may have to arrange outside financing (see Chapter 2) to cover the contract price.

Figure 1-1

Form **8594** (Rev. Jan. 1996) Department of the Treasury Internal Revenue Service	**Asset Acquisition Statement** **Under Section 1060** ▶ **Attach to your Federal income tax return.**	OMB No. 1545-1021 Attachment Sequence No. **61**

Name as shown on return | Identification number as shown on return

Check the box that identifies you: ☐ Buyer   ☐ Seller

Part I   General Information—To be completed by all filers.

1 Name of other party to the transaction | Other party's identification number

Address (number, street, and room or suite no.)

City or town, state, and ZIP code

2 Date of sale | **3** Total sales price

Part II   Assets Transferred—To be completed by all filers of an original statement.

4 Assets	Aggregate Fair Market Value (Actual Amount for Class I)	Allocation of Sales Price
Class I	$	$
Class II	$	$
Class III	$	$
Class IV	$	$
Total	$	$

5 Did the buyer and seller provide for an allocation of the sales price in the sales contract or in another written document signed by both parties? . . . . ☐ Yes ☐ No

If "Yes," are the aggregate fair market values listed for each of asset Classes I, II, III, and IV the amounts agreed upon in your sales contract or in a separate written document? . . . . ☐ Yes ☐ No

6 In connection with the purchase of the group of assets, did the buyer also purchase a license or a covenant not to compete, or enter into a lease agreement, employment contract, management contract, or similar arrangement with the seller (or managers, directors, owners, or employees of the seller)? . . . . ☐ Yes ☐ No

If "Yes," specify (a) the type of agreement, and (b) the maximum amount of consideration (not including interest) paid or to be paid under the agreement. See the instructions for line 6.

For Paperwork Reduction Act Notice, see instructions.   Cat. No. 63768Z   Form **8594** (Rev. 1-96)

Form 8594 (Rev. 1-96)

Page **2**

Part III **Supplemental Statement**—To be completed only if amending an original statement or previously filed supplemental statement because of an increase or decrease in consideration.

7 Assets	Allocation of Sales Price as Previously Reported	Increase or (Decrease)	Redetermined Allocation of Sales Price
Class I	$	$	$
Class II	$	$	$
Class III	$	$	$
Class IV	$	$	$
Total	$		$

8 Reason(s) for increase or decrease. Attach additional sheets if more space is needed.

9 Tax year and tax return form number with which the original Form 8594 and any supplemental statements were filed.

Be sure to have everything in place for closing. Give yourself a cash cushion to ensure that the seller meets all of his/her obligations by placing a portion of the sale price in "escrow." This means that a third party (typically an attorney for one side or both) will hold the money in trust until certain conditions are met.

IDEA 4: Buy a Franchise

You may be able to buy a pre-packaged business, known as a franchise. Currently, there are between 3,000 and 5,000 franchisors—companies that will sell you a franchise. In a franchise business, the concept is already there. In addition, there may be support in the form of advertising, products and advice from the franchiser. But buying a franchise it not like buying an existing business; it is more akin to starting from scratch.

Some franchises go in and out of favor (for example, yogurt shops, once hot, are now struggling). In addition, if you buy a franchise, you give up some autonomy because you are required to do things according to franchise policy.

Locating the Franchise For You

Newspapers and magazines, small business trade shows, reference books in your local library and even Internet web sites are some of the ways you can locate a franchise that may be right for you. What industry do you have experience in? What type of training will a particular franchise provide? Be sure you know the nature of the business you are getting into, and are prepared to put in the required time, training and effort.

You should also beware of scams masquerading as business opportunities. "Earn big money in your spare time." "With only a small investment, earn thousands each month." To protect yourself, ask to see a disclosure document. According to the Federal Trade Commission's Franchise and Business Opportunity rule, sellers of goods and services that enable a person to start a business must provide this document, called the Uniform Franchise Offering Circular (UFOC), if a buyer is required to spend at least $500 in the first six months and the seller has agreed to provide certain goods or services (such as finding ideal locations). The statement must be given to you at least 10 days prior to a sale.

The disclosure statement should include an audited financial statement. This is a statement prepared by a certified public accountant who is warranting the authenticity of the information provided. If the disclosure document contains earnings claims, they must be supported by separate written proof. The seller should also provide references. For example, if you are looking to become a distributor, ask for the names of ten existing distributors for the same seller. Make sure that they are within your area. Be wary if the seller only gives you the names of one or two distributors who may be across the country. These "distributors" may be *singers,* a term used to described liars paid by sellers to support their stories.

Check other terms and conditions carefully.

States Requiring Sellers to Register

Alabama
California
Connecticut
Florida
Georgia
Indiana
Iowa
Kentucky
Louisiana
Maine
Maryland
Michigan
Minnesota
Nebraska
New Hampshire
North Carolina
Ohio
Oklahoma
South Carolina
South Dakota
Texas
Utah
Virginia
Washington

- What are your territory rights (can the franchisor sell another franchise in your same area)? If you fail to get these rights clarified in your franchise agreement, you may be out of luck if the franchisor sells another franchise in your vicinity.

- What are your performance obligations? Do you have to do a certain amount of business? What time frame is provided for meeting performance standards?

- What cut does the franchisor get (for example, 3% of gross sales)? Are fees payable weekly? Monthly? Quarterly?

- What other fees does the franchisor charge (for example, an advertising fee of between $1/2\%$ to 2% of gross sales; grand opening charges; renewal fees; fees for site selection)?

- What does the franchisor provide in exchange for franchise fees? Do you enjoy the benefit of national advertising? Are you required to buy products from the franchisor?

- How can you terminate a franchise agreement (are there penalty clauses; any refund of the franchise fee)? A franchisee may be stuck in the business unless the franchisor commits some gross act (fraud, bankruptcy). On the other hand, you want be protected from having the franchisor terminate you too easily (for example, simply on 30 days notice). Unless it is someone you know well, check out the seller of a "business opportunity" through various sources:

  - Call your local Better Business Bureau. This will let you know if there have been any complaints lodged against the seller.

- Call the attorney general's office in your state. Many states have laws regulating business opportunities which may require sellers to register.

Still other states use general fraud statutes, consumer protection laws and securities laws to attack bogus business opportunities. You may want to steer clear of any franchisor that has numerous outstanding lawsuits. The franchisor is required to provide you with this information. Also, speak to existing franchisees to determine their satisfaction with the franchise.

Get Expert Assistance

While you can do the leg work on a franchise in which you are interested, it may be advisable to have an accountant review the financial materials. This will help you assess whether you can expect to make any money from the deal. Why put in all the capital and the work if you are required to share too much of the profit with the franchisor?

You may also want an attorney who specializes in franchise contracts to review the one that is proposed to you. You may be able to avoid additional fees or obtain some relief on certain clauses (such as the termination clause) if you have an attorney negotiate the changes for you.

For further information about franchises in general, check listings of franchise associations in Appendix A.

IDEA 5: Start Your Business on a Part-Time Basis

Operating on the theory that it is better not to put all your eggs in one basket, starting a business on a part-time basis allows you to test the waters. You can gradually introduce your product/services to the marketplace to see if the public is interested. You can hone the nature of your business while relying on outside income for support. Starting a new business on the side can be particularly helpful in turning a hobby into a business.

For those who do not have the luxury of being financially independent, there is also a financial plus to starting your business on a part-time basis. Starting a business entails a double financial burden—having enough funds to get the company rolling and also having sufficient cash to meet your living expenses and other personal obligations. New businesses generally do not generate sufficient revenue to meet an owner's personal needs for roughly eight months (some businesses may take less time; some considerably longer). This means that in raising money to start a business, you also need to raise the money to cover personal financial obligations (including, for example, your rent or mortgage payments, utilities, food, car payments, and health insurance premiums) for those eight months or so. If you are employed and can keep your current job while moonlighting at your own business, you can eliminate one of the burdens—the need to raise capital to cover your personal expenses. Your salary will continue to cover your personal needs while you put your available capital toward your business.

While starting your business on a part-time basis allows you to operate without the constraint of having to meet your own salary costs, there is an important drawback to consider. Starting part-time may mean not giving the sufficient time and attention needed to really get the business going. You may have a perfectly good idea that will never become viable because you did not give it a fair chance.

If you are working for a company but fear that downsizing might eliminate your job and would like to start your own business, begin your planning immediately.

Did You Know. . .

Current statistics show that managers age 45 and over who have been laid off opt to start a business (rather than try to re-enter the job market) nearly 90% of the time. The reason: Existing jobs just aren't there.

Don't wait until the ax falls to start planning your business. Use your current employment status to its best advantage by investigating your business opportunities. Also, begin to save now for start up capital.

IDEA 6: Write Your Own Business Plan

A business plan is a report describing your company—what you do (your product or service), what the market is like and how your business fits into it, how much you earn, who runs the company and more. A plan is important for a number of reasons. It serves as a road map for starting and growing your business. Developing your business plan forces you to think ahead and make projections: Where do you want your business to be in three years? In five years? How do you plan to get there? A business plan is also required if you are looking for outside financing (see Chapter 2). Prospective lenders or investors want to learn what your business is all about—whether your product or service is marketable, whether you have the vision to grow and whether you and your team have the talent to support your vision. Even if you already own a business or are planning to buy an existing business or franchise, you still need a business plan.

There are professionals who can write a business plan for you. They generally charge several thousand dollars for the service. In addition, since they do not know your idea or company as intimately as you do, they may not accurately convey your vision of the business. Therefore, you should write your own business plan. You will save a significant amount of money while producing a plan that best serves your needs. What is more, writing the plan yourself will serve as a learning experience. It will force you to think through all phases of the business, something you may not have done previously.

There are various formats for a business plan. You can learn about these alternative formats from books specifically on writing a business plan. These books can be found in your local library or bookstore. You can also use simple computer software programs on writing a business plan.

> ### $$Extra Savings
>
> The Small Business Administration (SBA) makes available numerous "shareware" software programs on writing a business plan. There is no charge for shareware programs. Shareware through the SBA can be found on the Internet at www.sbaonline.sba.gov/shareware/starfile.html.

The software programs lay out the necessary sections of the plan; all you do is fill in the numbers for your company. You can also tailor the plan as your needs dictate. Shareware programs can be downloaded on your computer. Be aware, however, that downloading is not always as simple as it would seem.

The General Contents of a Business Plan

The general contents of most business plans are fairly standard. The following list should help you to draft your own business plan.

Cover sheet

Prepare a cover sheet (title page) with the name, address and phone number of the business.

Statement of purpose

This is a one-page statement of purpose, the reason for which you wrote the plan. This could, for example, be the objective of obtaining start up capital or a loan for expansion.

Table of contents

Include in the table of contents the following parts.

- *Part 1: Business Description (sometimes called the Summary Description or Executive Summary):* This section of the business plan provides a summary of your business. State your company name and address and either the date it was formed or a sentence indicating that it is being formed. Include a statement about the legal organization of your business. For example, if you have incorporated and elected subchapter S status for federal income tax purposes (and for state tax purposes if applicable), state that you are an S corporation. (The various options for business organization are discussed in Chapter 3.) List your product or service and describe your goals and objectives. In effect, Part 1 of your business plan is like the first paragraph of any well-written news article. It contains the who, what, where, when and why of your business.

- *Part 2: Product/Service Description:* In this section, explain the core of the business—the product or service you are providing. Be specific, but concise.

- *Part 3: Marketing and competition:* Discuss the market for your product/service. How large is it? Who is the competition? If you do not know this information, find out. (Some tips for market research sources and assistance may be found in Chapter 4.) Explain how you are marketing your product/service. Are your prices/sales terms competitive?

- *Part 4: Personnel (Management):* Introduce your team: Who owns the business? Who runs the business? What qualifications do officers have? For example, if you are the sole owner of your business, state this. Then briefly describe your work experience and educational background that may be relevant or helpful to your business. Discuss what business functions you oversee (such as product development, finances or sales). Then explain how you now (or intend to in the future) meet the personnel requirements for other business functions. For example, you may have to rely on outside professionals or consultants for certain tasks (e.g., accounting, marketing). List all the people who contribute to the operation and success of your business as well as those you anticipate hiring or contracting with.

- *Part 5: Operating requirements:* Describe the equipment and facilities needed to make and market your products/services. For example, if your company sells gizmos, do you manufacture them or does some other company manufacture them for you? If you manufacture them, where are your facilities located? What equipment is necessary, and where is this equipment housed? Also, talk about how many people are required to produce the product. If your business is selling a product, discuss your sales force. Is it in-house? Multilevel? Do you rely on an outside sales force?

- *Part 6: Financial data:* A considerable number of different financial projections must be included in all business plans. The purpose of these projections is to show what capital you need and how you intend to repay it. If your business plan is for start up purposes, include:

1. Projected start up costs (including funds to cover your personal living expenses if necessary);

2. Expected return on investment (ROI), or profit, for the first year;

3. Projected income statements for two years (what revenue is expected to be generated during this period and what the business will net after expenses);

4. Projected balance sheets for two years (statements showing the assets and liabilities of the company); and

5. Projected monthly cash flow statement for 12 months (how much revenue will be earned and how money will be spent each month for one year). If you are beyond the start up phase and have been in operation for a while, you obviously do not need to include projected start up costs. However, you must include income statements and balance sheets for the last two years (sometimes lenders and investors will want to see statements for the last three years). Worksheets for these financial projections are included in this Chapter. In making financial projections, be realistic. While all projections are just estimates of future performance and lack certainty, do not expect lenders or investors to be impressed by highly inflated numbers. Also, do not delude yourself with hopes of overnight success. Do not, for example, think you can go from a revenue of $100,000 in the first year to $10 million in the second year. Your numbers must be based on something tangible, like experience or market research.

- *Part 7: Supporting documents:* Some of the following are required in all business plans that will be used to seek financing; other documents are included only if appropriate. The following required documentation is based on SBA loan program requirements. Other lenders or investors may want additional documentation. If you are trying to obtain a bank loan or investors to put money in your business, you must include a copy of tax returns of all owners of the business for the last three years in addition to an income statement for the past year (if the income tax return has not yet been prepared for this period). You must also include personal financial statements of all the owners (or at least those owning 20% or more of the company). Personal financial statements are simply balance sheets for individuals, showing their net worth (the amount by which their assets exceed their liabilities). Some other types of documents you may want to include:

proposed leases for premises or equipment; licenses, patents and other proprietary items; the franchise contract (if the business is a franchise); letters of intent from suppliers and manufacturers; other material that may be helpful in explaining your business (e.g., testimonials or scientific data showing that your product works).

In making your plan, remember that it reflects upon your business, so you want it to be clear, neat and professional. Even if you are writing it as an exercise to help you think through the business and are the only one who will ever see it, write it in such as way that you would be proud to show it to others. Make sure that it is complete. There is no rule on the length of the plan; it should be only as long as is necessary to provide a complete picture of your business and where it is going.

Even if you undertake to write the plan yourself, you may want to get professional help (from an accountant or other "numbers" person or a marketing firm) in preparing the financial data portion of the plan if you do not have the expertise. You may also want to have some outsider read your draft and give you constructive criticism before you submit your business plan to lenders or investors.

$$Extra Savings

You can have your business plan reviewed free of charge by SCORE, a volunteer organization under the auspices of the SBA, or by a state or local economic development center. Getting good advice on your business plan is discussed in Chapter 4.

Part A: Worksheets for Preparing Financial Information

The following pages provide you with worksheets to help you prepare the financial information required in a business plan. With each worksheet, you will find some explanation to help you in filling in the required information. You may adapt these worksheets as needed.

If you are starting a business from scratch, you want to know how much money you will need to open your doors. You may need to consider a number of items. A worksheet and explanation can be found in Chapter 2 (Worksheet for Projecting Start up Costs).

If you are buying an existing business, you do not need all the items listed in the worksheet. Many of them will have been included in the price you paid for the business. But even when buying an existing business, there are still some start up costs to consider. You will probably need to incur professional fees (attorneys and accountants) to change the ownership of the business. You will also need new stationery reflecting your ownership. You may need new licenses or permits.

WORKSHEET FOR INCOME PROJECTION STATEMENT

	Jan.	Feb.	Mar.	Apr.	May	Jun.	Jul.	Aug.	Sep.	Oct.	Nov.	Dec.	Total
Total revenue*													
Cost of sales**													
Gross profit													

*Revenue from sales of products after returns and markdowns/fees for services.

**In the case of inventory-based businesses, the cost of inventory.

Fixed expenses	Jan.	Feb.	Mar.	Apr.	May	Jun.	Jul.	Aug.	Sep.	Oct.	Nov.	Dec.	Total
Rent													
Utilities													
Insurance													
Licenses/permits													
Loan repayment													
Depreciation													
Miscellaneous													
TOTAL													

Variable expenses	Jan.	Feb.	Mar.	Apr.	May	Jun.	Jul.	Aug.	Sep.	Oct.	Nov.	Dec.	Total
Wages													
Payroll taxes													
Advertising													
T & E expenses													
Office supplies													
Legal/ acct'g fees													
Miscellaneous													
TOTAL													

Fixed expenses	Jan.	Feb.	Mar.	Apr.	May	Jun.	Jul.	Aug.	Sep.	Oct.	Nov.	Dec.	Total
Pre-tax profit													
Taxes													
Net profit/loss													

WORKSHEET FOR ONE-YEAR ESTIMATED CASH FLOW

	Jan.	Feb.	Mar.	Apr.	May	Jun.	Jul.	Aug.	Sep.	Oct.	Nov.	Dec.	Total
Cash in*													
Cash in bank													
Petty cash													
Cash sales													
Receivables													

continues

WORKSHEET FOR ONE-YEAR ESTIMATED CASH FLOW (continued)

	Jan.	Feb.	Mar.	Apr.	May	Jun.	Jul.	Aug.	Sep.	Oct.	Nov.	Dec.	Total
Total cash in**													
Disburse-ments***													
Cash balance ****													

*Amount on hand at the first of each month

**Total of cash in, cash sales and accounts receivable

***Payments for rents, wages, utilities and other expenses

****Difference between total cash in, etc. and disbursements as of the end of each month

WORKSHEET FOR BUSINESS BALANCE SHEET

Assets		*Liabilities and Equity*	
Cash	$____	Accounts payable	$____
Notes/accounts receivable	____	S.T. mortgages, notes, bonds	____
Inventories	____	Other current liabilities	____
Stocks, bonds, securities	____	L.T. mortgages notes, bonds	____
Real estate	____	Other liabilities	____
Depreciable assets	____	Owner(s) equity	____
Intangibles	____		
Other assets	____		
TOTAL ASSETS	$____	TOTAL LIABILITIES/ EQUITY	$____

A balance sheet is like a snapshot of a company's financial plusses and minuses. Obviously, in a start up situation, there is no need for a business balance sheet because the company has yet to be formed. However, if an existing business is seeking to attract additional investors or needs a loan, then a business plan should contain a balance sheet.

All businesses that are up and running should prepare a balance sheet at least once a year reflecting the company's assets and liabilities. For purposes of a business plan, an existing business can construct the balance sheet for the month immediately preceding the month in which the plan is being written. For example, if you are writing a business plan in May, you can use a balance sheet as of April 30th. Alternatively, you can use a balance sheet for the preceding quarter or even from the preceding year-end if that is the most definitive financial information on hand.

The dollar value of each item is the amount that is being carried for that item on the company's books. The following is an explanation of some items that should be included in a balance sheet (if they are applicable):

Assets

Notes/accounts receivable. These are amounts owed to the business for services, products or capital already furnished to clients or customers. This item should be reduced for any allowance made for bad debts.

Depreciable assets. This item includes equipment, a plant, and other depreciable property. In listing the amount of depreciable assets, reduce the amount by accumulated depreciation already claimed for these assets.

Intangibles. These include patents, trademarks, copyrights and good will. Again, in reporting the amount of intangibles, reduce the amount by accumulated prior amortization taken for these intangibles.

Liabilities

S.T. mortgages, notes, bonds. These are short-term obligations that are payable in less than one year.

L.T. mortgages, notes, bonds. These are long-term obligations that are payable in one year or more.

Owner's equity

This is the amount that owners have put into the business in order to receive stock (if the business is a corporation) or an ownership interest (if the business is a sole proprietorship, partnership or limited liability company). It does not include loans that owners have made to the business.

Part B: Worksheets for Supporting Documentation

WORKSHEET FOR PERSONAL BALANCE SHEET

Assets		*Liabilities*	
Cash on hand/in accounts	$_____	Accounts payable	$_____
U.S. government bonds	_____	Notes payable	_____
Listed marketable securities	_____	Mortgages	_____
Unlisted nonliquid securities	_____	Installment loans	_____
Real estate	_____	Life insurance loans	_____
Life insurance (cash value)	_____	Other liabilities	_____
Retirement accounts	_____	TOTAL LIABILITIES	$_____
Car	_____		
Furniture/fixtures	_____		
Notes/accounts receivable	_____		
Other liquid assets	_____		
TOTAL ASSETS	$_____	NET WORTH	$_____

The amounts listed in the personal balance sheet, which is another term for a personal financial statement, are simply total amounts derived from schedules attached to the balance sheet that explain the items in more detail. (A sample supporting schedule may be found below.) The following list will give you an idea of some of the information you are required to provide in separate schedules when preparing a personal balance sheet.

SAMPLE SUPPORTING SCHEDULE FOR CASH ACCOUNTS

Depository institution	In name of*	Account type**	Balance
			$

*Indicate whether the account is in the owner's name alone or in joint name.

**Indicate whether the account is checking, savings, money market or a certificate of deposit.

Assets

Cash accounts. You must list the depository institution (such as a bank, brokerage firm or money market fund) and the type of account (checking, savings, or certificates of deposit).

Listed marketable securities. These are stocks and bonds traded on public exchanges, such as the New York Stock Exchange, the American Exchange or NASD (over-the-counter stocks). In a schedule of listed marketable securities, describe the issuer (e.g., IBM, Ford, Intel) and the number of shares or the face amount of the bond. Also enter the current market value of the securities. It is the selling price of these securities (what you could get now if you sold the securities), not what you paid for them or their face amount, that is important in providing your current financial picture. Of course, the price fluctuates on a daily basis. Just use the value for the day you are preparing the personal financial statement or other recent convenient date.

Unlisted securities. If you own stock or hold bonds in privately held corporations, list the name of the issuer and the number of shares (or face amount of the bonds) as well as what you think their current value is. It may be necessary to explain what valuation method you used to arrive at the current value.

Real estate. If you own a house or other property, list the location and a description of the property (such as a personal residence on Elm Street or a commercial building on Main Street). Also, enter the date you acquired the property and what you paid for it. Finally, enter what you estimate to be its current value (what you would get if you sold it today).

Retirement accounts. List the type of retirement account you have: IRAs, Keogh plans, 401(k) plans and amounts vested in pension plans or other qualified retirement plans. In listing the value of these accounts, do not take into account the fact that you may be subject to penalty if you took a distribution at this time.

Notes/accounts receivable. If you have made loans to other parties, list the debtor's name, the purpose of the loan and the amount of monthly payments to you. Also list the remaining balance on the loans.

Liabilities

Notes payable. List the creditor's name and the purpose of the loan. Also include information about the monthly payment on the loan as well as any collateral. Finally, enter the remaining balance (the amount you still owe) on the loan.

Mortgages. If your house is subject to a mortgage, enter the name of the lending institution, the property (your house) that secures the mortgage, the original amount of the loan and the monthly payment (principal and/or interest). Finally, list the remaining balance on the mortgage. Repeat this procedure for mortgages you have on any other property.

Installment loans. Provide the same information required for notes payable: creditor's name, purpose of the loan, collateral, monthly payment and remaining balance. You can, for example, list your car loan in this category. Student loans may also fall within this category.

Other liabilities. List and explain any other liabilities you have. You can include credit card balances and loans taken on your life insurance. You do not have to include in your total liabilities or contingent liabilities (you may be called upon to satisfy liabilities for which there is no certainty about your expenditure). For example, if you have guaranteed a loan made to someone else, you are contingently liable for repayment. If the borrower fails to repay the loan, the lender can look to you for repayment.

Net Worth

Net worth is simply the difference between total assets and total liabilities. If assets exceed liabilities, then net worth is a positive number. If liabilities exceed assets, then net worth is a negative number.

PERSONAL INCOME STATEMENT

Type of Income	Amount
Salary	$_____
Commissions and bonuses	_____
Business income	_____
Dividends	_____
Interest	_____
Capital gains	_____
Net rental income (rentals less expenses and depreciation)	_____
Other income	_____
TOTAL	$_____

Generally, a personal income tax return operates as a personal income statement. However, a separate personal income statement is generally required to show income for the prior year if you do not have a tax return available to provide this information. For example, if you are preparing a business plan in November, you will not yet have completed a tax return for the current year.

The personal financial statement reflects income for a one-year period. If you are preparing it mid-year, then the statement is based on income for a fiscal year. In this case, list the month in which the fiscal year ends (e.g., November) and figure income based on the preceding 12-month period (e.g., from December through November). Most of the income items in the personal income statement are self-explanatory. If you have any other type of income you want to include, list it as "Other Income" and include an explanation.

CHAPTER 2
Raising Capital

Raising capital is, perhaps, the most important step in starting any business. It is also a necessary step for expansion. For small businesses, capital formation is critical. Business experts have identified the number one reason for business failures to be undercapitalization. Business owners simply do not raise enough money to start a business properly or to sustain the growth necessary to allow their companies to succeed.

Unfortunately, most small business owners are forced to start on a shoe string or not at all. Personal savings may be small or nonexistent. Owners' access to borrowing capital is limited because they lack "track records" or adequate collateral to command sufficient loans on favorable terms. According to the SBA, more than 80% of new business owners do not use any commercial loans or debt financing to get started, forcing them to rely on personal savings, family and friends. Still, despite the difficulties in raising capital, the entrepreneurial spirit will not be denied. Many are willing to take the risk of starting up, even though money may be short. While undercapitalization may be the number one reason for failure for businesses in general, it need not necessarily doom your venture. You can find the money you need for your business. There are many sources for raising funds if you know where to look.

In order to raise capital, you first need to project how much you need, whether it is to get your business off the ground or to grow it into its next phase. You cannot simply approach a lender and say "How much will you give me?" You must be prepared to ask for exactly what you think you need.

You must also know what type of financing you are seeking. There are two types of financing: equity and debt. "Equity" means that the party putting up the funds becomes an owner in the business. As such, there is a continuing participation in the ups as well as the downs of the company. An equity participant does not have to be repaid. They hope to share in the profits of the business. "Debt" means that the party putting up the funds is merely a lender (a creditor). As such, the lender will be repaid the amount of capital advanced, plus interest. Once the debt has been repaid, the lender is no longer connected to the business. The lender is repayed whether or not the business is doing well. In addition, there are some financing arrangements that combine elements of both debt and equity.

After you have determined the type of financing you want, you have to know where to look for it. There are a number of alternative sources under the categories of both equity and debt financing. Some are more suited for start up capital; others can be used only to grow existing businesses. There are also a number of programs designed specifically to assist small businesses in raising capital. Getting the funds from these programs is not, however, as easy as it may seem.

In this Chapter, you will learn how to estimate the amount of capital you will need to get started (whether you are starting from scratch or buying an existing business). You will also be introduced to the various sources of financing. The sources profiled throughout this Chapter are the most common ones you will encounter. But keep in mind that not every financing option has been covered. (For example, raising money by selling shares or interests to the public is beyond the scope of this book.)

IDEA 7: Project the Amount of Capital Needed for Start Up

In Chapter 1, you learned the necessary parts of a business plan. The purpose of the plan is not only to provide a blueprint for building the business. It also serves as a guide for determining how much capital is needed to get the business started. Even if you do not write a comprehensive business plan (a step that is not recommended to skip), you should at least complete the worksheet for figuring the amount of start up capital you require.

Worksheet for Projecting Start Up Costs

Start up items	*Estimated cost*
Equipment	$
Computers, telephones, copiers, faxes	
Office furniture and fixtures	
Machinery (for manufacturing businesses)	

Start up items	*Estimated cost*
Inventory (for product oriented businesses)	
Supplies	
Stationery, business cards, office supplies	
Professional fees	
Legal fees to set up a corporation, etc.	
Accounting fees to set up books and accounts	
Insurance	
Fire or liability insurance on property/products	
Workers' compensation	
Disability insurance	
Licenses/permits	
Occupancy costs	
Deposit on a lease	
Remodeling costs to ready the premises	
Deposit on utilities	
Initial operating expenses	
Salaries/wages (and payroll taxes)	
Utilities	
Advertising/promotion	
Unanticipated miscellaneous expenses	
TOTAL START UP COSTS	$

If you are starting a business from ground zero, you want to know how much you will need to open your doors and sustain your operations until such time as revenue can be expected to flow in.

Equipment

You need to look at several categories of equipment. First, all businesses today need to consider buying technological equipment—computers and peripherals, faxes, telephones, cellular phones, personal communication systems (PCSs), pagers, and copying machines. It is almost impossible to run a business—any kind of business—without a computer today. The kind of computer you want to get will depend not only on your budget but, more importantly, upon the type of business you are going into. For example, if you are starting a newsletter, your computer needs to be sophisticated enough to produce professional-looking documents. In order to achieve this, you may need certain software, a laser printer and perhaps a modem. If your business entails heavy number-crunching (if, for example, you are in marketing or financial services), your computer must be powerful enough to handle your projected workload. Take all this into account in making projections. You may be able to reduce your initial outlay if you can use equipment you already own (such as a cellular phone). There are many sources available which can help you determine what kind of computer would best serve your needs. Consult your library or a computer retail store for more information.

Another category of equipment to consider is office furniture and fixtures (e.g., lighting). Again, all businesses (manufacturing as well as service businesses) need an office in which to process bills, order supplies and handle other administrative tasks. How much you spend on office furniture and fixtures depends not only on your budget, but also on the type of business. For example, if the public will see your offices, then more money needs to be spent on furniture and fixtures than if the office is a back room used only by you for administrative tasks.

Other equipment needs depends upon your type of business. If you are in the retail business, for example, you will need a cash register or registers and display cases. If you are a craftsperson, you may need special tools. If you are manufacturing a product, you may need special equipment.

In projecting start up costs for equipment, keep in mind that the business need not necessarily buy all that is required. In many cases, it may be possible (and make good sense) to lease the equipment. Buying versus leasing is discussed in Chapter 7.

Inventory

If you are in a production business—a retail store, a wholesale operation, or a mail-order catalog—you need to stock up on items that you will be selling. How much inventory you need to start is an important question to consider. You do not want to order more than you need to get going because it will use up your limited capital too quickly. On the other hand, you do not want to order less than you need to get started because you may be paying more per unit than you would if you had ordered more. The larger the order, the greater the price reduction you can generally command from the supplier. In order to estimate closely the amount of inventory needed to open your doors (and the cost that this will entail), you should have an understanding of the "cash flow cycle." This is basically the time over which inventory is ordered, paid for, sold, and for which funds are received. The cash flow cycle is explained in Chapter 5.

Supplies

All types of businesses need various supplies. Most require office supplies (even where the business does not revolve around an office), such as stationery, business cards, staples, paper clips, file folders and paper. In Chapter 12, you will learn about a number of ways to reduce the cost of these supplies.

You may also need supplies that are specific to your business. For example, if you run a cleaning service, you need to start with a number of different cleaning supplies—cleansers, ammonia, mops, paper towels, sponges and other supplies. Again, as is true in the case of inventory, you need enough to get started but not too much. You do not want to tie up your capital in excess supplies that will not be used for months.

Professional Fees

If your business is set up in any way other than as a sole proprietorship (the type of entity that arises when a single individual goes into business and does not incorporate), you probably need the services of an attorney. This can be a significant start up cost. Ask the attorney in advance what professional fees will be charged and what services will be provided. Obviously, the fees will depend to some extent on the type of business you set up, your location and what other legal tasks you want the attorney to do. In addition to fees paid to attorneys, there may also be state filing or registration fees (such as incorporation fees).

You may also want an accountant to set up your books and records to get you going. Again, there is a fee for this service. You may want to have accounting or bookkeeping services continue on a monthly basis. Factor this cost (in the start up phase) into the amount of start up capital needed.

You may also need to incur other professional fees in the start up phase (e.g., assistance from marketing firms or someone to help you write the business plan).

Insurance

Today, a business needs a number of different types of insurance to start and operate. You need liability insurance to cover your business in the event of personal injury or damage to property on your premises. If you plan to operate the business from your home, be sure to adjust your homeowner's insurance in addition to obtaining the necessary business coverage. If the business has employees, you are required to have workers' compensation and disability insurance. The amount of this coverage is estimated by the carrier based on the nature of the business, the size of the payroll and the company's revenue. You also have to pay unemployment insurance for employees, although this type of insurance may be viewed as more of a payroll tax than as private insurance. This should be factored into initial operating expenses (discussed later in this chapter). Depending on the type of business, you may also be required to carry product liability insurance. For example, if you sell a product to a store that will sell it to the public, the store may require you to have product liability insurance as protection for the store against any possible claims from its customers. (If a customer sues the store because of a defect in your product, the store will, in turn, look to you for payment.) Insurance is covered in more detail in Chapter 11.

You may also want to consider "business interruption insurance" to cover your payroll, rent/ mortgage, utilities, and other operating expenses if the business is temporarily shut down because of a fire, hurricane or other natural disaster or other event.

In estimating start up costs for insurance, consider that you may be required to pay for an entire year's coverage for workers compensation or disability (even though you do not yet know the size of your payroll or your annual revenue.) At the end of the year, the carrier will conduct an insurance "audit" in which it looks at actual payroll and revenue and determines exactly what should have been paid. If you overestimated your payroll and/or revenue, you may be entitled to a refund (which is generally applied toward premiums for the following year). If you underestimated these amounts, you will have to pay the difference at that time. In making an estimate, it is advisable to err on the side of too little, rather than too much in order to minimize your start up costs.

It may be helpful to talk things over with a knowledgeable insurance agent. Make sure the agent is proficient in business insurance. The agent who sells you your personal car insurance may not be the best person to advise you on your business insurance needs.

Licenses and Permits

Some businesses may require special licenses or permits. Be sure to have all required licenses and permits in place when you start (so that you can avoid fines or penalties). Check with your state (or agency issuing licenses/permits) to determine costs. Also, check with your city or town to find out about local licensing and permit requirements.

If you are selling a product, you may have to get a manufacturer's ID code assigned to you by the Uniform Product Code Council. Some stores will not sell merchandise that does not have a UPI code. To find out about applying for your ID and for the fee schedule, call the Uniform Product Code Council at (513) 435-3870.

Occupancy Costs

In the start up phase, you may have to spend a significant amount of capital in getting the premises ready to open your doors for business. Consider a number of occupancy costs you may be required to pay:

- Deposit on a lease (first month/last month or some other arrangement)

- Deposit on utilities (electric company deposit/telephone deposit)

- Remodeling costs to get the premises ready for your business. This can include lighting, electrical work, plumbing, cabinetry, painting, tile, linoleum or carpeting and other fixtures and alterations.

In figuring occupancy costs, also consider any costs incurred to comply with zoning requirements (such as legal fees to obtain variances). Check with the building department for the city/town in which you plan to operate.

Initial Operating Expenses

Until the business can produce revenue to cover expenses, start up costs should be sufficient to pay for salaries (and payroll taxes—FICA, FUTA, state unemployment insurance), utilities, advertising, promotion and other short-term expenses. For example, if the business will be paying for the owner's gas and car expenses for business mileage, be sure to include this in the estimate.

If you borrow funds to start a business, factor into initial operating expenses the cost of debt service: what will be paid (principal and interest) to the lender on a monthly basis during the start up phase.

Finally, be sure to factor in your own salary. This is the amount that is necessary for you to live on. Unless you have another way to cover your personal expenses (such as a spouse's salary), you need to provide funds for this purpose.

Did You Know. . .

According to the National Bureau of Professional Management Consultants, those who start consulting businesses should be prepared to subsidize themselves 100% in the first year, 70% in the second year and 20% in the third year. Consultants should be self-sufficient (have enough income from the business to cover business expenses and their own salaries) after the third year.

Unanticipated Miscellaneous Expenses

Some expenditures defy classification. The business may have to pay for certain travel expenditures that come up unexpectedly. The types of miscellaneous expenses will naturally vary with the type of business. Be sure to allow for a sufficient cash cushion to carry you through the start up phase.

If you are buying an existing business, you probably do not need as much capital for your start up phase. You will not need most equipment and inventory; that is part of what you are paying for when you buy the business. You may not need many supplies. Still, there are some start up costs to consider. You will probably need to incur professional fees (attorneys and accountants) to change ownership. You will also need new stationery reflecting your new ownership. You will need initial operating expenses to cover payroll, utilities and advertising. Since the business is producing revenue, the estimates for these expenses should be substantially less for those who buy an existing business. Still, the company may undergo a period of reduced revenue while the change in ownership is being introduced. And you should budget for unanticipated miscellaneous expenses—even re-painting the name on the door to reflect the new ownership.

IDEA 8: Use Your Savings to Start the Business

Looking in your bank account may not reveal an amount equal to what you have projected to be your start up costs. Still, you may be surprised to find that you have personal savings that may not readily come to mind, but that you can tap for start up costs. The following section outlines some of your options.

Did You Know. . .

The SBA estimates that 80% of new businesses start up with only the resources of the owner or owners.

Home Equity Loans

If you have owned your home for some time and have paid your mortgage, or if your home has appreciated substantially, you may be sitting on considerable equity which you would be able to pocket if you sold your home today (after repaying existing mortgages). To get a rough idea of what your equity may be, ask a local real estate agent to provide you with an informal appraisal by telling you what homes comparable to yours in the area have sold for recently. With home equity loans, you can borrow against the equity in your home and use the funds for any purpose. Generally, a lender will make a home equity loan up to 75% or 80% of the present equity in the home because the loan is secured by the home itself.

Example: The market value of your home is $200,000 and you have a current mortgage balance of $100,000. A lender will make a home equity loan of 75% of the present equity. You would, under these circumstances, be able to borrow $75,000 against your home (current equity of $200,000−$100,000 mortgage × 75%).

Interest on the first $100,000 of home equity debt is fully deductible regardless of the purpose for which the funds are used. Generally, loans taken to start a business are treated like those made for investment regardless of the amount borrowed. As such, interest on these loans is deductible only to the extent of net investment income (e.g., income from interest and dividends). However, if it can be shown that the purpose for starting the business was to provide a current income (rather than a mere investment), you may be able to deduct all interest as business interest on which there is no limitation.

There is a great deal of paperwork involved in obtaining a home equity loan. Interest rates and terms of repayment vary with each lender. Interest rates on home equity loans (which are merely second mortgages on a personal residence) generally run higher than interest rates on first mortgages. However, there may be introductory interest rates or other breaks that make these loans attractive. There is usually a maximum 15-year repayment period, but again, repayment terms may differ. You may have the option of repaying interest for a certain number of years and then commence principal repayment. Before signing on with one lender, shop around for the best terms.

Of course, the drawback to borrowing against your home is the risk that you will be unable to repay the loan and could lose your home. Many people are adverse to jeopardizing their home ownership with a loan used for a business venture. Before taking out a home equity loan, make sure you fully understand this risk. Even if you decide to use a home equity loan, be aware that there may be loan fees and other closing costs associated with this type of borrowing. The amount you realize from this loan which can be put into your business may not be the full amount of the proceeds you must repay (the difference being those fees and closing costs).

Loans From Life Insurance Policies

If you have had a whole life or universal life policy in effect for some time, you may have built up cash surrender value in the policy. Ask your insurance agent how much cash you have in your policy. You can borrow from your life insurance policy on very favorable terms. Interest rates on policy loans are generally the lowest type of loans available. You do not even have to repay the amount borrowed; if you die before repayment, the outstanding balance is simply subtracted from the amount your beneficiary receives. Of course, your insurance may be intended to protect your family, so keep in mind that a loan diminishes your family's protection (until the loan is repaid). If you do repay the loan, you can do so whenever it is convenient to you (when you have the funds available).

A loan against your life insurance policy is very easy to arrange—simply ask your insurance company for it. After signing a simple form, a check is issued. Generally, a policy loan can be arranged (from the time of the request to the time the check is issued) within a week.

Loans From 401(k) Plans or Other Qualified Retirement Plans

If you have worked for an employer who maintains a 401(k) plan or other qualified retirement plan in which you have participated, you may be able to borrow against your vested benefits in the plan. Be sure the plan allows borrowing. Check with the plan administrator to determine whether you can borrow, how much you can borrow and what the repayment terms will be. In general, the greatest amount you can borrow from your plan is 50% of your vested account balance or $50,000, whichever is less. If you have already taken loans, then the $50,000 limit is reduced by the amount of prior loans that have not yet been repaid. To get a loan from a qualified retirement plan, ask your plan administrator (ask your employer who to contact). Generally, you must complete a simple application before the check is issued. Interest charged on the loan is usually at a favorable rate (less, for example, than interest on a personal bank loan).

In taking a loan from a qualified retirement plan, be sure that the loan meets the requirements necessary to avoid having it treated as a taxable distribution. The loan must be repaid in no more than five years (a longer repayment period applies only to borrowing for the purchase of a home). The loan must be in writing and require that principal be repaid in equal amounts over the term of the loan. Adequate interest must be charged on the loan. If these requirements are not satisfied, then the loan may be treated as a distribution from the plan, which is taxable.

Warning

Borrowing from a qualified retirement plan is generally advisable only if you are planning on using the funds for a sideline business. If you leave your employment to start a business, then you are required to repay the loan from the plan in full. If you do not, then the employer may reduce your vested account balance by the amount of the outstanding debt. This reduction is treated as a distribution which is taxable for income tax purposes and may even be subject to tax penalties as well.

Go "On Margin" Against Your Securities

Your savings may not be in the bank. Instead, you may own stocks and bonds, perhaps even a considerable portfolio. You do not have to sell these securities to raise capital. You may be able to borrow against their value at favorable terms. Simply sign a "margin agreement" consenting to the terms of the margin loan and a check can be issued. You can usually borrow up to 50% of the value of your equities (stocks) and up to 90% of government securities.

Example: You own publicly traded stocks worth $100,000 and Treasury bonds worth $50,000. You would be able to borrow $95,000 ($100,000 equities × 50% + $50,000 government securities × 90%).

Interest charged on margin accounts is only a small amount above the prime rate. Of course, if the value of your securities drops and you have borrowed the maximum, you may be forced to sell a portion of your securities to cover your "margin call." In other words, in the example above, if the value of the stocks drops to $90,000, then the maximum loan could only be $90,000 ($100,000 × 50% + $50,000 × 90%). You would have to sell sufficient securities to pay off $5,000 of the loan ($95,000 – $90,000).

Personal savings alone may not be sufficient to adequately support a business start up. If you find that your personal savings do not cover what you have projected to be your start up costs, you might not want to attempt to start on just what you have. You may well find that your business will go under (because you are undercapitalized) and you will have lost your savings. If you find your personal savings to be insufficient to get you started properly, you may have to use both personal savings and other sources of financing. Look at the other ideas in this chapter to find additional sources of financing.

IDEA 9: Get a Personal Loan

You may be able to a personal loan from your local bank or credit union. This is an unsecured loan based on your credit-worthiness. Do you have a good credit history? Will you be able to repay the loan? These are the two key things that any lender will want to know. If you are working and using a personal loan to start a sideline business, then your salary may be sufficient to convince a bank of your ability to repay.

A personal loan may be granted regardless of how sound (or unsound) your business concept may be. Of course, a bank cares about what the money is being used for (a bank will not, for example, lend money if it knows it will be used to gamble at the Atlantic City casinos). The loan application typically asks how the money will be used (to start a business, to buy a franchise), but a personal loan application does not get into details about the business in the same way as a business loan. The chief concern of the bank is your ability to repay.

There are two drawbacks to consider with a personal loan. First, you are personally liable to repay it. If the business fails, you must still repay the loan. If you are unable to repay the loan, the lender can look to your personal assets—your house, your stocks and bonds—for repayment. Second, the interest rate charged on a personal loan may be higher than the rate charged on other types of loans. A personal loan should not be the first type of financing to consider.

IDEA 10: Apply for a Business Loan

Commercial banks provide business loans both for starting a business and for expansion of an existing one. Savings and loan associations and thrifts do not offer business loans. While you may have your home mortgage with your neighborhood savings bank, you must go to a commercial bank for a business loan. If you are unfamiliar with commercial banks in your area (such as Bank of America, Wells Fargo, Chase, Citibank), look in the Yellow Pages for the listings of commercial banks near you.

To increase your chances of getting a loan, it is advisable to look for commercial banks that are aggressively looking to lend to small businesses. Some banks only deal with large, well-established customers. Others, such as Wells Fargo, have begun to aggressively seek customers wishing to receive small business loans.

Did You Know. . .

In 1995, Wells Fargo loans to small business owners increased 61% over the prior year by soliciting line-of-credit loans as small as $5,000 to small business owners. It offers a one-page application that cuts the time needed to prepare the application from 12 hours to just 15 minutes.

How do you know which banks will be most receptive to making a small business loan? Ask other small businesses in your area who handles their loans. Also ask at the SBA's Small Business Development Center in your area. Call the SBA for a referral to the Center nearest you (800) 827-5722.

There are two types of business loans: Short-term loans and long-term loans. A short-term loan is one that must be paid back within one year. A short-term loan is typically used for working capital, to carry accounts receivable and revolving lines of credit. Long-term loans last more than one year, with the length of time depending upon what the money is used for. Long-term loans can be used to cover start up costs, major expansion projects, the purchase of plants and equipment and even vehicle purchases. The rates charged on commercial loans depend upon the terms of the loan and on numerous other factors.

If you are seeking start up capital, be prepared to provide the bank with a sound loan proposal. A loan proposal is nothing more than another term for a business plan. (See Chapter 1 for details on preparing a business plan.) The plan should show how you intend to spend the money, and how you expect to pay it back. Be sure to include a number of ancillary documents requested by the lender, such as personal financial statements for all the owners.

The key to obtaining a business loan for a business that does not yet have a track record—a start up business—is the financial viability of the owners. Do the owners have a good personal credit history? Do the owners have assets (a house, stocks and bonds) that can be viewed as collateral for a loan?

Warning

Regardless of how the business is organized (e.g., a partnership, corporation), the bank will almost certainly require all owners to personally guarantee the loan. Thus, if the business fails to repay the loan, the owners must make good on the debt. This is a serious commitment on the part of owners. It could jeopardize their personal residence and life savings. Unfortunately, there is just no getting around this personal guarantee requirement. The only time that this requirement may be waived is if the loan proceeds are to be used to purchase assets that a bank could look to for repayment. Thus, if the loan proceeds are used to buy a plant or heavy equipment, the bank may be willing to forego the personal guarantee of owners.

If you are seeking capital for an existing business, the bank is primarily interested in the company's track record for the past three to five years. This is a strong indication of the company's ability to repay the loan. Again, a detailed loan proposal must accompany an application for a business loan.

The process for obtaining a business loan can be timely and complicated. There are numerous forms to complete, and banks generally do not make rapid decisions about business loan applications. It may be weeks before a loan commitment is made.

If you do not get a loan from the first bank, do not assume that no bank will give you a loan. Try to find out why your application was rejected. Maybe you can correct some problems and get a loan from another bank.

IDEA 11: Get a Small Business Administration Loan

There is no such thing as an SBA loan (a loan from the Small Business Administration). The SBA does not lend money directly to small businesses. SBA loans are loans "sponsored" by the SBA: they do not come directly from the government, they are given by commercial banks. The SBA induces banks to lend to small businesses by guaranteeing a percentage of the loan. The SBA will guarantee 75% of the loan, up to a maximum guarantee of $375,000 (for a $500,000 loan). (There are some lines-of-credit loans that can go higher.) For smaller loans of up to $100,000, the SBA will guarantee 80% of the loan.

Did You Know. . .

The average SBA guaranteed loan is $175,000.

There is also a relatively new "Microloan Program" sponsored by the SBA for loans up to $25,000. These loans are obtained through nonprofit organizations.

SBA guaranteed loans are both short-term and long-term (the distinction between these loans is explained earlier in this chapter). The average term of an SBA sponsored loan is eight years.

Common SBA Loan Programs

Currently there are several different SBA loan programs. The most common types include:

Commercial mortgages. The greatest percentage of SBA loans are taken to finance the purchase, construction or refinance of "owner occupied" commercial properties. Businesses looking to acquire a plant, for example, may be able to finance up to 90%

of the cost, with repayment over 25 years. In comparison, regular commercial loans will only finance up to 75% over much shorter periods of time. This type of loan cannot be used by a business that simply invests in commercial properties. However, the owner need only use up to 51% of the space to be considered "owner occupied"; the remainder of the property can be leased to third parties.

Capital term loans. These loans can be used to obtain capital to start a business or to buy a franchise. Thus, for example, they can be used for operating capital. There is usually a 7-year repayment period.

Equipment loans. Businesses that need to buy expensive equipment—heavy machinery, sophisticated computers, extensive telephone systems—may want to get this type of SBA sponsored financing. The repayment period is geared to the depreciable life of the equipment being acquired, up to a maximum period of 10 years. In comparison, commercial loans for equipment generally have a 3–5 year repayment period.

Greenline program. Existing businesses that need working capital can get a revolving line of credit. The line is based on the company's accounts receivable and/or inventory. The company borrows against these assets and, when it repays the loan, it can re-borrow as needed. The line of credit can run for 5 years. In comparison, lines of credit from commercial sources are generally payable on demand or for a term up to one year.

Low Doc loans. The Low Doc loans require only minimal documentation. It is not a separate type of loan, but a process that can be used for any of the loan programs discussed above, except for Greenline loans, for amounts up to $100,000. The application form is a one-page form. You attach to this the business plan, personal financial statements of owners and whatever other documentation is requested by the lending institution. The bank making the SBA guaranteed loan makes the loan determination by completing a one-page analysis of the loan request. The Low Doc not only makes the loan process easier, it also cuts the approval time to as short as 48 hours!

Fa$trak loans. Under a two-year pilot program that began in February 1995, another simplified process is available for loans of less than $100,000. Lenders use their own forms and can apply the SBA guarantee without first obtaining the SBA's approval for the loan. However, the guarantee is limited to 50% instead of the usual 80%.

   Getting an SBA loan is not as easy as it sounds. The process can be quite lengthy. Generally, you must apply for a regular business loan from a commercial bank. Then, if you are turned down, the bank will work with you to obtain an SBA guaranteed loan.

To apply for a loan, be prepared to show several things:

- *You must show that your have a reasonable stake in the business.* This means that you have already invested at least 25% to 50% of the amount of the loan you are requesting. The bank will not finance all of your business. You must first demonstrate that you are willing to put yourself on the line.

- *You must have a good credit rating.* This is proven by having a good credit report, a solid work history and, perhaps, letters of recommendation.

- *You need a good business plan.* The plan must show that you understand the business and are committed to its success. The business plan elements explained in Chapter 1 are modeled after the type of business plan required for an SBA guaranteed loan.

- *You should have the experience and training necessary to run your business.* Again, your prior work history can support this requirement.

- *You must show how you plan to repay the loan.* This means showing that the business will have sufficient cash flow to make monthly loan payments.

To inquire about SBA loan programs, call the SBA at (800) 827-5722 or visit its Internet web site at http://www.sbaonline.sba.gov/.

504 Loans

The SBA also sponsors a 504 loan program which is available not through banks, but from SBA Certified Development Companies. Certified Development Companies (CDCs) are private non-profit organizations in various localities that help small businesses. The 504 program is geared for small and medium-sized companies that need capital to acquire space or equipment. The loan is only for long-term fixed assets (e.g., plants and machinery). The company must already have a proven track record of profitability. Therefore, it is not suitable for seed money. Also, the loan cannot be used to refinance or restructure existing debt. Limits on the amount of a 504 loan can be increased under certain circumstances.

Typically, the 504 loan process takes between 60 and 90 days. A local Certified Development Company can advise you on the 504 loan package if you wish to apply. You can ask the SBA about a Certified Development Company near you. Or you can call the National Association of Development Companies at (800) 972-2504 for a referral to a Certified Development Company in your area.

Which SBA Loan Program Is Right for You?

SBA Loan Program	Dollar Limit	Start Up Money	Expansion Capital
Commercial mortgages	Up to $500,000	Yes	Yes
Equipment term loans	Up to $500,000	Yes	Yes
Capital term loans	Up to $500,000	Yes	Yes
Greenline program	Up to $750,000	No	Yes
Low Doc program	Less than $100,000	Yes	Yes
Fa$trak program	Less than $100,000	Yes	Yes
Microloan program	Up to $25,000	Yes	Yes
504 loans	Up to $500,000	No	Yes

IDEA 12: Check Out Grants and Awards for Which Your Business May Be Eligible

There are many different types of grants and awards that a business can apply for to obtain money to help you get started, to do research or to expand facilities. Private foundations and the government (federal, state and even local) provide grant money and awards to various businesses or business owners. The best part of getting a grant or award is that you do not have to pay it back. It is not a loan, but rather a source of funding that is to be used for the purpose intended—free money!

Foundations

Private foundations—there are thousands of them—are a source of capital to get your business going or to fulfill your expansion needs. Private foundations give grants to businesses that meet a specific criteria reflecting the foundations' areas of interest. For example, they may be looking to assist a certain type of business or foster minority ownership. It pays to investigate the grants for which your business may be eligible.

One of the prime sources of locating grant money over $5,000 is *The Foundation Directory*, published by the Foundation Center in New York City. It is updated annually, and can be found at local libraries. The book provides a complete listing of foundations by category and by state. The directory contains the foundations' fields of interest, allowing you to know whether your business fits their profile. It also provides a listing of guidebooks that tell you how to apply for the grant.

(Additional information about the Foundation Center, a list of its field offices, a publication catalog and more can be found at its web site at http://fdncenter.org.) Some grants are made for capital costs and for "seed money." Seed money can be used to cover salary and operating costs to start up new projects.

Typically, the application process for a grant is started by submitting a letter of intent to the foundation. The letter is a general outline of your proposed project, the nature of your business and a brief description of the key people involved. Explain how the grant money will be used and provide a general estimate of the total money requested.

There is no way to predict how long the grant process will take. Some foundations operate on a grant cycle (they make grants at certain times of the year) and will only consider applications submitted within specified periods. Others operate less formally and will consider applications when submitted. Some foundations will acknowledge a letter of intent and tell the applicant whether to continue the process; others may not even respond. If a foundation shows interest in a letter of intent, an applicant may be asked to submit a more complete proposal. Generally, a business plan (as explained in Chapter 1) will contain the necessary information to satisfy the foundation's requirements.

If you get a grant, be prepared to submit interim reports showing the foundation that the money is being used as expected. You will also be required to submit a final report at some point in addition to having an audit by the foundation to assure that the funds were used for the purpose for which the grant was given.

Another source of "free" funding is prizes and awards given by private organizations, as well as by government agencies, to existing businesses that have demonstrated a certain proficiency or otherwise meet special requirements. A complete listing of prizes and awards can be found in *Awards, Honors and Prizes* (Gale Research) which may be found in your local library system.

To receive an award or prize, a business must usually make an application. The process for obtaining the different awards or prizes varies, so investigate the requirements with the donor organization. In checking out sources of grant money or awards, be sure to note that some can be used by start ups, while others are only for established businesses.

If receiving a grant or award sounds too good to be true, there is a reason. Grants and awards are not easy to come by. Competition for grant money is stiff. Foundations give grants only for projects in which they are interested. You simply may not fit the profile. While the grant avenue should certainly be explored, do not count on it as your first source of funding.

Government Grants

The federal government also gives grants to small businesses engaged in certain areas or industries. For example, the Environmental Protection Agency (EPA) has recently made a number of grants to existing small businesses (not to startups) developing ways to reduce pollution (e.g., drinking water treatment, waste management, pollution prevention). These grants are limited to "small businesses" (defined as those with less than 500 employees). Similar grants may be forthcoming in the future. Check with the Small Business Innovative Research Program hotline at (919) 541-5293 or the EPA's web site at http://www.epa.gov/docs/ord.

State and local governments may also provide grants to small businesses.

Two guidebooks for locating government grant money are *The Action Guide to Government Grants, Loans and Giveaways* by George Chelekis (A Perigee Book 1993) and *Government Give-aways for Entrepreneurs* by Matthew Lesko (Information USA, Inc. 1992). These and other guidebooks can provide a good starting point for finding sources of government grants. However, be aware that the information contained in these guides is subject to frequent change, and may not be accurate by the time you read it.

IDEA 13: Get Woman/Minority/Handicapped Certification to Qualify for Special Programs

If you are a woman, a member of a minority, or are handicapped you may be eligible for special financing programs. Some of these programs are government sponsored while others are from private sources. If you think your business may qualify for special programs, be sure to check the eligibility requirements carefully.

Did You Know. . .

Women-owned businesses grew by 80% between 1990 and 1996.

Women and Minorities

If you meet the qualifications of the program, you may be able to get certification for business as a Woman or Minority Business Enterprise (W/MBE). This can qualify you for special programs, loans, grants and other assistance.

Each lending institution or organization offering special W/MBE assistance may have its own requirements for certification. As a general rule, however, most have the following requirements:

- *At least 51% ownership by women/minority individuals.* Look at the total equity ownership in the company. If the majority of the company is owned by women or minority individuals, then the ownership test is satisfied.

- *Women/minority individuals run the day-to-day operations of the business.* They must be involved in decision-making. They cannot simply be silent investors.

- *Women/minority individuals have a "real and substantial" investment in the firm.* The women or minority individuals cannot be "fronts" for non-minority owners. They cannot, for example, simply hold stock that is really owned by non-minority owners.

- *The company is "independent."* The company cannot be too closely tied with non-minority businesses. For example, if the sole client of the company is a non-minority company, then the company is not considered a W/MBE.

SBA's 8(a) Program

Financing assistance is available to certain minority enterprises. The program's definition of "minority" is a business at least 51% owned by individual(s) who are socially and economically disadvantaged citizens of the U.S., American Indians, or Alaskan natives. However, brokers, packagers and franchisers are not eligible for the 8(a) Program. The SBA conducts group seminars to explain the program in general and the certification process in particular.

National Association of Women Business Owners and Wells Fargo Bank

NAWBO and Wells Fargo Bank have made available a fund of about $1 billion for the purpose of offering financing to profitable women-owned businesses seeking money for expansion. For information, call (212) 916-1473.

Handicapped Individuals

The SBA provides a special loan program for businesses owned by disabled individuals as well as businesses operated in the interests of disabled individuals. Such individuals may be eligible for special financing under a program called HAL-2. Eligibility requirements include:

- The business qualifies as small under SBA criteria.

- The business is not engaged in the speculation or investment in rental real estate.

- It is 100% owned by one or more handicapped individuals. This is defined as a person who has a permanent physical, mental or emotional impairment, defect, ailment, disease or major disability. Such disability must keep the individual from competing on a par with non-handicapped competitors.

- The handicapped individual must actively participate in the management of the business (i.e., absentee owners are not eligible).

How the business is organized (sole proprietorship, partnership, corporation) is not a determining factor in eligibility.

Businesses operated in the interests of the handicapped

Another SBA financing program related to the handicapped is designed for businesses (both profit and nonprofit) that are specifically geared toward the handicapped. The program is called HAL-1. Eligibility requirements include:

- The business or organization must operate in the interests of the handicapped. This is evidenced by the business's by-laws, incorporation papers, certificate of tax-exempt status by the IRS or recognition by the U.S. Secretary of Labor or state vocational rehabilitation agency.

- At least 75% of the direct work involved is done by handicapped persons and the net income of the business cannot benefit any stockholder or other individual.

IDEA 14: Get a Private Loan

If your savings cannot carry you and you cannot get a loan from a commercial bank (business loan or SBA sponsored loan), consider seeking a loan from private sources. Your local newspaper probably contains advertisements from persons looking to make business loans. You can also find sources of loans on the Internet.

There are two main drawbacks to private loans. Generally, they will only be given where the proceeds are used to acquire equipment or other property that can serve as collateral for the loan. (If you have sufficient personal assets to serve as collateral for a loan, you probably can get a loan directly from a bank and do not need to go to a private source.) Thus, a private loan may not be the right source for getting start up capital if you are going into a business that needs to spend a lot on inventory or on promotion because there will be nothing from the proceeds to serve as collateral for the loan.

Second, the interest rate and pay back period on a private loan may not be on the most favorable terms. The interest rate is generally higher than the rate charged by banks. Also, the private lender may want to be paid back faster than a bank.

Still, if your credit rating is not good (so that a bank will turn you down for a loan), you might consider looking for a loan from a private investor.

Warning

As a general precaution, be sure to have an attorney review the loan agreement with a private lender before you sign it.

IDEA 15: Seek Financing Through a Small Business Investment Company or a Specialized Small Business Investment Company

The SBA licenses Small Business Investment Companies (SBICs), privately-managed firms, to provide financing for small business. These are not usually straight loans. Rather, SBICs make long-term loans that involve options to buy equity or are structured as convertible debentures (debt that can be converted to stock). Financing is tailored to a particular business's needs, so terms vary considerably.

In order to obtain funding, a business plan is required. (See Chapter 1 for details on writing a business plan.) However, if you just want to inquire about the possibility of financing, you do not need a plan. As a small business, you probably meet SBIC eligibility requirements. SBICs can lend to companies whose net worth is less than $18 million and whose average after-tax earnings are less than $6 million for the past two years.

For a listing of the SBICs in your area (there are about 175 nationwide), call the National Association of Small Business Investment Companies at (703) 683-1601.

Specialized Small Business Investment Companies can provide financing for companies that have a majority ownership by socially or economically disadvantaged persons. Generally, such financing is straight equity rather than loans. To find out more about SSBICs, contact the National Association of Investment Companies (NAIC) at (202) 289-4336.

IDEA 16: Bring in Other Investors

If you are unable to get outside financing on a reasonable basis to supplement your savings, you may want to bring in other investors. This allows you to put all the capital you raise into the business without having to worry about immediate repayment (making monthly payments of interest and principal on a loan). You may also want to bring in other investors if you think they can offer to the business the expertise that you are lacking. You may, for example, be knowledgeable about marketing but want to have a co-owner who knows about financial matters.

The extent to which other investors participate in the day-to-day operations of the business depends upon how you set up the arrangement. The investors may prefer to remain "silent partners" who do not get involved in daily business activities. Instead, they are looking for a return on their investment down the road, when the business can be sold or even "taken public" (with stock sold to the general public on a listed exchange).

Did You Know. . .

Typically, private investors are looking for a minimum internal rate of return of 30% and hope to realize their return within three to five years.

Alternatively, some investors may want to take a more active role. They may want to work with you in the business, reaping their reward from their investment both in the form of salary and benefits as well as a potential capital appreciation on their ownership interest. Even if they do not work in operations, it is common for an outside investor to demand a role on the board of directors.

The extent to which investors get to share in the ownership of the business depends upon what you negotiate. What are they demanding in exchange for their cash? What part of your ownership are you willing to give up in exchange for their investment? There are no set guidelines for making this arrangement.

There is a downside to bringing in outside investors. It dilutes your ownership of the company. You may not be able to unilaterally decide where the company is going and how it should get there. You may need the investors' approval.

While it is not uncommon for many outside investors to express interest in your company, getting one to actually give you cash is another matter. As a minimum, they want to see a business plan. They want to test out some of your claims in the business plan (perhaps looking at the market or trying the product). The process can be lengthy, with final agreement taking up to six months. However, this long waiting period can serve a useful purpose. It gives you time to get to know the investors, and vice versa. This can alert you to potential conflicts in business goals and philosophy that could pop up later on, giving you the opportunity to work out differences before joining forces or deciding to part ways before it's too late.

If you choose to bring in outside investors, be sure to use a buy-sell agreement or other document to restrict their ability to transfer their interests to others. You want to make sure that these investors do not sell their interests to others (perhaps bringing in parties that are unfavorable to you).

IDEA 17: Look into Venture Capital

As a practical matter, small businesses are not prime candidates for help from venture capital firms. These firms are looking for businesses that will be able to return to them a handsome profit in a relatively short period of time. They are not interested in investing in the corner deli or a consulting business.

If, however, your business is the type that is of interest to venture capitalists—a new technology, a hot product—you just might interest a venture capital firm. In seeking their infusion of cash, however, remember that in exchange for investing in your business, they take a sizable percentage of equity. Many small business owners do not want to give up control. Whether this preference makes sense depends upon the situation. It may be advisable for an owner to keep 10% of something rather than 100% of nothing. If the venture capital means the difference between making a business go or not, then the choice seems rather clear.

Venture capitalists do more than take a sizable ownership position in your business. They may also have a major say in how the business is run. Of course, venture capital firms differ widely, and some take more active roles than others. Understand that you will have an ongoing relationship with the venture capital firm for a long time, maybe ten years or more. Be sure that you can work with the firm and understand the synergy.

If you think your business may be attractive to venture capitalists, complete a business plan (as explained in Chapter 1). Be clear on what you want from them and what you are willing to give up. Venture capital firms see hundreds of business plans each month. Yours must stand out. For venture capitalists, perhaps the key element of a business is its management team. If they have confidence in you, they may think your business worthy of their capital.

To locate venture capitalists that may be interested in your type of business, contact venture associations or organizations listed in Appendix A.

Also check out *Pratt's Guide to Venture Capital* in your local library. Finally, check out Internet web sites for venture capitalists.

IDEA 18: Borrow from Family or Friends

If you do not have enough savings of your own or sufficient collateral to command a commercial loan, you may want to ask family or friends to help you out.

In borrowing from family or friends, be sure to observe formalities—primarily for their protection. Draw up a loan agreement, set up a repayment schedule, and specify an adequate interest rate. There are important tax-related reasons for these formalities. First, if no interest rate is charged, the loan may be viewed as a "below market loan." Under the tax law, the lender will be deemed to have received the amount of interest that should have been charged (and is taxable on this amount). The amount of interest that should have been charged is the "applicable federal interest rate" for the term of the loan. These rates are published by the IRS monthly and vary with the type of loan: long-term (over nine years), mid-term (over three years but not over nine years) or short-term (three years or less). In the case of demand loans, which are payable when the lender asks for payment, the short-term rate should be used. Also, if you are unable to repay the loan, the lender will want to claim a deduction for the loan as a bad debt, but will have a difficult time proving to the IRS that a loan, rather than a gift, was intended by the advance without a written loan agreement.

The downside to borrowing from family or friends is the friction and bad feelings that can ensue if the business fails and you do not repay the loan. Make sure that the party you are borrowing from can afford to lose the money if you fail to repay (that the party's standard of living would not be adversely affected by a default on your part). Also, be sure to explain the risk of making the loan to your relative or friend.

IDEA 19: Borrow Against Your Credit Cards

Many people may have heard stories of individuals successfully starting businesses by borrowing against their MasterCard and Visa. Spike Lee was able to produce his first film this way.

Did You Know. . .

Recent statistics show that nearly a quarter of all small businesses (defined here as those employing less than 19 people) have used credit cards for financing at some time.

Still, this is a very risky undertaking and should be considered only as a last resort. Why?

Credit card borrowing is the most expensive type of loan you can get. If you look at your monthly statement, you can determine the current rate of interest. Generally, credit card companies state this interest in monthly terms. If your card charges 1.5% per month, then you are paying 18% per year! This rate is not uncommon (and could go even higher). If you fail to make required monthly payments on your credit card debt, you can seriously damage your credit rating which will affect your ability to borrow money in the future.

CHAPTER 3

Setting Up Your Form of Business

There are several ways in which you can organize a business: as a sole proprietorship, partnership (either a general partnership or a limited partnership), limited liability company or corporation (either a C corporation or an S corporation). The way you choose to organize your business has an immediate impact on your start up costs since some forms of organization are more costly to get started than others. The way in which you organize your business also controls your bottom line—how much tax you will pay on profits (and what you can keep of those profits after taxes) and how you can write-off losses—because different forms of business are taxed in different ways. Where you locate your business is also an important decision; many are limited in their choice of location.

In this chapter, you will learn about the types of organization you can use for your business and the initial costs for setting up the organization. Your choices may be limited because of who you are in business with, what state you wish to reside in and other factors. This chapter will also show how your choice of business organization affects your taxes when the business is up and running as well as how your choice affects other matters that can impact you and your company's bottom line. Finally, you will learn how to determine where to locate your business and how to take the first step in getting started.

IDEA 20: Go It Alone

If you run a business by yourself and do not adopt any formal type of business organization (such as a corporation), then you are automatically a sole proprietorship. While the term "proprietorship" sounds like it covers only storekeepers, it technically applies to any unincorporated business owned by one person. It covers professionals in private practice like doctors, lawyers, and accountants in addition to consultants and those who are treated as "independent contractors."

What does being a sole proprietor mean? From a legal and tax perspective, simply that you and the business are virtually one and the same. You are personally liable for any debts that the business incurs. This means, for example, that if you sign a lease for store space for your business and you break the lease, the landlord can look to your personal assets—your house, your savings—to satisfy your contractual obligation. If a customer injures himself on your premises, he can sue you personally. Some states may provide homestead protection against lawsuits for a personal residence. Other than this, a sole proprietor's only easy and practical way of shielding personal assets from lawsuits related to a business is to carry adequate insurance to cover all possible liabilities.

Getting Started

A sole proprietorship does not require any legal attention to get started. You can simply decide to be in business and you are in business, although you may have to register your business with your local government. Call your town or county clerk for more information. There may be a small filing fee for registering your name.

> **Example:** Sue Smith opens a boutique called The Clothes Box. She may be required to register with her city or county as Sue Smith, doing business as The Clothes Box. This is sometimes referred to as a "DBA" (doing business as).

You can register your business on your own; you do not need the services of an attorney. Contact your town or county clerk's office to inquire about registration. That office should be able to provide you with all of the forms needed for registration. Why register? You may be legally required to register in order to conduct business in your area. Registration also protects the name of your business by preventing anyone else from using it in your area. (By the same token, you cannot use the name of a business that is already in use.) You may also need to be registered in order to open up a business bank account.

While a sole proprietorship is the least costly form of business to organize and get started, it may not necessarily save money down the road. If the business is profitable and you want to enjoy certain personal benefits on a tax-free basis—medical coverage or life insurance—other forms of business organization may make more sense since a sole proprietorship cannot provide these tax-free benefits to its owner. These other forms are discussed throughout this chapter.

Tax Impact

From a tax point of view, the business is not separate from you. You report all of the business's income and expenses on your individual income tax return (IRS Schedule C included below, or Schedule C-EZ which is not included; Schedule F, not included, is for farming businesses).

All of the business's profits are immediately taxable to you; all of the losses are yours as well. This is true whether you take money out of the business or reinvest it in equipment, additional inventory or other business-related purposes.

> **Example:** Your consulting business takes in $60,000 in fees and pays out $15,000 in expenses. Your net profit is $45,000 ($60,000 – $15,000). This profit is added to your other income from interest, dividends and capital gains and can be offset by adjustments to gross income, itemized deductions or the standard deduction, and personal exemptions. The net amount (taxable income) is then subject to income tax in your tax bracket. For example, if you are single and your taxable income is $50,000, you are in the 28% tax bracket. This means that your business income is, in effect, being taxed at as much as 28%.

In the start up phase of your business, you may not have any profits. In fact, you may have losses (expenses in excess of business income). As long as you have made an economic investment in the business and you operate it as a business, these losses can be used to offset your income from other sources (e.g., interest, dividends, capital gains). Losses from business means less tax paid on dividends, spouse's salary, or other income. There are several limitations on loss deductions; hobby loss rules, passive activity loss rules and at-risk rules are discussed in Chapter 12.

Chances of an IRS Audit

Type of Business	*Percentage of Returns Audited in 1995**
Sole proprietorships	
Under $25,000	5.85%
$25,000 to under $100,000	3.08%
$100,000 and over	3.47%
Partnerships	0.46%
S corporations	0.92%
C corporations (based on assets)	
Under $250,000	0.78%
$250,000 to under $1 million	2.18%

*1995 is the latest year for which these statistics are available.

Figure 3-1

**SCHEDULE C
(Form 1040)**

Department of the Treasury
Internal Revenue Service (99)

Profit or Loss From Business
(Sole Proprietorship)

► **Partnerships, joint ventures, etc., must file Form 1065.**

► **Attach to Form 1040 or Form 1041.**   ► **See Instructions for Schedule C (Form 1040).**

OMB No. 1545-0074

1995

Attachment
Sequence No. **09**

Name of proprietor

Social security number (SSN)

A Principal business or profession, including product or service (see page C-1)

B Enter principal business code
(see page C-6) ►

C Business name. If no separate business name, leave blank.

D Employer ID number (EIN), if any

E Business address (including suite or room no.) ► ....
City, town or post office, state, and ZIP code

F Accounting method: **(1)** ☐ Cash **(2)** ☐ Accrual **(3)** ☐ Other (specify) ► ....

G Method(s) used to
value closing inventory: **(1)** ☐ Cost **(2)** ☐ Lower of cost or market **(3)** ☐ Other (attach explanation) **(4)** ☐ Does not apply (if checked, skip line H)

	Yes	No

H Was there any change in determining quantities, costs, or valuations between opening and closing inventory? If "Yes," attach explanation.

I Did you "materially participate" in the operation of this business during 1995? If "No," see page C-2 for limit on losses.

J If you started or acquired this business during 1995, check here ► ☐

Part I Income

1	Gross receipts or sales. **Caution:** If this income was reported to you on Form W-2 and the "Statutory employee" box on that form was checked, see page C-2 and check here ► ☐	1
2	Returns and allowances	2
3	Subtract line 2 from line 1	3
4	Cost of goods sold (from line 40 on page 2)	4
5	**Gross profit.** Subtract line 4 from line 3	5
6	Other income, including Federal and state gasoline or fuel tax credit or refund (see page C-2)	6
7	**Gross income.** Add lines 5 and 6 ►	7

Part II Expenses. Enter expenses for business use of your home **only** on line 30.

8	Advertising	8	**19** Pension and profit-sharing plans	19
9	Bad debts from sales or services (see page C-3)	9	**20** Rent or lease (see page C-4):	
10	Car and truck expenses (see page C-3)	10	**a** Vehicles, machinery, and equipment	20a
11	Commissions and fees	11	**b** Other business property	20b
12	Depletion	12	**21** Repairs and maintenance	21
13	Depreciation and section 179 expense deduction (not included in Part III) (see page C-3)	13	**22** Supplies (not included in Part III)	22
			23 Taxes and licenses	23
14	Employee benefit programs (other than on line 19)	14	**24** Travel, meals, and entertainment:	
15	Insurance (other than health)	15	**a** Travel	24a
16	Interest:		**b** Meals and entertainment	
a	Mortgage (paid to banks, etc.)	16a	**c** Enter 50% of line 24b subject to limitations (see page C-4)	
b	Other	16b	**d** Subtract line 24c from line 24b	24d
17	Legal and professional services	17	**25** Utilities	25
			26 Wages (less employment credits)	26
18	Office expense	18	**27** Other expenses (from line 46 on page 2)	27
28	**Total expenses** before expenses for business use of home. Add lines 8 through 27 in columns ►			28
29	Tentative profit (loss). Subtract line 28 from line 7			29
30	Expenses for business use of your home. Attach **Form 8829**			30

31 **Net profit or (loss).** Subtract line 30 from line 29.

  • If a profit, enter on **Form 1040, line 12,** and ALSO on **Schedule SE, line 2** (statutory employees, see page C-5). Estates and trusts, enter on Form 1041, line 3.

  • If a loss, you MUST go on to line 32.

	31	

32 If you have a loss, check the box that describes your investment in this activity (see page C-5).

  • If you checked 32a, enter the loss on **Form 1040, line 12,** and ALSO on **Schedule SE, line 2** (statutory employees, see page C-5). Estates and trusts, enter on Form 1041, line 3.

  • If you checked 32b, you MUST attach **Form 6198.**

32a ☐ All investment is at risk.
32b ☐ Some investment is not at risk.

For Paperwork Reduction Act Notice, see Form 1040 instructions.   Cat. No. 11334P   Schedule C (Form 1040) 1995

Schedule C (Form 1040) 1995   Page **2**

Part III   Cost of Goods Sold (see page C-5)

33	Inventory at beginning of year. If different from last year's closing inventory, attach explanation . .	**33**	
34	Purchases less cost of items withdrawn for personal use	**34**	
35	Cost of labor. Do not include salary paid to yourself	**35**	
36	Materials and supplies	**36**	
37	Other costs	**37**	
38	Add lines 33 through 37	**38**	
39	Inventory at end of year	**39**	
40	**Cost of goods sold.** Subtract line 39 from line 38. Enter the result here and on page 1, line 4 . .	**40**	

Part IV   Information on Your Vehicle. Complete this part **ONLY** if you are claiming car or truck expenses on line 10 and are not required to file Form 4562 for this business. See the instructions for line 13 on page C-3 to find out if you must file.

41   When did you place your vehicle in service for business purposes? (month, day, year) ▶ ..../.........../........ .

42   Of the total number of miles you drove your vehicle during 1995, enter the number of miles you used your vehicle for:

a   Business ....   b Commuting ....   c Other ....

43   Do you (or your spouse) have another vehicle available for personal use? . . . . ☐ **Yes**   ☐ **No**

44   Was your vehicle available for use during off-duty hours? . . . . ☐ **Yes**   ☐ **No**

45a   Do you have evidence to support your deduction? . . . . ☐ **Yes**   ☐ **No**
 b   If "Yes," is the evidence written? . . . . ☐ **Yes**   ☐ **No**

Part V   Other Expenses. List below business expenses not included on lines 8–26 or line 30.

....	
....	
....	
....	
....	
....	
....	
....	
....	
46 **Total other expenses.** Enter here and on page 1, line 27 . . . . **46**	

✪ *Printed on recycled paper*

From a tax viewpoint, there is one major drawback to sole proprietorship status: You run the highest risk of getting an audit on your business income.

IDEA 21: Take in Partners

There are many reasons why you may not want to go it alone and, instead, take in partners. You may need the capital that others can bring to the business. You may lack expertise in certain areas that others can provide. You may just not want to shoulder all of the work and responsibility of running the business, preferring instead to share the burden with one or more partners.

Getting Started

Whatever your reason for joining with others, the simplest form of doing business with one or more parties is a partnership. You are not required to take any legal steps in forming a partnership. Simply joining together with the common business purpose of making a profit is enough to establish a partnership from a legal and tax view. Like a sole proprietorship, you may be required to register your business with your local government. Call your town or county clerk for more information. There may also be a small filing fee for registering your name.

As a practical matter, however, it is strongly advisable to make a formal partnership agreement. This agreement spells out all of the understandings between the partners: how profits are to be shared (equally or unequally), what happens in the event that one partner becomes disabled, retires or dies, and how long the partnership is to run. Generally, partnerships allocate items of income, gain, loss, deductions and credits on the basis of each partner's ownership interest. Thus, for example, in a 50/50 partnership, one half of these items is automatically allocated to each owner. However, this need not be the case. The partnership agreement can be used to detail special allocations for tax purposes of items of income, loss, deduction and credits of the partnership, provided that these allocations make economic sense. While all partners go into a business with the best of intentions and feelings for each other, when things go wrong, blame and resentment can cause problems. If things are put down on paper, there is less opportunity for misdealings.

There is nothing preventing you from writing your own agreement. However, it may be wise to spend the money to have an attorney draw up an agreement. The money you spend now may save you money down the road. An attorney who regularly handles these matters may be able to anticipate problems that could arise and provide solutions. Unfortunately, you can expect to pay an attorney anywhere from several hundred dollars and up for this service, depending upon the complexity of your situation.

If you wish to write your own partnership agreement, here are the main points that should be included:

General provisions

This section contains a description of the partnership. It includes the name of the partnership, the names and addresses of the partners, the business in which the partnership will be engaged, the place of business, the duration of the partnership (a term of years or the completion of a business objective), a statement providing that no partner shall sell, assign, pledge or mortgage his/her partnership without the consent of the other partners, and the circumstances under which new partners may be added.

Partnership capital

This section sets forth a description of partnership capital, or the amount contributed by each of the partners to form the partnership. This section contains a description of the initial capital contributed by each partner (cash, property), whether, in a special event, any property is to be returned to a partner, and additional contributions if required.

Management

This section sets forth the rules for running the partnership: Whether voting on partnership matters is to be controlled by majority vote or unanimous vote; designation of a managing partner who is given primary responsibility for decision making; and whether resolution of disputes between partners is to be decided by binding arbitration or by some other means.

Services to the partnership

This section explains what each partner will do and what each can expect to receive from the partnership. Discussed are duties of the partners (whether each is required to devote full time to partnership business or not); compensation (limited to share of partnership profits, guaranteed payments, otherwise); manner of payment (weekly, monthly, quarterly, annually; drawing account or otherwise); expense account (if any); and liability insurance to be maintained by the partnership to indemnify the partners against actions incurred by one or more partners in the good faith interests of the partnership.

Allocation of partnership items

This section deals entirely with the division of partnership profits and losses. In it, the partnership can specify equal allocations or any special allocations (provided there is some economic effect).

Accounting and tax matters

This section contains items that control the partnership (not the partners), such as the tax year (calendar year, fiscal year), accounting method (cash basis, accrual basis), location of the partnership's books and records and rights of inspection. It also names a partner to act as the "tax matters partner," who is the person who acts on behalf of the partnership in the event of an audit by the IRS.

Changes in and termination of the partnership

This section details how amendments can be made to the partnership agreement and what happens in the event that a partner withdraws from the partnership (how notice of withdrawal is to be given, how distributions to a withdrawing partner are to be made, and whether there is a covenant not to compete by the withdrawing partner). It also explains the circumstances under which a partner can be expelled, and what happens in the event of retirement, disability or death of a partner.

Transactions between partners and the partnership

This section allows or bars sales or other transactions between partners and the partnership.

> ### Warning
>
> Limited partnerships, special partnerships formed under state law which limit the personal liability of some owners, (discussed more fully below) must have a formal partnership agreement which conforms to state law requirements. Therefore, it is strongly advised that the services of an attorney be used to draft a limited partnership agreement.

Legal Consequences

A partnership has many of the same legal consequences that a sole proprietorship does. Generally, when a partner dies, the partnership automatically terminates. Of course, a partnership agreement can provide for this contingency in order to avoid disruption of the business. It can, for example, allow the partner's estate to become a partner and continue the business.

Also like a sole proprietorship, partners have personal liability for the debts of the business. Each partner is "jointly and severally liable" for the debts of the partnership.

Example: Let's say two people form a 50/50 partnership and rent office space. Each contributes $2,500 to get the business started. The business does not make it and there is still $10,000 remaining on the lease. The landlord can look to either partner to satisfy the obligation. Thus, either partner can be on the limb for $10,000. Should the landlord obtain a judgment against one partner and recover the $10,000, that partner can then look to the other partner for his or her share of the obligation.

There is a special kind of partnership that does limit the liability of some owners. It is called a limited partnership. In this type of organization, at least one owner is a general partner with unlimited personal liability. Other owners may be limited partners whose liability for partnership debts is limited to the amount of their contribution in the partnership.

Example: Same as the example above except that one of the 50% partners is a general partner while the other is a limited partner. In this case, the landlord can look to the general partner for the entire $10,000. The limited partner can only lose the $2,500 initial investment.

Limited partners do not have any say in the day-to-day operations of the business; they are "silent partners."

Tax Impact

In terms of taxes, a partnership is also similar to a sole proprietorship. Each partner reports his or her share of partnership profit or loss, gains and credits on an individual income tax return. Items that need to receive special treatment on an individual's return because of certain limits, such as charitable contributions (which are subject to a deduction limit based on income), a first-year expense deduction (which has dollar and taxable income limits) or capital gains and losses (gains may be taxed as special rates; losses are currently deductible only to the extent of gains and up to $3,000 of ordinary income) pass through to partners as separate items from a partnership's general profit or loss. The partnership itself does not pay any tax. It does, however, file an annual information return—Form 1065, U.S. Partnership Return of Income—with the IRS, reporting all of its income and expenses and detailing how partnership items are allocated to each partner. This allocation of items is contained in Schedule K-1, which is given to each partner.

Since each partner reports his or her share of partnership items on an individual income tax return, partners may pay different rates of tax on the same share of partnership items.

Example: The AB Partnership has two equal partners. Partner A's share of partnership profit is $25,000, as is Partner B's share. Partner A is married and her spouse earns a sizable income. Altogether, after factoring in deductions, Partner A's taxable income is $110,000. Partner A's share of partnership income is taxed at rates up to 31%. In comparison, Partner B is single and has no other significant income. After deductions, Partner B's taxable income is $20,000. Partner B pays only 15% on his share of partnership income.

Partners may be subject to special limits on deducting losses from partnership activities. These rules—at-risk rules and passive activity rules—are very complicated. In general, they seek to limit current deductions for losses to the extent of a partner's economic investment in the activity, provided that the partner sufficiently participates in the business. By definition, since limited partners are not involved in the day-to-day operations of the business, they are barred from deducting their

Figure 3-2

SCHEDULE K-1 (Form 1065)	**Partner's Share of Income, Credits, Deductions, etc.**	OMB No. 1545-0099
Department of the Treasury Internal Revenue Service	▶ **See separate instructions.** For calendar year 1995 or tax year beginning , 1995, and ending , 19	**1995**

Partner's identifying number ▶ | **Partnership's identifying number ▶**

Partner's name, address, and ZIP code | Partnership's name, address, and ZIP code

A This partner is a ☐ general partner ☐ limited partner
☐ limited liability company member
B What type of entity is this partner? ▶ ....
C Is this partner a ☐ domestic or a ☐ foreign partner?
D Enter partner's percentage of: (i) Before change or termination (ii) End of year
Profit sharing . . . . % .... %
Loss sharing . . . . % .... %
Ownership of capital . . . . % .... %
E IRS Center where partnership filed return:

F Partner's share of liabilities (see instructions):
Nonrecourse . . . . $ ....
Qualified nonrecourse financing . $ ....
Other . . . . $ ....
G Tax shelter registration number . ▶ ....
H Check here if this partnership is a publicly traded partnership as defined in section 469(k)(2) . . . . ☐
I Check applicable boxes: **(1)** ☐ Final K-1 **(2)** ☐ Amended K-1

J **Analysis of partner's capital account:**

(a) Capital account at beginning of year	(b) Capital contributed during year	(c) Partner's share of lines 3, 4, and 7, Form 1065, Schedule M-2	(d) Withdrawals and distributions	(e) Capital account at end of year (combine columns (a) through (d))
			( )	

	(a) Distributive share item		(b) Amount	(c) 1040 filers enter the amount in column (b) on:
Income (Loss)	**1** Ordinary income (loss) from trade or business activities . . .	**1**		See pages 5 and 6 of Partner's Instructions for Schedule K-1 (Form 1065).
	2 Net income (loss) from rental real estate activities	**2**		
	3 Net income (loss) from other rental activities	**3**		
	4 Portfolio income (loss):			
	a Interest	**4a**		Sch. B, Part I, line 1
	b Dividends	**4b**		Sch. B, Part II, line 5
	c Royalties	**4c**		Sch. E, Part I, line 4
	d Net short-term capital gain (loss)	**4d**		Sch. D, line 5, col. (f) or (g)
	e Net long-term capital gain (loss)	**4e**		Sch. D, line 13, col. (f) or (g)
	f Other portfolio income (loss) *(attach schedule)*	**4f**		Enter on applicable line of your return.
	5 Guaranteed payments to partner	**5**		See page 6 of Partner's Instructions for Schedule K-1 (Form 1065).
	6 Net gain (loss) under section 1231 (other than due to casualty or theft)	**6**		
	7 Other income (loss) *(attach schedule)*	**7**		Enter on applicable line of your return.
Deductions	**8** Charitable contributions (see instructions) *(attach schedule)* . .	**8**		Sch. A, line 15 or 16
	9 Section 179 expense deduction	**9**		See page 7 of Partner's Instructions for Schedule K-1 (Form 1065).
	10 Deductions related to portfolio income *(attach schedule)* . . .	**10**		
	11 Other deductions *(attach schedule)*	**11**		
Investment Interest	**12a** Interest expense on investment debts	**12a**		Form 4952, line 1
	b (1) Investment income included on lines 4a, 4b, 4c, and 4f above	**b(1)**		See page 7 of Partner's Instructions for Schedule K-1 (Form 1065).
	(2) Investment expenses included on line 10 above	**b(2)**		
Credits	**13a** Low-income housing credit:			
	(1) From section 42(j)(5) partnerships for property placed in service before 1990	**a(1)**		⎫ Form 8586, line 5
	(2) Other than on line 13a(1) for property placed in service before 1990	**a(2)**		
	(3) From section 42(j)(5) partnerships for property placed in service after 1989	**a(3)**		
	(4) Other than on line 13a(3) for property placed in service after 1989	**a(4)**		⎭
	b Qualified rehabilitation expenditures related to rental real estate activities	**13b**		⎫
	c Credits (other than credits shown on lines 13a and 13b) related to rental real estate activities.	**13c**		See page 8 of Partner's Instructions for Schedule K-1 (Form 1065).
	d Credits related to other rental activities	**13d**		
	14 Other credits	**14**		⎭

For Paperwork Reduction Act Notice, see Instructions for Form 1065. Cat. No. 11394R **Schedule K-1 (Form 1065) 1995**

Schedule K-1 (Form 1065) 1995   Page **2**

	(a) Distributive share item		(b) Amount	(c) 1040 filers enter the amount in column (b) on:
Self-employment	**15a** Net earnings (loss) from self-employment	15a		Sch. SE, Section A or B
	b Gross farming or fishing income	15b		See page 8 of Partner's Instructions for Schedule K-1 (Form 1065).
	c Gross nonfarm income	15c		
Adjustments and Tax Preference Items	**16a** Depreciation adjustment on property placed in service after 1986	16a		
	b Adjusted gain or loss	16b		See pages 8 and 9 of Partner's Instructions for Schedule K-1 (Form 1065) and Instructions for Form 6251.
	c Depletion (other than oil and gas)	16c		
	d (1) Gross income from oil, gas, and geothermal properties . .	d(1)		
	(2) Deductions allocable to oil, gas, and geothermal properties	d(2)		
	e Other adjustments and tax preference items *(attach schedule)*	16e		
Foreign Taxes	**17a** Type of income ▶			Form 1116, check boxes
	b Name of foreign country or U.S. possession ▶			
	c Total gross income from sources outside the United States *(attach schedule)*	17c		Form 1116, Part I
	d Total applicable deductions and losses *(attach schedule)* . .	17d		
	e Total foreign taxes (check one): ▶ ☐ Paid ☐ Accrued . .	17e		Form 1116, Part II
	f Reduction in taxes available for credit *(attach schedule)* . . .	17f		Form 1116, Part III
	g Other foreign tax information *(attach schedule)*	17g		See Instructions for Form 1116.
Other	**18** Section 59(e)(2) expenditures: **a** Type ▶			See page 9 of Partner's Instructions for Schedule K-1 (Form 1065).
	b Amount	18b		
	19 Tax-exempt interest income	19		Form 1040, line 8b
	20 Other tax-exempt income	20		
	21 Nondeductible expenses	21		See page 9 of Partner's Instructions for Schedule K-1 (Form 1065).
	22 Distributions of money (cash and marketable securities) . . .	22		
	23 Distributions of property other than money	23		
	24 Recapture of low-income housing credit:			
	a From section 42(j)(5) partnerships	24a		Form 8611, line 8
	b Other than on line 24a	24b		

Supplemental Information

25 Supplemental information required to be reported separately to each partner *(attach additional schedules if more space is needed):*

....

....

....

....

....

....

....

....

....

....

....

....

....

....

....

....

....

....

....

....

....

....

✪ *Printed on recycled paper*

share of business losses because of the passive activity loss rules. For further details on these rules, see Chapter 12 and IRS Publication 925, Passive Activity and At-Risk Rules.

Like a sole proprietorship, a partnership cannot offer partners tax-free fringe benefits such as medical plans and group term life insurance. Profitable partnerships that want to offer fringe benefits to owners must consider the corporate form of business organization.

Partnerships run an extremely low risk of being audited. As you can see from the audit statistics mentioned earlier in this chapter, partnerships are rarely audited. When they are, it should be noted that the IRS does not go after individual partners to question a partnership item. Instead, it audits the partnership itself (even though the partnership is not a taxpayer). Then, after an audit of the partnership, an adjustment can be made to the partnership item (a portion of which passes through to each partner). At that point, each partner must then adjust his/her individual tax return to reflect the change in the treatment of the partnership item.

IDEA 22: Organize as a Limited Liability Company

A relatively new type of business organization is called a limited liability company (LLC for short). An LLC is a creature of state law (these laws vary from state to state).

> ### Did You Know. . .
>
> All states and the District of Columbia have enacted special laws to allow a hybrid type of business organization to be formed.

A limited liability company is owned by its members and combines the best features of a partnership and a corporation. It can offer the pass-through income tax treatment of a partnership where business income is taxed on the partners' individual returns (instead of the double taxation of a corporation as explained below). It also offers the limited personal liability afforded by a corporation (in comparison to unlimited personal liability for partners in a partnership).

In addition to those starting their own businesses, professionals—for example, lawyers and accountants—may also be able to form limited liability partnerships (LLPs) for their practices.

Getting Started

As creatures of state law, LLCs must be formed according to the laws of a particular state. There may be filing or registration fees upon organization in addition to some miscellaneous fees. For example, in New York, newly formed LLCs are required to place public notices in local newspapers for a certain number of weeks. There may be ongoing annual fees as well.

In view of the relative newness of limited liability companies, it may be advisable to use the services of an attorney to organize one if this is the type of organization desired. Again, while an attorney is not required, it certainly is wise to use one who is knowledgeable in the area. The attorney should, following organization, help the limited liability company set up its articles of organization and bylaws because some states permit flexibility in their statutes that may cause the entity to be treated as a corporation rather than as a partnership for federal income tax purposes. An attorney can ensure that the company's articles of organization and bylaws comport with the requirements to ensure partnership treatment for federal income tax purposes.

> **Warning**
>
> While limited liability companies have attracted great interest in recent years, it should be cautioned that they are still new and many issues have not yet been resolved by statute or case law.

Legal Consequences

As already mentioned, an LLC is more like a corporation than a partnership for legal purposes. It can be structured to have "continuity of life"; this corporate attribute means that the business continues unaffected by the death, retirement or withdrawal of a member. It can also be structured to have another corporate attribute: "free transferability of interest." This means that interests in an LLC can be sold to third parties without the consent of other members. It can, and generally is, structured to have "centralized management" like a corporation. Decision-making for daily operations can be left to one person or a small group of members who function as managers.

Also like a corporation, a limited liability company affords members limited personal liability. Just like shareholders in a corporation, members do not risk their personal assets when starting an LLC. However, also like a corporation, members may be required to become personally liable on company debts. Members may be required to co-sign loans and/or leases to their LLC. Thus, while technically free from unlimited personal liability for business debts, members may become personally liable for some business debts.

Tax Impact

As mentioned earlier, if the limited liability is classified as a partnership for federal income tax purposes, then it is taxed in the same way as a partnership. This means that the LLC files a partnership return—Form 1065, U.S. Partnership Return of Income, with members reporting their share of LLC items on their individual income tax returns (as reported to them on Schedule K-1; see page 60).

> ### Did You Know. . .
>
> The IRS has proposed rules to allow unincorporated businesses with two or more owners, such as limited liability companies, to elect their tax treatment—partnership or corporation. Most LLCs are expected to choose partnership treatment, but a possible reason for choosing corporation tax treatment over partnership tax treatment may be the availability of certain fringe benefits (tax-free group health insurance) which is not an option for members in LLCs using partnership treatment. Before choosing corporation tax treatment for a limited liability company, discuss the matter with a tax professional.

Since LLCs are relatively new, there are no audit statistics for them as yet.

IDEA 23: Incorporate Your Business

Whether you own the business yourself or with others, you can choose to organize the company as a corporation. A corporation is a separate legal entity formed under state law. Once the entity is formed, it is essentially separate from its owners. It files its own tax return and pays its own taxes; it can sue and be sued. It stays in existence until it is dissolved in accordance with state law. Thus, whether its owners sell out or die, the corporation can continue indefinitely. A corporation may or may not be more costly to operate than an unincorporated business. There are numerous factors that influence the net cost of operating a business as a corporation.

Getting Started

Like an LLC, a corporation is a creature of state law. It cannot exist until it is formally established under state law.

From a dollar perspective, a corporation is more costly to set up than other entities. It may cost several hundred dollars or more to incorporate. This is because there are state incorporation fees.

Self-Incorporate

You can incorporate yourself. Use special software that provides you with the forms necessary for incorporation in your state. You can even incorporate online (e.g., http://corp@incorporate.com).

The cost for self-incorporation is considerably less than the cost for incorporating with the help of an attorney. However, incorporation may not be the place to be saving a few dollars (at most a few hundred dollars).

To find out about incorporating in your state, call your state's Department of Commerce or Department of State. There are also a number of services that will help you self-incorporate relatively inexpensively. Some of these services are listed in Appendix A.

Use an attorney to incorporate

You are not required to use an attorney to incorporate your business and there are numerous sources that can help you do it yourself. However, attorney's fees for incorporation may not be too high and may be well worth the money. Attorneys will not only take you through the incorporation process, they will also help prepare the corporation's bylaws and minutes to get the corporation up and running. For example, an initial board of directors meeting must be held to elect corporate directors and officers. An attorney can inform you about who can serve in these positions (and who cannot). Attorney's fees for incorporation vary widely, so ask around.

Attorneys may also provide additional services along with incorporation. Shareholders in small corporations may want to restrict to whom other shareholders can sell their stock. They may also want to provide for such contingencies as disability, retirement or death of a shareholder. These issues can be addressed in a contract called a "buy-sell agreement." Generally, the agreement prevents a shareholder from selling his or her shares during life to outsiders without at least first offering the shares to other shareholders or to the corporation itself. The agreement also details what happens when a shareholder becomes disabled, retires or dies. It fixes the price (or the mechanism for fixing the price) of shares to be bought on disability, retirement or death. It also determines whether the corporation will buy back the shares or whether the other shareholders will acquire the stock directly from the outgoing shareholder (or that shareholder's estate).

A buy-sell agreement is another document which has important legal and tax consequences. Again, while you are not required to use the services of an attorney to draft an agreement, it may be advisable to do so. The attorney can address the personal concerns of shareholders and advise about the legal and tax consequences of various alternative arrangements. Funding buy-sell agreements is discussed in Chapter 11.

Where to incorporate

Many large corporations incorporate in Delaware or in Nevada because corporation laws in these states favor management over outside shareholders. Thus, a number of public corporations incorporate in these states to make it more difficult for shareholders to bring suits against them. If you operate in New York or Texas, for example, should you also incorporate out of state? The answer is generally no. Small, privately held corporations do not need the same protection from shareholders as publicly held corporations. In small corporations, shareholders are management.

If you do choose to incorporate in one state and then do business in a different state, there may be added expenses to consider. Even if you do incorporate out of state, you may still be required to register and pay state corporation taxes if you do business in-state. Thus, for most small corporations, it is advisable to incorporate in the state in which they do business.

The costs of getting started are not the only costs to factor in when deciding to use the corporate form of business organizations. A corporation may also entail additional costs to operate. There may be annual state taxes and/or fees (e.g., franchise taxes). If you pay for accounting services, there is the added expense of maintaining the corporation's books and records. The tax treatment for organizational expenses is discussed in Chapter 7.

Legal Consequences

A corporation offers owners an important legal protection—limited personal liability. Since the corporation is a separate legal entity, it can make its own contracts and be held responsible for them. This means that the shareholders of the corporation are not responsible for the corporation's debts. Lenders, suppliers and other creditors of the corporation must look to the corporation for satisfaction; they cannot look to the shareholders.

Technically, shareholders are not personally liable for corporate debts. However, shareholders can become personally liable in two instances. First, they are personally liable for any corporate debts that they guarantee. Many lenders will require owners of small businesses to co-sign or guarantee loans to a corporation. (See Chapter 2 for a discussion of when lenders require personal guarantees by business owners.) Also, landlords may require owners of small businesses to co-sign or guarantee a lease to the corporation. Shareholders can also be held personally liable for corporate debts in payroll tax issues. Shareholders who are treated as "responsible persons" under the Internal Revenue code may be held 100% personally liable for their corporation's unpaid "trust fund taxes." These are income taxes withheld from employees' wages and Social Security and Medicare taxes on wages. These taxes and potential liability are explained in greater detail in Chapter 6.

Tax Impact

Since a corporation, called a C corporation, is a separate legal entity, it is subject to its own tax. This is a corporate income tax that operates in much the same way (but not identically to) the individual income tax. The corporation files its own tax return—Form 1120, Corporate Income Tax Return—to report its income or loss. The federal corporate tax brackets are different from those for individuals. The corporate rates range from a low of 15% to a high of 35% as follows:

If taxable income is: Over—	But not over—	Tax*is	Of the amount over
$0	$50,000	15%	$0
$50,000	$75,000	$7,500 + 25%	$50,000
$75,000	$100,000	$13,750 + 34%	$75,000
$100,000	$335,000	$22,250 + 39%	$100,000
$335,000	$10,000,000	$113,900 + 34%	$335,000
$10,000,000	$15,000,000	$3,400,000 + 35%	$10,000,000
$15,000,000	$18,333,333	$5,150,000 + 38%	$15,000,000
$18,333,333		35%	

*Note: The top tax rate is 35%. The rates of 38% and 39% are used to phase out the benefit from the lower brackets. A corporation will never pay more than 35% of its taxable income in federal income tax.

Those corporations engaged in the fields of health, law, accounting, engineering, architecture, actuarial science, performing arts or consulting and that meet certain ownership and service tests are subject to a flat tax rate of 35%. (Large corporations also pay a flat 35% rate.) This compares with individual income tax rates ranging from 15% to 39.6%.

The rate at which your corporation's income is taxed depends not only on how much the business earns but also on how much you take out of the corporation in various forms—salary, benefits, dividends. Thus, if you have a consulting business (which is usually classified as a personal service corporation) and you take out most of the profits in the form of salary, the balance of the profits are taxed at a flat 35%. The salary you have withdrawn is taxed to you at your individual income tax rates. If you have a retail business and you take out most of the profits in the form of salary, you may only be paying a tax of 15% on the balance of the profits. Of course, as in the case of the consulting business, the salary you take out of the retail business is still taxed to you at your individual income tax rates.

Remember that the use of a corporation entails "double taxation." Income earned by the corporation (and not taken out in the form of salary or other deductible payments to owners) is taxed first to the corporation. Then, when the owner takes distributions from the corporation in the form of dividends (which are not deductible by the corporation), the owner also pays tax on this amount. This double taxation increases the cost of doing business as a corporation. Of course, careful tax planning can ensure that most if not all of the profits are withdrawn as deductible amounts, thereby eliminating tax at the corporate level.

Accumulated earnings

Suppose that instead of distributing funds from the corporation as dividends, the money is left in the corporation. Accumulations of earnings may be desirable for a number of reasons. If the corporation is liquidated, each shareholder's portion may be taxed as capital gains (which are subject to more favorable tax rates than the rates on ordinary income). Similarly, if the corporation buys out one shareholder (by redeeming his or her shares), again the proceeds may be treated as capital gains. In view of the desire for capital gains, the law limits the amount of funds that a corporation can accumulate before being subject to a penalty tax. The corporation can accumulate up to $250,000 without any worry ($150,000 for personal service corporations). If there are excess accumulations, no penalty will be imposed if it can be shown that the excess accumulations were for the reasonable needs of the business. This may include, for example, funds to expand the business or to buy out retiring owners.

Tax-free fringe benefits

A C corporation can take advantage of tax rules that permit a number of tax-free fringe benefits for owners who work for their corporations ("owner-employees"). These include, for example, medical reimbursement plans, health insurance, dependent care assistance and group term life insurance. Use of these fringe benefits allows owners to enjoy a variety of corporate-paid personal expenses on a tax-free basis.

> **Example:** A C corporation adopts a medical reimbursement plan to pay employees (including owner-employees) up to $5,000 in out-of-pocket medical expenses for themselves, spouses and dependents. In 199X, George, the sole owner/employee of C, incurs $3,000 of out-of-pocket expenses. The company reimburses George and deducts the payment. George did not have to pay for the expenses himself. (Had there been no medical reimbursement plan he might have been able to deduct a portion of the expenses as an itemized medical deduction, depending on his overall personal tax picture.)

Warning

In addition to federal corporate tax, corporations may be subject to state corporate income tax or franchise tax. This increases the tax cost of doing business as a corporation.

IDEA 24: Elect to Be an S Corporation

How does a business organize to obtain limited liability for owners with the pass-through tax treatment for federal income tax purposes (to avoid double taxation)? One alternative is to use an S corporation. (Another alternative already discussed is a limited liability company.) However, a one-person company that wants to obtain pass-through income tax treatment must use an S corporation. While some states permit the formation of one-person limited liability companies (New York, for example), the IRS will not guarantee that these one-person companies will be afforded pass-through tax treatment for federal income tax purposes.

Did You Know. . .

About half of all U.S. corporations are now S corporations. Of these, about half have only one shareholder; 89% of S corporations have 3 or fewer shareholders and 99% of all S corporations have 10 or fewer shareholders.

Note that at the time this book was being prepared the IRS was considering a measure to allow businesses regardless of the number of owners to choose whether to be taxed as partnerships (i.e., pass-through entities) or as corporations. It is not certain whether and when this measure will be adopted.

Getting Started

An S corporation is a regular corporation for state law purposes. It is formed in the same way as a C corporation. Then the corporation, with shareholder consent, elects to be taxed as an S corporation by filing IRS Form 2553, Election by Small Business Corporations to Tax Corporate Income Directly to Shareholders.

Warning

Some states also allow an S election and these states have their own forms that need to be filed. They are different from IRS forms and may have their own time limits for filing.

Figure 3-3

Form **2553** (Rev. September 1993) Department of the Treasury Internal Revenue Service	**Election by a Small Business Corporation** (Under section 1362 of the Internal Revenue Code) ▶ For Paperwork Reduction Act Notice, see page 1 of instructions. ▶ See separate instructions.	OMB No. 1545-0146 Expires 8-31-96

Notes: 1. This election, to be an "S corporation," can be accepted only if all the tests are met under **Who May Elect** on page 1 of the instructions; all signatures in Parts I and III are originals (no photocopies); and the exact name and address of the corporation and other required form information are provided.

2. Do not file **Form 1120S**, U.S. Income Tax Return for an S Corporation, until you are notified that your election is accepted.

Part I **Election Information**

Please Type or Print	Name of corporation (see instructions)	**A** Employer identification number (EIN)
	Number, street, and room or suite no. (If a P.O. box, see instructions.)	**B** Date incorporated
	City or town, state, and ZIP code	**C** State of incorporation

D Election is to be effective for tax year beginning (month, day, year) . . . . ▶ / /

E Name and title of officer or legal representative who the IRS may call for more information

F Telephone number of officer or legal representative ( )

G If the corporation changed its name or address after applying for the EIN shown in **A,** check this box . . . . ▶ ☐

H If this election takes effect for the first tax year the corporation exists, enter month, day, and year of the **earliest** of the following: (1) date the corporation first had shareholders, (2) date the corporation first had assets, or (3) date the corporation began doing business . . . . ▶ / /

I Selected tax year: Annual return will be filed for tax year ending (month and day) ▶ . . . .
If the tax year ends on any date other than December 31, except for an automatic 52-53-week tax year ending with reference to the month of December, you **must** complete Part II on the back. If the date you enter is the ending date of an automatic 52-53-week tax year, write "52-53-week year" to the right of the date. See Temporary Regulations section 1.441-2T(e)(3).

J Name and address of each shareholder, shareholder's spouse having a community property interest in the corporation's stock, and each tenant in common, joint tenant, and tenant by the entirety. (A husband and wife (and their estates) are counted as one shareholder in determining the number of shareholders without regard to the manner in which the stock is owned.)	**K** Shareholders' Consent Statement. Under penalties of perjury, we declare that we consent to the election of the above-named corporation to be an "S corporation" under section 1362(a) and that we have examined this consent statement, including accompanying schedules and statements, and to the best of our knowledge and belief, it is true, correct, and complete. (Shareholders sign and date below.)*		**L** Stock owned		**M** Social security number or employer identification number (see instructions)	**N** Shareholder's tax year ends (month and day)
	Signature	Date	Number of shares	Dates acquired		

*For this election to be valid, the consent of each shareholder, shareholder's spouse having a community property interest in the corporation's stock, and each tenant in common, joint tenant, and tenant by the entirety must either appear above or be attached to this form. (See instructions for Column K if a continuation sheet or a separate consent statement is needed.)

Under penalties of perjury, I declare that I have examined this election, including accompanying schedules and statements, and to the best of my knowledge and belief, it is true, correct, and complete.

Signature of officer ▶   Title ▶   Date ▶

See Parts II and III on back.   Cat. No. 18629R   Form **2553** (Rev. 9-93)

Form 2553 (Rev. 9-93)   Page **2**

Part II   **Selection of Fiscal Tax Year (All corporations using this part must complete item O and one of items P, Q, or R.)**

O   Check the applicable box below to indicate whether the corporation is:

    1.   ☐   A new corporation adopting the tax year entered in item I, Part I.

    2.   ☐   An existing corporation retaining the tax year entered in item I, Part I.

    3.   ☐   An existing corporation changing to the tax year entered in item I, Part I.

P   Complete item P if the corporation is using the expeditious approval provisions of Revenue Procedure 87-32, 1987-2 C.B. 396, to request: **(1)** a natural business year (as defined in section 4.01(1) of Rev. Proc. 87-32), or **(2)** a year that satisfies the ownership tax year test in section 4.01(2) of Rev. Proc. 87-32. Check the applicable box below to indicate the representation statement the corporation is making as required under section 4 of Rev. Proc. 87-32.

    1. Natural Business Year ▶ ☐ I represent that the corporation is retaining or changing to a tax year that coincides with its natural business year as defined in section 4.01(1) of Rev. Proc. 87-32 and as verified by its satisfaction of the requirements of section 4.02(1) of Rev. Proc. 87-32. In addition, if the corporation is changing to a natural business year as defined in section 4.01(1), I further represent that such tax year results in less deferral of income to the owners than the corporation's present tax year. I also represent that the corporation is not described in section 3.01(2) of Rev. Proc. 87-32. (See instructions for additional information that must be attached.)

    2. Ownership Tax Year ▶ ☐ I represent that shareholders holding more than half of the shares of the stock (as of the first day of the tax year to which the request relates) of the corporation have the same tax year or are concurrently changing to the tax year that the corporation adopts, retains, or changes to per item I, Part I. I also represent that the corporation is not described in section 3.01(2) of Rev. Proc. 87-32.

Note: *If you do not use item P and the corporation wants a fiscal tax year, complete either item Q or R below. Item Q is used to request a fiscal tax year based on a business purpose and to make a back-up section 444 election. Item R is used to make a regular section 444 election.*

Q   Business Purpose—To request a fiscal tax year based on a business purpose, you must check box Q1 and pay a user fee. See instructions for details. You may also check box Q2 and/or box Q3.

    1. Check here ▶ ☐ if the fiscal year entered in item I, Part I, is requested under the provisions of section 6.03 of Rev. Proc. 87-32. Attach to Form 2553 a statement showing the business purpose for the requested fiscal year. See instructions for additional information that must be attached.

    2. Check here ▶ ☐ to show that the corporation intends to make a back-up section 444 election in the event the corporation's business purpose request is not approved by the IRS. (See instructions for more information.)

    3. Check here ▶ ☐ to show that the corporation agrees to adopt or change to a tax year ending December 31 if necessary for the IRS to accept this election for S corporation status in the event: (1) the corporation's business purpose request is not approved and the corporation makes a back-up section 444 election, but is ultimately not qualified to make a section 444 election, or (2) the corporation's business purpose request is not approved and the corporation did not make a back-up section 444 election.

R   Section 444 Election—To make a section 444 election, you must check box R1 and you may also check box R2.

    1. Check here ▶ ☐ to show the corporation will make, if qualified, a section 444 election to have the fiscal tax year shown in item I, Part I. To make the election, you must complete **Form 8716,** Election To Have a Tax Year Other Than a Required Tax Year, and either attach it to Form 2553 or file it separately.

    2. Check here ▶ ☐ to show that the corporation agrees to adopt or change to a tax year ending December 31 if necessary for the IRS to accept this election for S corporation status in the event the corporation is ultimately not qualified to make a section 444 election.

Part III   **Qualified Subchapter S Trust (QSST) Election Under Section 1361(d)(2)***

Income beneficiary's name and address	Social security number
Trust's name and address	Employer identification number

Date on which stock of the corporation was transferred to the trust (month, day, year) . . . . ▶   /   /

In order for the trust named above to be a QSST and thus a qualifying shareholder of the S corporation for which this Form 2553 is filed, I hereby make the election under section 1361(d)(2). Under penalties of perjury, I certify that the trust meets the definitional requirements of section 1361(d)(3) and that all other information provided in Part III is true, correct, and complete.

_____   _____
Signature of income beneficiary or signature and title of legal representative or other qualified person making the election   Date

*Use of Part III to make the QSST election may be made only if stock of the corporation has been transferred to the trust on or before the date on which the corporation makes its election to be an S corporation. The QSST election must be made and filed separately if stock of the corporation is transferred to the trust after the date on which the corporation makes the S election.

♲ *Printed on recycled paper*

The cost of setting up an S corporation, then, is identical to a C corporation. There are the same state incorporation fees and attorney's fees associated with incorporation.

Legal Consequences

You are not required to use the assistance of a tax professional to make an S election, but you may want to use an attorney or accountant to complete the form (with the related cost for professional fees). You can complete the form yourself and file it with the IRS. You will note that in completing the form, you need an "employer identification number." Getting this number is discussed later in this Chapter. There is no filing fee for making the S corporation election.

The election must be filed with the IRS no later than the 15th day of the third month of the corporation's tax year.

> **Example:** Your corporation is on a calendar year (it closes its books each year on December 31st). If you want an election to be effective for 1997, you must file it no later than March 15, 1997.

If you miss this deadline, the election is automatically effective for the following year. Alternatively, a corporation can simply decide to make a prospective election by filing at any time during the year for the following year.

> **Example:** Your corporation wants an S election to be effective in 1998. It can file an election at any time during 1997 and it will automatically become effective on January 1, 1998.

An election can be filed by a new corporation or a corporation that has been in existence for many years. However, an election cannot be filed before the corporation is formed. The board of directors of the corporation must agree to the election. This agreement should be reflected in the minutes of a board of directors meeting. If you do use an attorney to file an S election, the attorney should also prepare the minutes. If you do not use an attorney to file an election be sure to prepare minutes to be included in the corporation's minutes book.

The following are samples of minutes that comply with all requirements for minutes of New York corporations making an S election. Before using these samples for your corporation, check with an attorney to see that your state's requirements are met.

If state law permits S corporation status, be sure that the corporate minutes reflect a state S election.

Since the filing date of an S election can become critical, be sure to file all elections using certified or registered mail. This is the only way to have prima facie proof that a timely election was made.

SAMPLE MINUTES FOR APPROVAL OF AN S ELECTION

MINUTES OF SPECIAL MEETING

OF THE BOARD OF DIRECTORS

OF

_____(Insert name of your corporation)_____

A special meeting of the Board was held on the date, time and at the place set forth in the written Waiver signed by all the Directors, fixing such time and place, and affixed to the minutes of this meeting.

All of the members of the Board being present, the meeting was called to order by the Chairperson. The Chairperson advised that all of the shareholders had executed IRS Form 2553 (and insert State Form number if a state election is also made) consenting to the election by the Corporation to be treated as a small business corporation for tax purposes. The Chairperson stated that the Corporation met all of the requirements for qualification and he/she recommended that such action be taken. Upon motion duly made, seconded and unanimously carried it was

> RESOLVED, that the Corporation elect under the provisions of Section 1362 of the Internal Revenue Code of 1986 to be treated as a small business corporation for income tax purposes; and it was further

> RESOLVED, that the appropriate officers are hereby directed to take any and all action necessary to comply with all of the requirements for making the election.

There being no further business to come before the Board, upon motion duly made, seconded and unanimously carried, the meeting was adjourned.

_____

Secretary

Approved:

_____

President

SAMPLE WAIVER OF NOTICE OF SPECIAL MEETING

WAIVER OF NOTICE OF SPECIAL MEETING

OF THE

BOARD OF DIRECTORS

OF

_____(Insert name of your corporation)_____

WE, the undersigned, being all of the Directors, hereby waive notice of a special meeting of the Board and consent to its being held on the date and time and at the place set forth below, and do hereby waive all notice of any adjournments thereof.

We do further consent that any and all lawful business may be transacted at such meeting or at any adjournments thereof as may be deemed advisable by the Directors present at such meeting.

PLACE OF MEETING: (Insert the place of the meeting)

DATE OF MEETING: (Insert the date of the meeting)

TIME OF MEETING: (Insert the time of the meeting)

PURPOSE OF MEETING: To approve an election under Section 1362 of the Internal Revenue Code of 1986 to be treated as a small business corporation for income tax purposes.

Dated: _____

_____
                                                    Director

_____
                                                    Director

_____
                                                    Director

Tax Impact

An S election means that the corporation's income passes through to its owners and is taxed directly to the owners. In essence, it is similar to a partnership. The corporation files an annual income tax return—Form 1120S, U.S. Income Tax Return for S Corporation. Then Schedule K-1 of this form is sent to each shareholder telling the shareholder of his/her share of each corporate item to be reported on the shareholder's individual tax return.

However, there is one difference between the taxation of partnerships and S corporations. In limited circumstances, an S corporation can itself become a taxpayer (a partnership can never be a taxpayer). Three different tax rules attempt to recoup some of the benefit that a corporation can realize from converting from C to S status. However, if a corporation is formed and immediately elects S status, it will never be subject to tax at the corporate level.

IDEA 25: Change Your Form of Business to Save Money

If you are already in business and operating in one form, you may find that another is more appropriate at this time. For example, you may have started as a sole proprietor but it is now time to incorporate. Or perhaps you started alone and now want to bring in partners, forming a partnership, a limited liability company or even incorporating. A change of business form can, under certain circumstances, save you money in the long run.

Tax Impact

If you decide to change your form of business, or are forced to change, be sure to understand the tax costs, if any, in going to the new type of organization. Generally, there is no tax cost to changing from a sole proprietorship to another form of business. For example, incorporation of a sole proprietorship can usually be done on a tax-free basis (assuming that there are no liabilities of a sole proprietor being taken over by the new corporation).

Warning

A corporation (whether it is a C corporation or an S corporation) that wants to adopt another form of organization (such as a limited liability company) must undergo a formal liquidation. This can result in immediate income tax to the business and to its owners. It is strongly advisable to discuss a proposed change of business form with an experienced tax professional.

Tax costs are not the only consideration. Also take into account any legal and accounting costs involved. There may also be fees to the state for registering a formal dissolution of the corporation.

Comparison of Types of Business Organization

The following chart can help you assess the advantages and disadvantages of operating in the various forms of organization.

Sole Proprietorships

Advantages	*Disadvantages*
Ease of formation	Unlimited liability
Minimal start up costs	Lack of continuity
Owner has direct control	Difficult to raise capital
Tax advantages for small owners	Problems on death of owner
Owner reaps all the profits	Owner shoulders all the losses
Least government regulation	

Partnerships

Advantages	*Disadvantages*
Ease of formation	Unlimited liability (for general partners)
Low start up costs	Lack of continuity
Management base	Divided authority
Greater sources of capital	Difficult to raise additional capital
Tax advantages	Difficult to find good partners
Limited government regulation	

Limited Liability Companies

Advantages	*Disadvantages*
Limited liability	Newness of type of entity
Tax advantages (if properly structured)	More costly to organize

C Corporations

Advantages	Disadvantages
Limited liability	Most expensive to organize
Continuity of existence	Most regulated
Ease of ownership transfer	Double taxation
Easiest to raise capital	Charter (legal) restrictions

S Corporations

Advantages	Disadvantages
Limited liability	Most expensive to organize (see C corporations)
Continuity of existence	Most regulated (see C corporations)
Tax advantages	Limits on who can be owners
Easiest to raise capital (see C corporations)	Charter (legal) restrictions

The number of owners involved in the business dictates to some extent the type of business organization you can choose.

Number of Owners

One owner	Two or more owners
Sole proprietorship	Partnership
C corporation	Limited liability company**
S corporation*	C corporation
	S corporation*

*S corporations can have up to 35 shareholders. However there are restrictions on who those shareholders can be. In general, S corporation shareholders must be individuals who are U.S. citizens or resident aliens.

**Some states permit one-person limited liability companies but it is doubtful that one-person limited liability companies would be able to enjoy the pass-through tax treatment accorded to limited liability companies with two or more members.

IDEA 26: Decide Where to Locate Your Business

Many business owners do not have a choice in the organization of their business. They are locked in by personal circumstances: They do not want to leave family and friends. They have a working spouse who cannot or does not want to relocate. They own a home and have roots in a community they simply will not give up.

But others may be free to move anywhere to start a business. Where there is this freedom to relocate, there are a number of factors that should be weighed in deciding where that new location should be. Some locations are more conducive for doing business than others.

Here is a listing of some considerations:

Cost of doing business

What taxes does the locality impose on a business? Here are just some of the business taxes you should check out:

- Corporate tax rate. Does the locality impose a tax on corporations?

- Unemployment tax rate.

- Workers' compensation costs.

- Sales taxes.

- Personal property taxes.

Local laws and regulations

Some localities regulate business activities more closely than others. Obviously, the greater the regulation, the higher the cost of doing business since it becomes a matter of dollars and cents to comply with regulations.

Also see if the locality you are considering will accommodate you. For example, if you plan to organize your business as a limited liability company, make sure that you do not pick one of the two states that still do not have LLC laws on the books.

If you are planning to operate a business from home, check out local zoning restrictions to see if your business is permissible.

Inducements

Some localities try to attract new businesses by offering a variety of inducements. They may offer property tax breaks, low-interest loan programs and more. Some areas are federally designated as "empowerment zones" which allow businesses to claim certain tax breaks.

Available workforce

If you are going to be working by yourself, this is not an issue. But if your business requires a trained workforce, check out the labor pool in any area you are considering.

Personal concerns

What is the personal income tax picture in the area? This will affect what you, as a business owner, will be able to retain from your business on an after-tax basis. It also affects the cost-of-living in an area, which translates not only into your own buying power but also into what you have to pay workers to attain a certain standard of living. What is the crime rate in the area? If crime is high, it becomes not only an unsafe and unpleasant place to be, but also a more costly place to do business (higher insurance costs, more security precautions required).

IDEA 27: Get Your Employer Identification Number and Get Started

Just as individuals have Social Security numbers to identify them, so too do businesses need special identification numbers for various purposes. Once you decide how you want to organize your business, the next step in setting up your form of business is getting an employer identification number from the IRS. You need an employer identification number to:

- Open a business bank account.

- Elect S corporation status.

- Make deposits of employment taxes.

- File tax returns.

- Set up company qualified retirement plans.

Your business's employer identification number can be obtained by filing IRS Form SS-4 according to the instructions accompanying the form.

To get a number, complete IRS Form SS-4 (an example of which is on the following page). Submit the form to the appropriate IRS service center listed in the instructions. You can even get a number assigned to you over the telephone by following the special instructions accompanying the form.

Your state may also assign you an employer identification number for state unemployment insurance purposes. Alternatively, you may simply be able to use your federal employer identification number on state forms.

Figure 3-4

Form **SS-4**
(Rev. December 1995)
Department of the Treasury
Internal Revenue Service

Application for Employer Identification Number

(For use by employers, corporations, partnerships, trusts, estates, churches, government agencies, certain individuals, and others. See instructions.)

▶ **Keep a copy for your records.**

EIN

OMB No. 1545-0003

Please type or print clearly.

1 Name of applicant (Legal name) (See instructions.)

2 Trade name of business (if different from name on line 1)

3 Executor, trustee, "care of" name

4a Mailing address (street address) (room, apt., or suite no.)

5a Business address (if different from address on lines 4a and 4b)

4b City, state, and ZIP code

5b City, state, and ZIP code

6 County and state where principal business is located

7 Name of principal officer, general partner, grantor, owner, or trustor—SSN required (See instructions.) ▶

8a Type of entity (Check only one box.) (See instructions.)

☐ Sole proprietor (SSN) _____
☐ Partnership   ☐ Personal service corp.
☐ REMIC   ☐ Limited liability co.
☐ State/local government   ☐ National Guard
☐ Other nonprofit organization (specify) ▶ _____
☐ Other (specify) ▶

☐ Estate (SSN of decedent) _____
☐ Plan administrator-SSN _____
☐ Other corporation (specify) ▶ _____
☐ Trust   ☐ Farmers' cooperative
☐ Federal Government/military   ☐ Church or church-controlled organization
(enter GEN if applicable) _____

8b If a corporation, name the state or foreign country (if applicable) where incorporated

State

Foreign country

9 Reason for applying (Check only one box.)

☐ Started new business (specify) ▶ _____
☐ Hired employees
☐ Created a pension plan (specify type) ▶

☐ Banking purpose (specify) ▶ _____
☐ Changed type of organization (specify) ▶ _____
☐ Purchased going business
☐ Created a trust (specify) ▶ _____
☐ Other (specify) ▶

10 Date business started or acquired (Mo., day, year) (See instructions.)

11 Closing month of accounting year (See instructions.)

12 First date wages or annuities were paid or will be paid (Mo., day, year). **Note:** *If applicant is a withholding agent, enter date income will first be paid to nonresident alien. (Mo., day, year)* . . . . ▶

13 Highest number of employees expected in the next 12 months. **Note:** *If the applicant does not expect to have any employees during the period, enter -0-. (See instructions.)* . . . ▶

Nonagricultural	Agricultural	Household

14 Principal activity (See instructions.) ▶

15 Is the principal business activity manufacturing? . . . . ☐ Yes   ☐ No
If "Yes," principal product and raw material used ▶

16 To whom are most of the products or services sold? Please check the appropriate box.   ☐ Business (wholesale)
☐ Public (retail)   ☐ Other (specify) ▶   ☐ N/A

17a Has the applicant ever applied for an identification number for this or any other business? . . . . ☐ Yes   ☐ No
Note: *If "Yes," please complete lines 17b and 17c.*

17b If you checked "Yes" on line 17a, give applicant's legal name and trade name shown on prior application, if different from line 1 or 2 above.
Legal name ▶   Trade name ▶

17c Approximate date when and city and state where the application was filed. Enter previous employer identification number if known.

Approximate date when filed (Mo., day, year)	City and state where filed	Previous EIN

Under penalties of perjury, I declare that I have examined this application, and to the best of my knowledge and belief, it is true, correct, and complete.

Business telephone number (include area code)

Fax telephone number (include area code)

Name and title (Please type or print clearly.) ▶

Signature ▶

Date ▶

Note: *Do not write below this line. For official use only.*

Please leave blank ▶	Geo.	Ind.	Class	Size	Reason for applying

For Paperwork Reduction Act Notice, see page 4.   Cat. No. 16055N   Form **SS-4** (Rev. 12-95)

CHAPTER 4

Getting Good Advice

One of the keys to success in starting and running a business is being knowledgeable about your company in particular and business in general. Surveys of successful and unsuccessful businesses reveal that the vast majority of successful businesses were run by owners who had taken business courses, regularly read business books and magazines and used professionals—lawyers and accountants—in the start up phase. You need to educate yourself about all aspects of business operation— marketing, finance, personnel and more. You also need to know how and when to call in professional help.

In this chapter, you will learn about different kinds of help available for your business. Some of this help is free and very good. Much of the free help comes from government sources—the Department of Commerce, Department of Labor and the Treasury Department. Some help can be costly, but is still very worthwhile. Paid help can come from attorneys, accountants, business consultants and other professional advisors.

IDEA 28: Get Referrals to Information Sources from the Small Business Answer Desk

Don't know where to start looking for help? A number of important sources are discussed in this Chapter. However, if you want to cut to the chase and get a personal referral to the appropriate agency or office for help in starting a business, try the Small Business Answer Desk at

(800) 8-ASK-SBA. This is a toll-free information referral service of the SBA. To speak to a representative, you should select any of your choices (e.g., starting a business, financing a business, help for minorities), listen to the recorded message and then key in the number for the representative.

> **Warning**
>
> Be prepared for a lengthy electronic phone menu. Write down the numbers that you have an interest in and keep them on hand for future reference.

The phone lines are manned between the hours of 8:30AM and 5:00PM (Eastern time) during the work week. The answer desk can also be reached by fax (202-205-7064). There is a special number for the hearing impaired seeking referral assistance (202-205-7333).

IDEA 29: Send for Free Information

The SBA provides a free "Small Business Start up Information Package" for prospective business owners. The package is a booklet that includes:

- A brief list of questions to determine whether entrepreneurship is for you.

- Government regulations for small business (and referrals to other agencies that can help you with compliance).

- What you need to know if you have employees (and referrals to other agencies that can help with federal and state regulations regarding the protection of employees).

- How to prepare a business plan, section by section, with commentary on which parts of the plan are most critical.

- How to finance the start up of your business and a list of some financing options.

- Small business resources in your area, including Business Information Centers (BICs).

- Small Business Development Centers (SBDCs) in your area.

- Small Business Institutes (SBIs) in your area.

- A description of SBA financing programs (e.g., guarantied loan programs, low documentation (LOWDOC) programs and micro-loan programs).

- Information about the Minority Enterprise Development Program for companies that are at least 51% owned by people who are either socially or economically disadvantaged citizens of the United States, American Indians, or Alaskan natives and who have management and technical expertise related to their company's product or service.

- Service Corps of Retired Executives (SCORE), including a list of SCORE chapters in your area.
- Active SBA lenders in your area (including banks and other lenders with SBA loan guaranty agreements and LOCDOC lenders).

The kit is available from your local SBA office (in person or by mail). If you cannot locate the local office in your telephone directory, then call the central SBA number (202-205-7701) or the Small Business Answer Desk (1-800-8-ASK-SBA) for assistance. Do not call the central SBA number for information other than the number of your local SBA office; they will simply refer you to the local office.

$$Extra Savings

The SBA has more than 60 free publications that may address particular problems or questions you face.

IDEA 30: Get Free High Tech Assistance

Under the auspices of the SBA, Small Business Information Centers (BICs) provide electronic bulletin boards, computer data bases, on-line information exchange, computer tutorials, application software as well as counseling, reference materials (audio and video cassettes and monitors) and start up guides. For example, BICs maintain more than 250 sample business planning guides that can be used to mold a new business. BICs can also refer you to personalized counseling through SCORE offices (discussed below).

See Appendix A for a listing of the SBA Business Information Centers. In addition to these main BIC offices, there may be other mini-BICs in your area. Mini-BICs also provide assistance to prospective and existing small business owners with planning, accounting, financing and more. If you cannot find a listing for a mini-BIC in your area, call the BIC in your state and ask for a local referral.

IDEA 31: Ask SCORE for Help

SCORE stands for the Service Corps of Retired Executives Association. They provide free counseling and training to small business owners and enjoy a high reputation of quality and helpfulness.

Did You Know. . .

SCORE is a voluntary organization of more than 13,000 retired executives nation-wide. SCORE operates under the auspices of the SBA.

Seminars offered by SCORE cover a wide range of topics. They include workshops on whether business ownership is right for you, getting financing from various sources and complying with business licensing requirements, and special considerations for exporting and women or minorities in business. There is usually a small registration fee ($20–$25) to attend a workshop.

You can also schedule a personal appointment to have a retired executive review your business plan or to discuss any other business issues. However, SCORE suggests that a business owner attend a workshop before scheduling a personal appointment.

Some local chapters of SCORE also show videotapes on certain topics, such as "Basics of Exporting." The tapes are run on a regular basis, free of charge.

IDEA 32: Check Out the Small Business Development Center (SBDC) in Your Area

The SBA sponsors Small Business Development Centers (SBDCs) in association with state and local governments in addition to academic and private communities. Currently, there are more than 900 SBDCs throughout the 50 states.

SBDCs offer low-cost assistance and counseling as well as training programs and conferences. They also provide reference libraries. Call the SBDC in your area to schedule a personal appointment.

IDEA 33: Get Special Assistance for Minority and Women Businesses

There is a national policy of encouraging the growth in number of businesses owned by minorities and women in this country. To this end, several federal agencies provide assistance to specific groups.

Minority Business Development Agency

There is a special federal agency designed specifically to provide information and assistance to minority entrepreneurs. The agency is called the Minority Business Development Agency (MBDA).

MBDA provides management and technical assistance on starting, managing and expanding a business to qualified entrepreneurs (those who meet MBDA eligibility). For example, MBDA can help with business planning, management and marketing, bid estimating, construction bonding, and loan applications. MBDA does not provide any funding; it does not offer loans, grants or loan guarantees to start or expand a business. Assistance can be found in Business Development Center Programs especially designed for minority entrepreneurs. In addition to Minority Business Development Centers (MBDCs), there are Indian Business Development Centers (IBDCs). These Centers are located in areas with the largest concentrations of minority populations.

Entrepreneurs eligible for MBDA assistance are socially or economically disadvantaged individuals. Classes of such individuals include: Hispanic Americans, Asian and Pacific Americans, Alaska Natives and Native Americans, African Americans and Hasidic Jews.

To locate a local MCDC or IBDC, contact the MBDC Region nearest you (listed in Appendix A) or get more information via the Internet (http://www.doc.gov/resources/BCDA_info.html).

Asian American Business Development Centers

The SBA has also created special development centers for Asian Americans. These centers provide information and assistance in obtaining financing for start ups and expansion.

National Association of Women Business Owners

This private organization provides information and assistance to women who start or run their own business. It also participates in certain financing programs (see Chapter 2). Call them at (212) 779-7504.

IDEA 34: Find Out About Assistance from Various Federal Agencies

Many U.S. Government Departments offer a variety of special assistance options to small businesses. There are also independent agencies that provide assistance to small businesses. The following is a partial list of federal and independent agencies that may be helpful in providing information and assistance to small businesses.

Department of Commerce

U.S. Export Assistance Center—Provides guidance on exporting.

Federal Trade Commission—Provides guidance on advertising and merchandising.

Small Business Office—Listing of major federal executive procurement agencies that offer small business information on procurement opportunities, guidance on procurement procedures and identification of both prime and subcontracting opportunities. Many of these agencies have women-owned business representatives to provide special assistance to women-owned businesses. (202) 482-2000.

Minority Business Development Agency—Provides guidance for minority-owned businesses (discussed earlier in this Chapter).

Department of Justice

U.S. Immigration and Naturalization Service—Helps in complying with the Federal Immigration Reform and Control Act of 1986 which requires all new employees to complete Form I-9, Employment Eligibility Verification, attesting to the fact that they are U.S. citizens or legal aliens.

Department of Labor

Federal Occupational Safety and Health Administration—Provides guidance on compliance with OSHA (health and safety standards).

Treasury Department

Internal Revenue Service—Information on tax obligations, educational programs for small business owners, tax forms and publications (see later in this Chapter for more details on IRS assistance).

Independent Federal Agencies

Environmental Protection Agency (EPA)—Handles requests for information, problem resolution, etc. Call the Small Business Ombudsman at (800) 368-5888.

NASA—Engineering help from the Technology Outreach Office (up to 40 hours free). Call (407) 867-1356 or see http://technology.ksc.nasa.gov.

IDEA 35: Check Out Your State, County or City Economic Development Office

State and local governments try to promote business development to bring in jobs and widen the tax base. In order to accomplish this, they have set up economic development offices. State, county and city economic development offices can provide you with free information to help you start or expand your business. They can tell you about:

- Loan programs
- Job programs
- Tax incentives
- Information about the market place

They can also help you formulate your business plan or review a business plan you have already drafted. Why is their help with your business plan so invaluable? They know what the business plan must contain in order to be successful in obtaining financing.

To find the economic development office (EDO) near you, call the central number listed for your state in Appendix A.

IDEA 36: Check Out Other State, County or City Assistance

A number of state, county or city agencies can provide small business owners with help on complying with various regulations. Here is a list of some of the agencies that may be of help to you. (Each locality may have a slightly different title for the agency.)

Department of Labor

- Programs to help business owners determine whether they are in compliance with OSHA requirements. Help in abating existing or potential hazards.
- Information on your state's unemployment laws.

Department of Taxation and Finance

- Information on state income tax withholding requirements (for states that have income tax on wages).
- Information on state income tax on business income (e.g. franchise taxes).
- Help in getting a resale certificate (also referred to as a resale number) for state sales tax purposes.

Department of State

- Information about incorporating your business or forming a limited liability company.
- Help in registering your company's name.

County and local government

- Help in getting business licenses.
- Help in registering your company's name.
- Guidance in building costs, permits and zoning.

IDEA 37: Get Free Help from the Internal Revenue Service

When you run a business, you cannot avoid the IRS. You will have to pay income taxes on profits (either directly on your individual income tax return or by filing special returns for your company). If you have employees, you will have to pay payroll taxes—income tax withholding on wages, Social Security and Medicare taxes (FICA) and perhaps even federal unemployment insurance (FUTA). You may also have to pay excise taxes for certain fuels or luxury tax on some items.

Taxes are an integral part of your business. The IRS offers various forms of free assistance to help you understand your tax obligations. By understanding what taxes you have to pay and when you have to pay them, you can avoid penalties as well as interest charged on tardy or insufficient payments.

Visit your local IRS office and ask for assistance. At the office, you will find all the forms that you may be required to file along with filing instructions. You may also find IRS publications that provide general information. Call the IRS for its tax forms and publications at (800) 829-1040.

Warning

Be prepared to keep trying this number since the line is almost always busy.

Here is a partial list of IRS publications that may be of help to you with your small business:

IRS Publication Number	*Publication Title*
15	Circular E, Employer's Tax Guide
334	Tax Guide for Small Business
463	Travel, Entertainment and Gift Expenses
533	Self-Employment Tax
534	Depreciation
535	Business Expenses
541	Tax Information on Partnerships
587	Business Use of Your Home
589	Tax Information on S Corporations
911	Tax Information for Direct Sellers
917	Business Use of a Car
937	Employment Taxes

Instead of calling, you can write to the IRS Forms Distribution Center to request forms or publications.

If your business is based in:	Mail your request to:
AK, AZ, CA, CO, HI, ID, MT NV, NM, OR, UT, WA, WY	Western Area Distribution Center Rancho Cordova, CA 95743-0001
AL, AR, IL, IN, IA, KS, KY, LA, MI, MN, MO, NE, ND, OH, OK, SD, TN, TX, WI	Central Area Distribution Center P.O. Box 8903 Bloomington, IL 61702-8903
CT, DE, DC, FL, GA, ME, MD, MA, NH, NJ, NY, NC, PA, RI, SC, VT, VA, WV	Eastern Area Distribution Center P.O. Box 85074 Richmond, VA 23261-5074

Attend a Free Seminar

In addition to publications, the IRS offers free seminars to individuals who start businesses. They are designed to tell you about your rights and responsibilities in the hopes of keeping you out of trouble. In addition a packet of information, the seminars provide workshops which detail steps for obtaining help from the IRS in various situations. Some of the specific topics covered in the seminars include:

- *Recordkeeping requirements for business owners.* Find out what records you should maintain and how long you should keep them. For example, find out what records can be kept on computer.

- *Tax filing requirements.* Businesses other than sole proprietorships must file tax returns or information returns separate and apart from their owners. Learn about the type of return required for your particular business entity, under what circumstances you must file and filing deadlines.

- *Employment taxes* (**also called payroll taxes**). If you have employees, you have to pay FICA on your employees' wages and other compensation (Social Security and Medicare). You may also have to pay FUTA (federal unemployment insurance tax) on employees' wages. Further, as an employer you are required to withhold income tax and the employees' share of FICA from employees' wages. Find out an employer's obligations for employment taxes...and the penalties that can be levied if you fail to meet these obligations.

- *Federal tax deposit rules.* Payroll taxes are generally *not* mailed directly to the IRS. Instead they are deposited with a bank or other financial institution eligible to accept tax deposits.

Some businesses are required to deposit payroll taxes via electronic transfers. Find out *where* deposits can be made and *when* they must be made. (Payroll taxes deposit requirements are discussed more fully in Chapter 6.)

- ***Filing electronically.*** More and more corporations and other businesses are required to file certain returns via computer. Understand *if* your business is subject to electronic filing and for *which* returns.

- ***Special rules for various types of businesses.*** (e.g., self-employed individuals; partnerships).

In addition to general seminars, some areas may offer specialized seminars geared to a specific type of business owner. For example, the IRS may offer a seminar solely for owners of S corporations.

When you form a business and apply for a federal tax identification number for the business, the IRS will send you information on local seminars to which you are invited. If you do not receive information but are interested in finding out about the seminar schedule in your area, call the IRS's Taxpayer Education Coordinator in your area (listing in the blue pages of your local phone book). If you do not find such a listing, call the IRS's general number, (800) 829-1040.

Get Help Off the Internet

The IRS has gone on-line. You can download federal tax forms and instructions, check out the law yourself and get advice. State information is also available. In addition, on-line servers have their own tax help sites, a number of which are listed in Appendix B.

Did You Know. . .

As a small business owner, your voice can be heard on tax issues. If you want to get the IRS to change its policies (or even the tax law), send your ideas to the IRS Office of Small Business Affairs PC, Room 1313, 1111 Constitution Ave. NW, Washington DC 20224.

IDEA 38: Visit Your Local Library

Your local library can provide you with a wealth of information to help you start or grow your business—all free of charge! Here are some of the resources that may be helpful to you. (Each library has difference resources, so check with your local library and seek a referral to another library for the resources of interest to you.)

Business planning books. Want to more information about writing a business plan? About accounting? About marketing? The stacks are full of books that can guide you in all phases of your business. One word of caution: Be sure to check the publication date of the books; books tend to remain on the shelves even though the information contained in them may be outdated.

Census information. Your library may have books on federal, state and local census information. Why is this important to you? It is a very good starting point for market research for your product or service. It can tell you about the number of households in a particular area and their income. It may also tell you a little about how they spend their income (what goes for housing, health care, etc.).

Internet. Your library may be tied into the Internet, allowing you to access information on-line. Typically there is no charge for this service, but your on-line time may be limited. This is a developing area, and not all libraries may have this resource yet.

Newspapers. *The Wall Street Journal, Investor's Daily, Crane's Business* (in Chicago and New York) and other business newspapers may provide you with invaluable information. You may be able to discern trends, pricing guidelines and other information to help you start and run your business.

Periodicals. Numerous magazines are geared toward business in general and to certain industries in particular. Some general business magazines of possible interest to you include:

- *Business Week*
- *Crane's Small Business*
- *Entrepreneur*
- *Forbes*
- *Fortune*

- *Home Office Computing*
- *Inc.*
- *Self-Employed Professional*
- *The Economist*

Reference assistance. Can't find what you're looking for? The reference librarian can help you. It may well be that your library does not have the information you need but another library in a participating library system can loan you the resources. All you have to do to get the help you want is to ask for it!

Seminars. The library may host a variety of seminars given by private parties (either during library hours or after-hours). These seminars may address general business concerns (e.g., starting a business) or specific issues (e.g., the latest technology).

College and university libraries. If you are lucky enough to be near a college or university library, you may be able to use the facilities even though you are not a student there. These libraries have much of the same material as local libraries; they may have even more. Some college and university libraries are "federal repositories" which means that they house federal documents that may be of help to you. Of course, the librarians in these libraries may not be able to give you the same level of service that you can get at local libraries since they are there to help students.

IDEA 39: Tap into the Internet

On-line computer information seems to be limitless. Each day the number of businesses, organizations, governmental agencies and individuals who log on and add their expertise is multiplying. Much of this information is free and is very helpful. Some information can be of direct use for your business—information on financing sources, listings of attorneys and accountants in your area, information on exporting, new products and more.

The Internet allows users to download "shareware" or free software programs. These programs can provide help in writing a business plan, keeping track of inventory, making financial statements and more.

Warning

Downloading may not be as easy as it would seem. It may require special software (which can also be downloaded). You may need the help of a computer expert to get you going with this task.

The Internet also has "chat rooms" and "business forums" that allow you to interact with others across the country on topics of mutual interest. For example, you may want to participate in a business forum on complying with the Americans With Disabilities Act. You can join in the forum or just "listen in." However, caution is advised. Take all information from these chat rooms and forums with a grain of salt and be sure to verify it with other sources.

In Appendix B, you will find a number of web sites for starting and running a business. These serve only as a jumping-off point. Once you get on the information highway, you must map your own course.

Warning

Web sites change on an almost daily basis. All of the sites listed in Appendix B, as well as those mentioned throughout the book, were verified at the time this book went to press. By now, however, they may be out of date (and many more may be available).

On-line Service Providers

To use the Internet, you need to have a service provider. There are two types of service providers: On-line providers and direct providers. There are three major commercial on-line providers: America Online (1-800-827-3338), CompuServe (1-800-848-8990), and Prodigy (1-800-776-3449). Each of these providers charge for your time, with a certain number of hours for a fixed fee and additional hours at additional cost. For example, America Online, CompuServe and Prodigy each currently charges $9.95 for the first 5 hours and $2.95 for each hour thereafter.

The Internet is increasingly being accessed by direct providers. These smaller providers offer access to the Internet at a fixed monthly rate (e.g., $19.95/month) and there may be no on-line time limit. AT&T and other telecommunications companies are also beginning to offer (or are considering offering) inexpensive Internet access.

$$Extra Savings

In figuring the overall costs of using the Internet, you must figure not only your on-line charges by the provider, but also your telephone charges. Check to see that your provider has a local telephone connection.

Not all the information found on-line is free. Some electronic bulletin boards (EBBs), for example, may charge a monthly or annual charge. For instance, the Economic Bulletin Board from the U.S. Commerce Department (Telenet address: ebb.stat-usa.gov; telephone 202-482-1986) has current economic statistics, analysis of foreign markets and trade leads. The cost of this EBB: $45 per year in addition to connect charges.

Warning

Use caution in giving your credit card number over the Internet. There have been cases in which these numbers have been intercepted and used by others to make unauthorized purchases.

IDEA 40: Use Your Telephone

There is an abundance of information out there for the asking. Just use your telephone to find out what you need to know. You will save time tracking things down via the telephone. You can use your telephone for numerous sources of information and advice. Here is just a partial listing of how you may be able to use your telephone:

- Finding guidance on organizing your business

- Locating lending programs

- Doing market research

- Finding professionals (attorneys and accountants)

In using your telephone, check with 800 directory assistance first. Many of the organizations that may be helpful to you have 800 (or 888) telephone numbers that are free of charge. Then, if you fail to find the organization you are looking for through the toll-free directory, try directory assistance for Washington, D.C. (area code 202). You will find that many national organizations have headquarters (or at least offices) in our nation's capital. If this proves unsuccessful, try other major commercial cities. Some of these include:

City	Area Codes
Boston	617
Chicago	312
Dallas	214
Los Angeles	213/310/818
New York	212
Philadelphia	215
San Francisco	415

Did You Know. . .

There are many ways to use directory assistance at low costs or no cost to you. Some of these ways are explained in Chapter 12.

IDEA 41: Join a Trade or Professional Association

Regardless of the type of business you are starting or running, there is a trade or professional association for you. These groups can provide tremendous assistance in terms of information and support. They often act as advocacy groups to propose or change legislation beneficial to the group.

They even offer special discounts and products to members (discussed in Chapter 12). Consider joining one or more groups to get information and other benefits offered to members.

Trade associations can provide information of interest in a particular sector (e.g., Homeopathic Pharmaceutical Association for information on homeopathic medicine). Professional organizations, on the other hand, are comprised of professionals (e.g., attorneys, accountants, engineers) who provide referrals to those seeking the services of member-professionals.

Associations for Small Business Owners

The associations and organizations discussed earlier may provide help for your business. But what about you as a business owner? How can you find out about groups to help you personally? There are groups that provide certain benefits (such as health insurance, travel and entertainment discounts, pre-paid legal services, electronic bulletin boards) as well as lobbying on issues affecting small and home-based businesses (such as zoning changes, increased tax breaks). Some national organizations that may be of interest are listed in Appendix A.

IDEA 42: Use an Attorney

Mention the word "attorney" and some people have an instant negative reaction. Whatever your personal bias, do not hesitate to use the services of an attorney in helping you get started and for some ongoing activities. If your attorney is good, you will certainly get your money's worth. Perhaps you will even get more. You may avoid certain pitfalls that can result to those who go it alone.

Here is a partial list of services for which you may want to consult an attorney:

- How to organize your business

- Incorporating your business

- Drawing up a partnership agreement

- Forming a limited liability company

- Drafting a buy sell agreement

- Drafting and reviewing contracts used by your business (e.g., agreements with suppliers, employment contracts)

- Reviewing leases

Your attorney may also serve as an important referral source to obtain financing or make other business connections. Attorneys who regularly deal with small businesses may have contacts with lenders and be able to provide valuable referrals.

<hr>

Warning

The attorney you may have used to prepare your will or do the closing on your home may not be the best attorney to help your business. Do not hesitate to use a different attorney for help with your business.

<hr>

The best way to find an attorney who is knowledgeable in business matters, reasonable in price and accessible (i.e., will return phone calls and handle matters expeditiously) is to ask other business owners in the area for referrals. If you are unsuccessful in getting some names in this manner, call your county or state bar association (listed in the Yellow Pages) for a listing of attorneys in your area who handle the type of matters you need attended to. Alternatively, you can call the American Bar Association at (800) 285-2221 to find a lawyer referral service in your area.

Once you find an attorney with whom you are comfortable, inquire about the fees you will be charged. Get specific. Will you pay a flat fee for incorporation? Will you be charged an hourly rate? Get this information in writing.

Using an Attorney Versus Doing it Yourself

In some cases, you may use an attorney for certain services; in others you may wish to do it yourself. How do you decide when to use an expert? The decision should be made based on how competent you feel about the job at hand. Can you write your own contracts? Are you sure the lease you are signing does not contain restrictions that could hamper your business?

Books and Software Packages

Today, there are many form books and software packages designed to let small business owners be their own attorneys. The good side of using these products is that they contain the basics for carrying on business activities such as a bill of sale, an invoice, and a limited warranty.

They can also be used to cut down on an attorney's billable hours. You do the basics (draft an agreement using the software) and then let the attorney simply review it. The downside to using these products: They may not suit your situation exactly and you may not know if or how to alter them accordingly. Also, you may come to rely on them too much and not seek out the advice you really need.

IDEA 43: Consult an Accountant

Like an attorney, an accountant will cost you money. In the long run, however, using an accountant may wind up saving you even more money than an attorney. An accountant can help you with the financial aspects of your business. An accountant can:

- Advise you on the tax and financial implications of choosing your form of business organization.

- Assist you in completing the financial parts of loan applications.

- Set up your books and accounts.

- File your tax returns with the IRS and with state agencies (including income tax, payroll taxes and sales tax).

- Counsel you on inventory issues.

- Prepare cash flow projections.

Many business owners are familiar with the names of the "Big Six" nationwide accounting firms (Arthur Andersen, Coopers & Lybrand, Deloitte Touche, Ernst & Young, KPMG Peat Marwick, and Price Waterhouse). Do you need, or are you better off with, one of these firms as opposed to another accountant? The answer depends on your business needs and the costs involved. For the most part, startups and small businesses need not pay the higher fees generally charged by these firms for routine accounting services.

Most accountants are certified public accountants, or CPAs. To hold this title, they must have passed state licensing tests and meet continuing education requirements. Accountants that do not have this certification are called public accountants. These individuals have generally completed accounting courses and may even hold accounting degrees. They, too, can provide financial assistance to small business. Other financial professionals that may be of assistance to small business are called enrolled agents. They are individuals who have passed a written test given by the IRS. Enrolled agents do not necessarily have accounting backgrounds, but can provide some similar services such as preparation of tax returns.

Warning

The professional you may use to prepare your individual income tax returns may not be the best person to help your business. Do not hesitate to use different professionals to meet your personal and business requirements.

As in the case of finding an attorney, your best source in finding an accountant is word-of-mouth. Ask other small business owners in your area who they use. If you cannot locate a CPA in this way, call your state CPA society for a list of accountants in your area. These numbers can be found in Appendix A.

To obtain a referral to a public accountant in your area, call the National Society of Public Accountants at (800) 966-6679. Referrals to enrolled agents may be found through the Association of Enrolled Agents at (202) 775-1800.

Did You Know. . .

Instead of looking for an accountant, an accountant may be looking for you. Once you organize your business, you may be surprised to receive numerous solicitations in the mail by accountants offering you their services. Accountants may market their services by buying lists of newly organized corporations or "doing business as" filings.

After you have selected an accountant—one you feel comfortable with and confident of—be sure to get the fee arrangement clarified. Will you pay an hourly rate for services? Will you be charged a fixed rate for specified services (monthly accounting services)? Additional amounts for special services (valuation of the business)? Get the fee arrangement in writing.

IDEA 44: Consult Other Business Professionals

Attorneys and accountants are not the only types of professionals that can help you start your company and make it grow. There are numerous types of experts in their fields who can offer specialized assistance. It may be advisable for you to seek them out. While you may be an expert in a certain aspect of your business, it is doubtful that you are skilled in all phases of the business (marketing, production, management). True, you generally must pay for this assistance. However, you may have little choice. You simply cannot do it all.

Here is a rundown of some of the types of experts you may want to consult. Of course, not all may be relevant to your business. Scan the list to see which types of experts can be most helpful to you.

- *Business plan consultant.* You learned in Chapter 2 about writing a business plan and were encouraged to develop one on your own. However, your final product can benefit from the expert eye of a business plan consultant. This expert can "test" your projections to see if they make sense and are within reasonable parameters. The expert can also help to tailor a plan for a specific loan program, knowing which aspects to emphasize and which to delete.

- *Insurance agent.* An insurance agent who is knowledgeable in business insurance matters can be invaluable in starting and growing your business. Insurance can protect you and your business in case of accidents, natural disasters and other unexpected events. An insurance agent should save you money by recommending the most cost effective insurance for you.

- *Media buyer.* If you plan to advertise your product or services on the radio and/or television, you might want to work with a media buyer. This person can develop an ad campaign that will take maximum advantage of ad placement within the constraints of your budget. A media buyer typically commands better per-spot prices from the stations that you could buy as a single purchaser coming off the street. The reason: Since a media buyer works with several clients at the same time, he/she can buy spots in greater volume, thereby warranting more generous discounts.

- *Product broker.* Do you have a product that you want to get on the shelves of stores? Of course, you can approach the stores directly and you may or may not have much success in putting your product on the selves. Competition for shelf space is fierce, particularly in well-known chain stores like supermarkets, pharmacies or office supply companies. A better way to break into retail establishments may be to use the assistance of a product broker. This type of expert acts as an intermediary between you and the stores. Typically, a product broker receives a percentage of the profits of the products placed on the shelves. For example, if each item you place on the shelf costs the store $10, the broker may take a 10% commission, or $1 per item. The broker may be willing to accept any reasonable fee arrangement that you can suggest. Be sure to understand fully the fee arrangement that the product broker is charging.

Warning

An insurance agent does not get paid for giving advice, only for selling insurance. Therefore, unless you know the agent personally, you may want to shop around to avoid overbuying coverage (buying more coverage than you really need).

How to Pay for Expert Assistance

Some experts have a flat fee for a project or assignment while some bill for their time (an hourly fee). Before asking someone to perform any services, be sure that you understand the costs involved. Have the expert put his/her fee arrangement in writing. This will avoid any misunderstandings about billing that can easily arise.

Depending of the type of business you are in, it may be possible to barter for services. You provide the expert with some needed service or product and, in turn, the expert performs a service for you. This allows you to obtain valuable services without any cash outlay.

Warning

The barter arrangement still entails tax consequences. The business is taxable on the product or service it provides. How do you value that product or service? What you must report as business income is the value of the services you received. This is essentially what the expert would have charged a cash-paying customer.

In some cases, where one particular expert provides an invaluable service and your resources are particularly low, he/she may be willing to take a small ownership interest (a hope of future profits) in lieu of a current fee. Decide whether and how much you are willing to give up of your equity position in the company. If you own 100%, you may be inclined to forego a 1% or 2% interest to someone who provides an important service and who may continue to be helpful to the business. Do not give away too much of your ownership interest instead of paying for services. If your business succeeds, then you will probably have overpaid for the service by giving away a piece of the company.

CHAPTER 5

Keeping Inventory Costs Down

If you are in a service business—as an interior decorator, a computer consultant, or a professional—you do not have to be concerned with inventory. However, if you manufacture and/or sell products, whether wholesale or retail, you must learn to manage your inventory. For a product-oriented business, inventory represents a heavy financial commitment. For businesses that start up and run on tight budgets, inventory control is especially crucial.

You must understand the cash flow cycle. This is the period from buying the material, to making the products or buying the products from a supplier, to selling the products to clients or customers, and, finally, to receiving payment for the sale. Obviously, you must expend money to make or acquire a product, and you must wait some period of time (each business's collection is different) until you receive payment. Understanding your business's cash flow cycle will help you to control inventory most efficiently.

In this chapter, you will learn about inventory methods and how to choose the method that will be most advantageous to you. You will also learn about cost-cutting measures to reduce inventory costs.

IDEA 45: Choose the Inventory Method Most Advantageous to Your Business

"Inventory" means the items you have on hand to sell. (Consignment items are not part of inventory because you have no obligation to pay for them; the obligation arises only when they are sold.) Inventory may be manufactured by you or purchased from suppliers and resold by you to others. In starting a business that will have inventory, you must choose a method of figuring your profits and losses on the sales of your products. There are two inventory methods: FIFO (first-in, first-out) and LIFO (last-in, first out).

FIFO means that the first items made or purchased are the first items sold. The "cost of the goods sold" (a term used to denote the cost of the inventory) will reflect the earliest items made or purchased.

Example: A company holds 1,000 units of item X in inventory that it purchased from a supplier in four equal lots as follows:

Lot Number	Cost per unit	Total cost
Lot 1 (January): 250 units	$1.00	$250.00
Lot 2 (February): 250 units	$1.25	$312.50
Lot 3 (March): 250 units	$1.50	$375.00
Lot 4 (April): 250 units	$1.75	$437.50

In June, the company sells 300 items. Using FIFO, it is considered to have sold the units beginning with the earliest lots. Thus, it is considered to have sold 250 units from Lot 1 and 50 units from Lot 2. In figuring gain or loss on the sale, it uses the following inventory costs:

Item Quantity	Cost
250 @ $1.00	$250.00
50 @ $1.25	$ 62.50

If the items were sold at $2.00 each ($2.00 × 300 units = $600.00), then profit on the sale is $287.50 ($600.00 – $312.50).

LIFO means that the most recent items purchased or made are treated as the first items sold. As long as prices continue to rise, use of LIFO assures a high cost of goods sold since the items sold will be the most recent (and presumably the most expensive) items made or sold.

Example: The situation is the same as above except that LIFO was used instead of FIFO. In figuring gain or loss on the sale, the company uses the following inventory costs:

Item Quantity	Cost
250 @ $1.75	$437.50
50 @ $1.50	$ 75.00

If the items were sold at $2.00 each ($2.00 × 300 = $600.00), then profit on the sale is only $87.50 ($600.00 − $512.50).

It is apparent that use of LIFO inventory resulted in a substantially smaller profit (on which there will consequently be less tax). In effect, when prices continue to rise, LIFO acts as a tax deferral mechanism since taxes will continue to be figured with respect to the most recently acquired items while tax is deferred on the earliest items. However, there is more to the choice.

$$Extra Savings

Toward the end of the year, your company's inventory may run low, requiring it to sell lower priced goods and thereby generating extra taxable profits. To avoid this and to minimize taxes, consider accelerating year-end inventory purchases to boost the holding of higher priced items. Of course, in deciding whether to take this step for tax savings, balance the savings against the cost of carrying the extra inventory.

If you need to borrow funds, be aware that banks and other lenders look more favorably on accounts receivable and cash than upon inventory. Therefore, in order to make year-end financial statements more appealing to lenders, consider year-end additions to inventory very carefully.

Valuing Inventory

FIFO inventory can be valued at cost or it can be valued at lower than cost or market value. Thus, where there is a market decline, FIFO inventory will show a lower value if cost is used.

LIFO inventory is generally valued at cost. However, a special method of valuing LIFO inventory, called dollar value LIFO, can be used to simplify valuation. Instead of valuing each item in inventory separately, a pool of dollars is used to value the items. This method figures cost using a "base year" rather than the quantity and price of units. Only small businesses, those with average annual gross receipts for the three prior years (or a portion of the period if the business has not been in operation for the entire period) of $5 million or less can use a simplified dollar-value LIFO method that allows inventories to be grouped according to certain major categories.

Warning

Large companies, those with gross receipts over $10 million for three preceding years, are subject to the uniform capitalization rules (called the UNICAP rules) that require all direct costs like material and labor and some indirect costs (e.g., repairs, rent, utilities, insurance) to be included in the cost of inventory rather than being separately deductible. As small businesses grow, they should be aware of this requirement.

Under general accounting rules, the same inventory method used for tax accounting (to figure gain and loss for tax purposes) must also be used for financial statements. Thus, a company's profit and loss statement for getting loans must reflect the same inventory method used for tax purposes.

The choice of inventory method is not a simple one. Talk to your accountant before making any choices. You can change from LIFO to FIFO.

$$Extra Savings

Switching inventory methods can generate a net operating loss that can be used to produce a tax refund via a carryback of the loss. Net operating losses are explained in Chapter 12.

Usually, IRS approval is required to change inventory methods. However, advance approval is not needed to change to LIFO. A company need only file a form (IRS Form 970) along with its tax return for the year in which LIFO is first used. A switch from LIFO to FIFO—a change that might be warranted in deflationary times—requires IRS approval in the year in which the change is made.

IDEA 46: Control Inventory Closely

Inventory is a cost you expend and do not recoup until you sell. It does not make much sense to acquire inventory that will simply sit around for a long time before being sold. This will needlessly tie up funds that could have been available for other purposes. By the same token, however, you do not want to run short of inventory that could be sold.

Therefore, keep a close eye on inventory. Make sure that you do not overstock or understock your shelves.

Keep Good Records of Inventory

Today, computer programs simplify inventory record keeping considerably; there are many commercial programs available at reasonable cost to assist you. The SBA has numerous "shareware" programs for inventory that can be downloaded from the Internet (http://www.sbaonline.sba.gov) at no cost. Choose the inventory program best suited to your type of business. For example, if you run an antique store, each item in inventory is a unit. You do not require the same type of program as a hardware store that carries hundreds of the same type of screw. Advanced cash registers can also be useful in tracking inventory.

Take a Physical Inventory

You should periodically take a physical inventory (make an actual count) of items on hand to make sure that your records are accurate. (The frequency that you should take a physical inventory is determined by the inventory system used, as discussed below). Suppose, for example, that your records show that you have 1,000x on hand but a physical inventory shows there are only 800x. You are short some inventory, requiring you to reorder earlier than you had anticipated. (You also want to determine what happened to the 200x inventory not accounted for. Are your records simply in error? Is there employee theft going on?)

Track Inventory Turnover

How fast do you sell your products? The ratio of sales to inventory determines how quickly inventory is being transformed into cash and accounts receivable. An efficient business has a high ratio as there is less need for short-term debt to carry inventory.

There are various ways to track inventory. Here are some common inventory systems:

- *Periodic inventory system.* This system requires that a physical inventory be taken at set times (typically quarterly). This type of system is easy and inexpensive to operate. However, it does not provide the best control over inventory. Actual inventory and materials are not known until the count is made. Thus, loss through theft may go unnoticed for quite some time. In addition, the plant or store must be closed for the time necessary to make the physical inventory.

- *Perpetual inventory system.* This system avoids the need for frequent physical inventory while maintaining daily accounting inventory. The control is done via documents or computer (e.g., counts of inventory cards). The data must, of course, be verified by taking a physical inventory at least once a year (at any convenient point). This system affords better control and permits more sophisticated cost analysis and other management techniques. The down side to this system: higher cost.

- *Retail inventory system.* Small retail stores may lack the computer equipment necessary for keeping a close rein on inventory. Still, there is an easy and inexpensive way to track inventory "by the book." In a notebook, an owner records all purchases at both cost and retail. The owner also figures the markups (and markdowns) to arrive at a "maintain markup percentage." At the register, the owner records all sales in the book. Then, at year end, sales (figured using the maintain markup percentage) are subtracted from opening inventory to arrive at the cost of goods sold. The owner also periodically counts all items (using a retail figure) and compares this with a retail control. The difference is called "shrinkage." All retail businesses expect a certain amount of shrinkage. The percentage varies with each business; there is no commonly acceptable amount of shrinkage.

Using this last method, most retail store owners know, more or less, what has been bought and what is on hand at any given time. The only cost to using this system is the cost of the book (and the costs associated with physically counting the inventory periodically—weekly, bi-weekly, monthly, etc.).

Note: There are different inventory systems for different types of merchandise.

Plan Restocking (or Production)

One of the purposes of tracking inventory is to allow a business to restock or produce new goods as needed. In reordering products, be sure to take into account seasonal or cyclical factors. For example, a hardware store that finds its stock of snow shovels low in March may not want to restock at that time, waiting instead until summer or even fall.

There are many different systems that can be used to make decisions on ordering or producing goods. Different systems are more suitable to different types of businesses. Here are some systems used by retailers and wholesalers to consider:

- *Two-bin system.* Goods are placed in two bins. When the first bins have been sold out, a reorder can be placed. This system is suitable for high-volume, low-cost items.

- *Min-max system.* A minimum shelf quantity is established. When stock falls to this level (the minimum), an order can be placed. The order brings the stock up to the maximum level, plus an optimum order lot size (the amount of an order that will command the best price).

- *ABC system.* Inventory items are assigned a category, A, B or C. A represents the "critical" items that have high value and/or high usage. The most stringent records and controls are applied to this category. Items in categories B or C receive less scrutiny since they are less critical.

- *Reorder point system.* Forecasts of demand and the time needed for replacement are calculated. Inventory is then stocked according to these calculations. In other words, reordering takes place when stock on hand dips below the level calculated to meet fore-casted demands, taking into account the time needed for replacement. As a variation on this system, a reservation system uses the same factors except that ordering is keyed to "available" inventory—items on hand less those reserved to meet existing forecasts.

IDEA 47: Reduce Inventory Costs

The less you pay for your inventory, the better. As a small business, it may not be easy to convince suppliers to give you the same terms they might offer to major corporations. Still, there are a number of approaches you can take that may cut the cost of inventory that can help your cash flow or improve your bottom line.

If you are short of cash, consider the following options:

Get suppliers to carry you. If you are cash-short, you may not be able to command reduced prices for acquiring inventory. Still, you may at least be able to put off payment to suppliers until you sell the goods you've purchased. It may be possible to negotiate with suppliers to delay payment until you have collected on your sales. Obviously this payment plan may not be easy to arrange. What is in it for the suppliers? They may be willing to wait for payment if you pay a premium for the inventory. This is a trade off—pay late, but pay more. If you are short of cash, you may have no choice but to try for this arrangement. In the start up phase of a business where each penny counts, this may be an important beginning strategy. As the business grows and cash flow improves, other strategies discussed below may come into play.

Get favorable repayment terms. Typically, inventory is sold on fixed terms—net 10 days, 30 days, or upon receipt. If you cannot get suppliers to wait until you've collected on sales, then at least try to negotiate more favorable terms, such as 60 days or 90 days. These longer terms will more closely equate with the time that you need to sell the items and collect payment. Find out what others in your industry are paying suppliers for similar items. This will give you some frame of reference for negotiation.

If you are not short of cash but are still looking for ways to reduce inventory costs:

Pay cash. Cash talks. Ask for a discount if you pay for the items immediately. For example, you may pay a portion of the charges at the time of ordering and pay the balance immediately upon delivery. Negotiate with suppliers. Some may be willing to give a discount while others may not.

Pay early. Typically, sales of goods are net 30 days (or some other stated time period). This means that you must pay for the goods in full by that date. Failure to pay in full can result in interest charges if the supplier takes them on. It can also adversely affect the company's credit rating. Ask for a discount if you pay for the items earlier than the date called for. For example, if you plan to pay upon receipt of the invoice for the items, ask for a discount (say 2%). Again, negotiate with suppliers. If they are experiencing cash flow problems, they may be interested in bargaining with you for quick payment.

Offer an exclusive. If you buy your inventory from a number of suppliers, you may be able to negotiate better terms if you offer one supplier an exclusive. Promise to buy solely from that supplier for a set period (e.g., a year). In return for this exclusivity (and increased sales for the supplier), ask for better prices.

$$Extra Savings

It may even pay to borrow money (which entails an interest cost) in order to enjoy a discount. Remember that a 2% monthly discount, when viewed on a yearly basis, works out to a 24% savings! Borrowing at substantially below this rate is a way to take advantage of this saving opportunity.

IDEA 48: Store Inventory Where There Is No Property Tax

Some states impose a property tax on inventory. For some businesses, it may be possible to physically move inventory to another state to avoid this tax. In deciding whether to use this idea, see whether it is practical. Determine the cost of moving and storing inventory in a neighboring state. Measure this cost against the tax savings to be realized from the move.

IDEA 49: Donate Excess Inventory

Suppose you have too much inventory to carry—inventory that you will probably never sell. You can receive an immediate tax benefit by donating the inventory to charity. The donation reduces the amount of your income subject to tax. The value of the deduction depends on your tax bracket. For example, if you are a sole proprietor in the 31% tax bracket and make a $1,000 donation, you will save $310 in taxes that would otherwise have been paid. The amount of the deduction for the donation of inventory depends on the nature of the charity.

General Rule

You can deduct donated inventory at its cost. For example, if your inventory is currently worth $2,000 but only cost you $1,000, your donation is limited to $1,000, its cost. However, your income may further limit your current deduction.

If you are an owner of an unincorporated business (a sole proprietorship, partnership or limited liability company) or a shareholder in an S corporation, your share of the business's charitable contribution is deductible on your individual return. As such, it is limited to 50% of your adjusted gross income. Unused deductions from the 50% limit can be carried forward for up to five years.

C corporations have a different limit. They can deduct charitable contributions up to 10% of taxable income (figured before the donation and certain other adjustments). Unused charitable contributions due to the 10% limit can also be carried forward for up to five years.

Inventory Donations for the Needy

C corporations that donate inventory to an organization that uses the inventory for the care of the ill, the needy, or children can deduct more than just the cost of the inventory. They can add to the cost of the inventory 50% of the difference between the cost and the value of the inventory. The donation cannot, however, exceed twice the cost of the inventory. Be aware that the increased deduction does not apply if the charity exchanges your inventory for money, other property, or services. It must use the inventory in its exempt purpose.

> **Example:** You own a bakery that is incorporated as a C corporation. You donate your day-old breads and cakes to a neighborhood soup kitchen that feeds the hungry. The corporation can deduct the cost of the inventory plus 50% of the difference between the cost and the value of the inventory.

Donations of Scientific Equipment

C corporations that donate new equipment that it manufactures to educational organizations within two years of its manufacture can also increase its deductible amount by 50% of the difference between the inventory's cost and its value. To qualify for this increased deduction, the equipment must be used by an educational institution for research in the U.S. in physical or biological science.

Warning

To claim the increased deduction for donations of scientific equipment, the corporation must receive a written statement from the educational organization attesting to the use of the inventory.

IDEA 50: Barter Distressed Inventory

Suppose you have inventory that you believe you can no longer sell—last year's items or items that just haven't moved. This is referred to as "distressed inventory." You want to dispose of these goods without hurting your financial statement. In other words, you want to receive something of value for these goods. One strategy is to barter the goods. There are two ways to accomplish this strategy.

- *Direct bartering.* You can exchange your distressed inventory with a company that is interested in acquiring it. That company may offer you its goods and services in exchange.

- *Barter exchange companies.* You can exchange your distressed goods with a barter exchange company and receive credits that can be used to purchase goods or services from others participating in the exchange company.

Warning

Bartering is a taxable transaction. The amount you must report as income for the distressed inventory is the value of the goods and services you receive in exchange.

6

CHAPTER

Meeting Personnel Needs

If you are a consultant, you may be the only worker your business needs to succeed. However, for most businesses, a one-person shop simply will not do. Businesses need people to run them, but the cost of this help can be considerable.

Payroll costs are a significant part of most businesses. What is meant by the term "payroll costs?" Payroll costs include all that you pay to employees for salary and benefits. Small companies may not be able to afford to offer benefits like medical insurance or pension plans. In order to attract qualified employees, wages at small businesses may have to be higher than those offered by the larger companies that are able to provide such benefits. But payroll costs are more than just the wages and benefits you provide. They also include payroll taxes for which you, as an employer, are liable. In addition, payroll costs include certain state insurance requirements for unemployment and workers' compensation.

In this chapter, you will learn about various payroll costs and strategies to keep them down. You will also learn about ways to make your payroll costs go farther, how to hire effectively and inexpensively and how to deposit payroll taxes timely to avoid penalties.

IDEA 51: Understanding Income Tax Withholding

An employer is required to withhold income taxes from employees' wages and deposit them with the IRS. The employer does not actually pay for the income tax withholding; the employee's paycheck reflects the amount that the employer retains from that check to deposit with the IRS. Thus, for example, if an employee's gross paycheck is $300 and income withholding is $45, the employee receives a check for $255; the $45 that the employer withholds is then credited toward the employee's income tax payment.

An employer figures income tax withholding for an employee based on the employee's marital status and withholding allowances claimed. The employer uses the information provided by the employee on the IRS Form W-4 to calculate income tax withholding according to IRS tables. These tables may be found in an IRS publication called Circular E.

If you are self-employed (whether a sole proprietor, a partner or a member of a limited liability company), compensation paid to you from the business (your fixed weekly or monthly payments or draw) is not treated as wages since you are not an employee of the company. Therefore, no income tax withholding is taken. Instead you are taxed on your share of profits from the business. You must satisfy your personal income tax obligations with respect to profits from the business by making quarterly estimated tax payments to the IRS. Tax deposit requirements for income tax withholding on employee wages are explained below.

FICA

As an employer, you are required to pay the employer portion of FICA for employee's wages. There are two parts to FICA: Social Security and Medicare. The employer's share of the Social Security section of FICA is 6.2% of compensation up to a wage base amount. In 1996, the wage base for this purpose was $62,700. The employer's share of the Medicare part of FICA is 1.45% of all compensation. There is no wage base limit.

> **Example:** You form a corporation and pay yourself an annual salary of $30,000. The corporation must pay the employer share of FICA, which is $2,295 (6.2% of $30,000 = $1,860 plus 1.45% of $30,000 = $435). The same amount is withheld from your salary to cover the employee's share of FICA (which is the same as the employer's share). Now assume that in 1996 you can afford to pay yourself an annual salary of $75,000. In this case, the corporation's share of FICA is $4,974.90 (6.2% of $62,700 = $3,887.40 plus 1.45% of $75,000 = $1,087.50).

FICA applies to all "covered wages." This includes not only base compensation, but also sick pay, vacation allowances, bonuses, commissions and many fringe benefits. Excluded from the category of "coverage wages" are the following:

- Health insurance coverage paid by an employer on behalf of employees

- Services provided to employees at no additional cost to employers

- Employee discounts on employer goods and services

- Working condition fringe benefits

- Minimal value fringe benefits (e.g., occasional cab rides for overtime workers)

- Qualified transportation fringes (e.g., public transit passes, monthly parking).

Again, if your business is not a corporation, then payments to you will not be treated as wages subject to FICA. Instead, you are liable for both the employer and employee share of the Social Security and Medicare taxes (called "self-employment tax"). As a result, you pay 12.4% of your net earnings from self-employment (up to the wage base amount) for the social security portion and 2.9% of all your net earnings for the Medicare portion. Net earnings from self-employment are not limited to the funds you withdraw from the business for your own purposes. Net earnings from self-employment means the profit from your business (or the net profit allocated to you from a partnership or limited liability company along with any guaranteed payments). You pay self-employment tax as part of your income tax; generally, this means that you pay the tax through quarterly estimated tax payments.

FUTA

The Federal Unemployment Insurance Act (FUTA) provides unemployment benefits to employees in conjunction with state unemployment systems. The employer pays the FUTA tax with respect to an employee's wages; nothing is withheld from the employee's pay for this purpose. The FUTA tax rate is 6.2% of the first $7,000 of wages per employee. However, a credit of up to 5.4% can be taken for state unemployment insurance. Thus, the FUTA rate can drop to as low as 0.8%.

If you are self-employed (a sole proprietor, a partner or a member of a limited liability company) you cannot be covered for unemployment, even if you want to. Therefore, you do not have to pay any FUTA for yourself; your FUTA liability applies only to your employees. (Of course, this means that you have no income protection in the event your work dries up.)

State Unemployment Insurance

In addition to federal unemployment tax (FUTA), you may also have to comply with state unemployment insurance requirements. Check with your state Department of Labor or employment division. Telephone numbers can be found in Appendix A.

IDEA 52: Hire Extra Help to Increase Your Billable Hours

If you are a consultant or otherwise earn your living by the services you personally provide, but have been "doing it all"—the bills, the scheduling, the ordering—you may be pennywise, pound foolish. True, you are not paying wages to another, thereby saving the wages and payroll costs, but you may be shortchanging your earning potential. You can maximize your income by hiring someone to handle your clerical needs. This will free you to devote your time to clients and customers, and allow you to bill for your services.

> **Example:** You hire someone to do clerical work (filing, letters, bookkeeping entries, ordering supplies) for five hours a week at $10 per hour (inclusive of payroll costs). This will cost you $50 per week, but if you bill your time out at $50 per hour or more, then you make back the expenditure in just one hour! If you can cover the clerk's expenditure and bill an additional four hours each week (the time you do not have to spend doing the clerical work yourself, which is probably less time than the clerk takes), then over the course of a year, you will have earned more than $10,000 additional income!

If you operate your business from a home office, be sure that local zoning laws permit the hiring of employees. Many areas still have outdated zoning laws that do not reflect the abundance of home-based businesses. They may preclude hiring employees who do not live in the home.

If you find that your zoning laws bar you from hiring an employee (or limit the number of employees), consider asking for a zoning variance or special permit to allow you to staff as needed.

IDEA 53: Hire Your Spouse and/or Children

Putting a spouse or child on the payroll instead of hiring from the outside has a number of advantages, fiscal and otherwise.

Exemption From Certain Payroll Taxes

If you hire your child (who is under age 18) to work for your unincorporated business, wages paid to the child are not subject to FICA. The exemption applies to a child under the age of 21 for FUTA. Thus, if your 20-year old works for your sole proprietorship, you do not have to pay FUTA on his/her wages but you and your child are liable for FICA taxes.

> **Warning**
>
> If you are in a partnership, the exemption applies only if both partners are the parents of the child (and there are no other partners).

If you hire your spouse to work for your sole proprietorship, wages are subject to FICA but not to FUTA. However, there may be an exemption from state unemployment coverage. For example, New York exempts from state unemployment coverage for both the spouses and the children under age 21 of sole proprietors.

If you have a corporation, employing a spouse or child will not save any money in payroll taxes. FICA and FUTA are due on wages paid to a spouse or child.

Other Considerations

Whether or not you will save payroll taxes by employing a spouse or child, there are other points to consider. There may be family tax planning advantages. Payments to a child are virtually free of any income tax. In 1996, for example, a child could earn up to $4,000 before any income tax was due on the earnings. The earnings can be increased to $6,000 if a child puts $2,000 into an IRA. The $2,000 IRA contribution avoids immediate income tax on the funds and starts the child on a lifetime habit of saving.

A sole proprietor who hires a spouse can turn the cost of health coverage, which is largely a nondeductible personal expense, into a deductible business expense. In 1996, for example, a sole proprietor could only deduct 30% of health coverage as a personal deduction. However, if a spouse is employed, the sole proprietor can provide health coverage for employees, their spouses and their dependents. Since the spouse is an employee (and the sole proprietor is a spouse of an employee), the cost of medical insurance for the family becomes a fully deductible business expense.

IDEA 54: Use Temporary Workers

Instead of putting workers on your payroll, which entails a more permanent commitment, hire workers through temporary employment agencies. The workers remain the employees of the agencies. As employers, these agencies handle all payroll taxes and workers' compensation obligations. You simply pay a flat fee for their services.

Did You Know. . .

Today there are more than 7,000 temporary agencies nationwide, nearly double the number from just five years ago. According to the U.S. Department of Labor, Bureau of Labor Statistics, the number of temporary and leased employees increased by more than 300% during the period from 1982 through 1993, while gains in employment in general were only 23%. The Bureau of Labor Statistics anticipates additional growth in the area of temporary employment through the year 2005 to be in the area of 56%, a statistic expected to be substantially greater than increases in actual employment.

In the past, temporary agencies were known for providing clerical help and laborers. Today, an increasing number of agencies supply professionals, many of whom have been the victims of corporate downsizing. Whether you need a bookkeeper, secretary or a professional (a chemist, an accountant), consider using temporary workers.

When is the use of temporary employees advisable? There are a number of times when expanding payroll may be premature or needless.

- *Start-up phase.* If you need help getting started, you may not want to commit to permanent employees. You may not even know how many employees you really need. You can fine-tune your personnel needs by staffing with temporary workers at the outset. Then you will be able to see whether and which type of employees you will require over the long haul.

- *Periods of expansion.* Your business seems to be growing and you are shorthanded. Before taking on employees, see if the business can sustain the growth or whether the expansion is only a temporary phenomenon. It is much more difficult to lay off permanent workers than temps.

- *Short-term projects.* If you have a special project, such as a grand promotion of a new product, you may want to use temporary workers for the project.

- *Seasonal needs.* Instead of hiring workers and then laying them off during slow seasons (and paying high unemployment insurance costs), consider using temporary workers for your busy seasons. For example, if you are particularly busy during the holiday season and need extra sales staff, use workers hired through a temporary agency.

There are additional benefits to using temporary workers. It is a way to "test drive" a worker to see if he/she can do the job and fits within the organization. Also, turning temporary workers into permanent employees saves on hiring costs (such as help-wanted advertising or employment agency fees otherwise used to get new employees).

The term "temporary worker" connotes someone who provides services for your business on a short-term basis. This need not be the case. You can keep a temporary worker on your staff indefinitely if you contract with a staffing or leasing company. The staffing or leasing company continues to be the employer, handling all payroll taxes. You may even be able to select your workers and then refer them to the staffing or leasing company.

To find a staffing or leasing company in your area, check with the National Association of Temporary and Staffing Services, 119 S. Asaph Street, Alexandria, VA 22314; phone (703) 549-6287.

Areas of Concern

Just because you hire temporary workers does not mean that you will not also be labeled an "employer" for certain purposes. State law may, in fact, recognize that a worker can have two employers: a general employer (temporary agency or staffing/leasing company) and a special employer (you). Why is the status of "employer" important? It affects not only responsibility for employment taxes and workers' compensation insurance, it can also affect whether a company is subject to certain federal regulations. For example, a company that regularly employs 50 or more workers for at least 20 weeks is subject to the Family Medical Leave Act, requiring the employer to grant up to 12 weeks of unpaid leave for the birth or adoption of a child, the care of a child, spouse or parent because of a serious health condition or the worker's own health condition. Most small businesses are far from the 50-employee threshold, but if a company uses temporary workers, are they counted for purposes of the 50-worker threshold? Where there is a "joint employment relationship" (as can be the case with temporary workers), then only the primary employer is responsible for the leave under the Family and Medical Leave Act. This is one case where the law regarding dual employers is clear. Other situations are not so clear.

The Americans With Disabilities Act (ADA) bars employers with 15 or more employees from certain discriminatory practices related to a person's disability. Instead, employers are required to provide training, advancement and special assistance to those with disabilities. The cost of compliance with ADA can be high. Again, if you use temporary workers, are they counted toward the 15-employee threshold? The answer is not yet clear (the law is too new). Just be aware of the situation. Get advice if your business expands and you take on an increasing number of workers—permanent or temporary.

IDEA 55: Use an Outside Sales Force

If the nature of your business is selling a product, you probably need a sales force to push the product. However, you may be able to avoid all employment costs for sales personnel while still enjoying outstanding sales performance. How? Use an outside sales force that is already established. There are marketing companies that can sell your product for you. Of course, there is a cost involved in this service. (How you arrange payment depends on the type of product being sold and the customary sales arrangements for your industry.) For example, if you are selling a hand cream, you may pay the sales company a per-jar amount.

You may be able to find a company with a product that is complimentary to yours. With its existing sales force, that company may be able to market your product line along with its own. There may be a downside to this arrangement: the other company's sales force may not be as motivated to sell your goods. It all depends on the compensation arrangements that the sales force enjoys.

When negotiating to use an outside sales force, consider a number of factors:

- *Length of arrangement.* Will the arrangement work out? Who knows. It is, of course, impossible to know before hand. You always hope for the best (and plan for the worst). In view of this uncertainty, it may be advisable to keep the initial term to a minimum (such as six months) with renewal options specified.

- *Exclusivity.* Can you continue to sell your product? Can you use other marketing companies? Be sure that exclusivity is discussed and clearly understood. For example, you may grant exclusivity in a particular area (such as the East Coast, or the Asian market). Or you may grant exclusivity to a market segment (such as the industrial market) while continuing to sell to the consumer market yourself.

- *Compensation.* What are the terms of payment for the arrangement?

IDEA 56: Hire Students

You may be able to get good help for your business at little or no cost. If you are near a local college or university, you may be able to hire an undergraduate or even graduate student looking for work experience.

Advantages

One of the key advantages to hiring students is cost. If you structure the arrangement in such as way that you provide training and feedback to the school, you may be able to use an "intern" at no cost (other than your time to supervise the student). Even if you do not want to formalize an internship with the school, you may only have to pay minimum wage for a student worker. Compare this cost with what you would have to pay for someone else and you can see the savings mount.

> **Warning**
>
> Watch out for increases in the minimum wage. Congress just increased the minimum wage to $4.75 per hour effective October 1996 and to $5.15 per hour effective July 1997.

Another advantage to hiring students is the opportunity to train a worker in your methods. A student with limited work experience may not have preconceived ideas about the ways to do things. You can mold an employee as you see fit.

Yet another reason for hiring a student is the potential for a future full-time employee. The student may work only part-time or during the summer while still in school. But if your business and the student make a good match, you may want to offer permanent employment following graduation. Both you and the student know what each is getting. Further, you save on not having to spend on outside hiring.

Disadvantages

In most cases, you are hiring inexperienced help. Therefore, it will take longer for work to get done, at least in the beginning. It will also require more explanation and supervision on the part of your staff or by you.

Where to Find Student Workers

Call placement offices of colleges and universities located near you. Also check out local youth employment departments. Some programs may even provide you with free workers.

> **$$Extra Savings**
>
> Check to see whether your company can participate in programs that pre-screen and pay wages for high school seniors and college students to enable them to gain useful experience.

IDEA 57: Use Hiring Methods That Keep Costs Down

As an employer, you want to minimize both the cost of hiring employees and the amount of turnover. The cost of hiring includes advertising, agency fees or other costs. You also want to make sure that you hire the right employees to avoid turnover. Turnover costs you money in several ways. First, you must incur hiring costs all over again. Then, too, there is loss of productivity because it usually takes some time for a new employee to get up and running.

Clearly Define Personnel Needs

Just because the amount of work increases does not necessarily mean you require additional employees. Remember that the cost of an employee is more than just the salary you pay. It includes payroll taxes, workers' compensation, other insurance costs, desk space, another telephone, perhaps another computer and on and on.

You may be able to stay with your current staff size by improving productivity. Compensate your current staff for additional work or productivity. You not only save on employment costs, you also increase the moral of your current staff. Or you may be able to use outside personnel (temporary workers, consultants, and other ideas discussed throughout this chapter) to meet your increased workload.

Do you need a secretary? In the past, the first employee hired was a secretary to answer calls, handle correspondence and organize the office. Today, this employee may no longer be a necessity. Technology has provided more cost efficient substitutes. "Follow-me phone systems" can answer calls, forward messages, track down the owner of the business and more. The cost of such systems is usually under $50 per month. With the wide-spread use of computers, many individuals who formerly used secretaries to type letters and reports are now doing it themselves. Computers also allow you to organize your office—schedule appointments (with reminders), pay bills and more. Obviously, the cost of this technological assistance is substantially less than the cost of hiring a secretary.

Hiring the Right Employee

You want to be sure that the person you hire is right for the job. Hiring the wrong person is costly. If the company hires the wrong person it may mean that the job will not get done properly and that there will be turnover, thereby costing the company in both lost productivity as well as duplicative hiring and training costs. Here are some tips to help you hire smart.

- *Write a job description.* You cannot expect an employee to do everything. To find the person that will be best able to do the things that you need to have done, be specific; write a job description for a position detailing tasks and expectations. This exercise will also help you define exactly what you are looking for.

- *Understand the interview process.* It is generally not advisable to hire the first person who answers an ad. You need to take the time to "comparison shop" prospective employees. Perhaps the first applicant will turn out to have been the best and will be the one who is offered the position, but you need to give yourself an opportunity to see who is out there. In today's job market (with corporate downsizing), there is an abundant supply of applicants for many different positions so you can afford to be choosy. Narrow down the field, schedule second interviews if appropriate, check references and then make your selection.

- *Explain the job thoroughly.* You may have decided on a particular individual. Now make sure that that person will be satisfied with you. Explain the job thoroughly. Do not fail to mention unpleasant or difficult aspects of the job. For example, do not minimize the need for travel if, in fact, you anticipate that there will be substantial travel. If you do not, you will only wind up hiring a discontented employee or an employee that will not stay on for long.

- *Check references.* You may have found someone who you think would be the ideal employee. Do not skip the important step of checking references. It is better to find out up front about any problems (some of which may be explainable by the prospective employee) than to find out after the person is on the payroll.

Did You Know. . .

Also be sure that you know the Equal Opportunity in Employment law. You do not want to be guilty of discriminatory practices that can come back to haunt you. Understand what questions you can and cannot ask. For example, you cannot ask about marital status, children, national origin, or religious observances. To find out more about what practices are considered illegal, contact your state Employment or Labor Department.

Minimizing Hiring Costs

There are various ways to go about hiring employees. Which method you use may depend upon the type of employee you are looking for. You may be less willing to expend agency fees to hire clerical help but are willing to do so for technical or professional people.

Use state unemployment offices as a source for help. You may be able to list job openings with these offices. Some even offer on-line listings. There is no cost to you for using these listing services. For the phone number of your state unemployment office see the listing of state unemployment offices in Appendix A. Also consider using temporary workers, part-timers, or students as a way of testing potential employees (discussed earlier in this Chapter).

$$Extra Savings

State programs can help you minimize training costs. If you hire certain employees—displaced homemakers, veterans, handicapped workers—you may be eligible for special training assistance. For example, under a program in New York called the Service Members Occupational Conversion and Training Act, employers can receive reimbursement of up to $10,000 for a employee's wages during a training period (up to $12,000 if the worker is a veteran with a service-connected disability rating of 30% or more). Check with the Department of Labor in your state to find about special training programs or other employer incentives for which you may be eligible. (Again, call the unemployment office for your state listed in Appendix A).

IDEA 58: Comply with Federal Laws and Regulations to Avoid Penalties

One of the biggest problems facing small businesses is compliance with federal laws and regulations. The failure to comply with these restrictions can lead to costly penalties. Unfortunately, a small business owner may not even know there are laws and regulations that require compliance.

Did You Know. . .

In 1996, after 16 years, the Regulatory Flexibility Act was made more effective in providing relief to small business. Federal agencies are now required to publish guides in "plain English." Federal agencies must consider the special needs and concerns of small business when proposing new regulations (they must prepare an analysis of the impact of the regulations on small business before going forward with the regulations). Congress now has an expedited procedure under which it can review proposed rules and, if necessary, veto them before they take effect.

Here are some of the regulated areas that you should be aware of for your business. Some laws and regulations apply to all businesses, regardless of size while others apply only to larger businesses. Be careful, however, because the definition of "small business" varies with each area of the law. Your business may be exempt from one law but required to comply with another.

Immigration Reform and Control Act

All businesses, regardless of size, are permitted to hire only individuals who are legally in this country to work: citizens and nationals of the U.S. and aliens authorized to work. The penalty for hiring an illegal worker is between $250 to $2,000 for the first violation and up to $10,000 for subsequent violations.

When you hire a new employee, you are required to verify his/her legal status by having the employee complete Form I-9 from the Immigration and Naturalization Service. All employers are subject to this rule; there is no exemption for small employers. However, you need not have this form completed by an independent contractor. (Independent contractors are discussed later in this Chapter.)

See the following page for the form that must be completed. To obtain a Handbook for Employers that provides instructions for completing the form, call the Immigration and Naturalization Service at (800) 870-0777.

Warning

Note that the requirement to have a prospective employee complete the form does not mean that you can discriminate against anyone on the basis of national origin or citizenship status. Such discrimination is prohibited under all circumstances.

OSHA (the Federal Occupational Safety and Health Administration)

Businesses are required to provide safe workplaces for employees. Employers must comply with published safety and health standards, allow inspections of the workplace, keep records of and report accidents and illnesses in the workplace and post certain information for employees to see. Employers in some states are subject to federal standards; in about half the states, state rules control safety and health in the workplace.

In general, most employers are subject to OSHA. Exempt are self-employed persons and those not engaged in interstate commerce. However, you are treated as being engaged in interstate commerce (and subject to OSHA) if you buy materials from out of state. Employers who regularly employ less than 11 employees may be exempt from reporting requirements and inspections. If violations by "small employers" are found, they may be subject to reduced penalties.

Small business owners can borrow training programs from an OSHA office to learn about potential hazards in the workplace. To find out about borrowing a training program, call (301) 763-1896.

Figure 6-1

U.S. Department of Justice
Immigration and Naturalization Service

OMB No. 1115-0136
Employment Eligibility Verification

Please read instructions carefully before completing this form. The instructions must be available during completion of this form. ANTI-DISCRIMINATION NOTICE. It is illegal to discriminate against work eligible individuals. Employers CANNOT specify which document(s) they will accept from an employee. The refusal to hire an individual because of a future expiration date may also constitute illegal discrimination.

Section 1. Employee Information and Verification. To be completed and signed by employee at the time employment begins

Print Name: Last	First	Middle Initial	Maiden Name
Address *(Street Name and Number)*		Apt. #	Date of Birth *(month/day/year)*
City	State	Zip Code	Social Security #

I am aware that federal law provides for imprisonment and/or fines for false statements or use of false documents in connection with the completion of this form.	I attest, under penalty of perjury, that I am (check one of the following): ☐ A citizen or national of the United States ☐ A Lawful Permanent Resident (Alien # A_____ ☐ An alien authorized to work until_____/_____/_____ (Alien # or Admission #_____
Employee's Signature	Date *(month/day/year)*

Preparer and/or Translator Certification. *(To be completed and signed if Section 1 is prepared by a person other than the employee.) I attest, under penalty of perjury, that I have assisted in the completion of this form and that to the best of my knowledge the information is true and correct.*

Preparer's/Translator's Signature	Print Name
Address *(Street Name and Number, City, State, Zip Code)*	Date *(month/day/year)*

Section 2. Employer Review and Verification. To be completed and signed by employer. **Examine one document from List A OR examine one document from List B and one from List C** as listed on the reverse of this form and record the title, number and expiration date, if any, of the document(s)

List A	OR	List B	AND	List C
Document title: _____		_____		_____
Issuing authority: _____		_____		_____
Document #: _____		_____		_____
Expiration Date *(if any):* ___/___/___		___/___/___		___/___/___
Document #: _____				
Expiration Date *(if any):* ___/___/___				

CERTIFICATION - I attest, under penalty of perjury, that I have examined the document(s) presented by the above-named employee, that the above-listed document(s) appear to be genuine and to relate to the employee named, that the employee began employment on *(month/day/year)* ___/___/___ and that to the best of my knowledge the employee is eligible to work in the United States. (State employment agencies may omit the date the employee began employment).

Signature of Employer or Authorized Representative	Print Name	Title
Business or Organization Name	Address *(Street Name and Number, City, State, Zip Code)*	Date *(month/day/year)*

Section 3. Updating and Reverification. To be completed and signed by employer

A. New Name *(if applicable)*	B. Date of rehire *(month/day/year) (if applicable)*

C. If employee's previous grant of work authorization has expired, provide the information below for the document that establishes current employment eligibility.

Document Title:_____ Document #:_____ Expiration Date (if any):___/___/___

I attest, under penalty of perjury, that to the best of my knowledge, this employee is eligible to work in the United States, and if the employee presented document(s), the document(s) I have examined appear to be genuine and to relate to the individual.

Signature of Employer or Authorized Representative	Date *(month/day/year)*

Form I-9 (Rev. 11-21-91) N

Americans with Disabilities Act (ADA)

Employers are prohibited from discriminating against workers on the basis of physical or mental impairments or conditions. However, this law goes beyond a simple rule against hiring discrimination. Employers must reasonably accommodate a worker's limitations by making the physical surroundings accessible (for example, by providing ramps for wheel chairs). Employers must also help a worker with limitations to do the job, for instance providing special equipment for hearing- or sight-impaired workers. The ADA applies to employers who regularly employ at least 15 workers.

Family Medical Leave Act

Employers must give employees 12 weeks leave for the birth or adoption of a child, or the illness of a family member. Such leave need not be paid; the law is designed to protect a worker who needs time off from being replaced. (Details of this law were discussed earlier in conjunction with leasing employees.) This law applies to employers who regularly employ 50 or more employees.

Age Discrimination in Employment Act (ADE)

This law prohibits job discrimination on the basis of age. It specifically prohibits forced retirement before age 70. This law applies to employers who regularly employ 20 or more employees.

Civil Rights Act Amendments of 1991

This amendment to Title VII of the Civil Rights Act of 1964 bans discrimination in employment on the basis of race. This law applies to employers who regularly employ 15 or more employees.

COBRA

Employers are not required to provide health insurance for employees. But employers who do must offer continuation coverage for workers who leave employment (voluntarily or otherwise) and their family. COBRA is not supposed to cost employers money since they are permitted to charge former employees 102% of the actual cost of the insurance (presumably the 2% over the insurance cost should cover the administrative costs of COBRA). This law applies to employers who regularly employee 20 or more employees.

Worker Adjustment and Retraining Notification Act (WARN)

Employers must give 60 days written notice of large scale layoffs and plant closings. This law applies to employers who regularly employ 50 or more employees.

IDEA 59: Use Performance-Based Incentives

One of the most difficult cost issues for small business owners is paying compensation to employees that approximates the amounts paid by larger companies. Those larger companies may well offer numerous fringe benefits on top of generous vacation time and personal leave time. Small businesses may not be able to compete dollar-for-dollar. What is a small business owner to do in order to attract and retain qualified employees? Use performance incentives to boost compensation. The employees will be rewarded for superlative performance. A small business will not have financial difficulty paying these bonuses since they are tied to increases in revenue. Here are some performance-based incentives you might consider:

Profit-sharing Plans

Use this type of qualified retirement plan to reward employees. The business deducts contributions made to employee retirement accounts, thereby reducing its cash outlay (the cost of the contributions is offset by tax savings). The employees are not taxed currently on these contributions, nor on earnings on the contributions. Instead, they pay tax only when funds are withdrawn.

The plans must comply with IRS and Labor Department requirements (e.g., who is allowed to participate in the plan, how contributions are figured). There are some administrative costs to consider (e.g., filing annual reports with the IRS).

Business contributions to employee accounts are tied to overall business profits (and are limited by tax rules that place caps on annual deductions). Thus, the business is required to make contributions only if it has the funds to do so because it has been profitable. But, since contributions relate to total profits, individual workers whose performance alone may be responsible for increased profits are not singled out for reward; all employees enjoy the fruits of their labors.

Bonuses

Give year-end bonuses for increased sales or some other measure of outstanding performance. This type of reward is immediate to employees (as compared with a profit-sharing plan which is not enjoyed until retirement).

Businesses on the accrual method of accounting (which includes all inventory-based businesses) can claim a current deduction for a year-end bonus even though it is not actually paid until the following year. This special rule allows accrual-based businesses to come up with the cash up to $2^1/2$ months after the close of the tax year. For example, say the business reports on a calendar year ending December 31 and wants to give a $1,000 bonus to a particular employee. The business can declare the bonus on December 21, 1996. The business has until March 15, 1997 to pay the bonus while still deducting it for 1996.

Warning

This special rule, however, does not apply to bonuses paid to owners. Payments to owners and employees related to owners are not deductible until actually made.

Other Incentives

Instead of rewards that require the business to make a cash outlay, consider other ways to compensate outstanding employees. Give praise. This may seem like a meaningless gesture, but it may be appreciated more than you imagine. Praise can be on a personal level—a thank you for a special job well done. It can also be public recognition, like a plaque for employee of the month, or an announcement to other employees.

There are some other ways to reward employees without substantial cost. For example, consider giving an employee an extra day off or a personal dinner on the company. Use your imagination to recognize when employees are going above and beyond the job description.

IDEA 60: Hire Employees That Entitle You to Tax Breaks

The tax laws allow employers to claim tax credits for hiring employees that fall into special categories. Tax credits are valuable because they reduce taxes on business profits dollar-for-dollar. Thus, each dollar of credit saves one full dollar of taxes.

Work Opportunity Credit

This new credit can be claimed for hiring workers from a "targeted group" (qualified recipients of public assistance or Supplemental Security Income; qualified veterans; qualified ex-felons; high-risk youths; vocational rehabilitation referrals; qualified food stamp recipients; and qualified summer youths). The credit is 35% of qualified first-year wages up to $6,000 ($3,000 for summer youth employees), provided the employee works a minimum amount of time. The top credit is $2,100 ($1,050 for summer youth employees). The credit applies for those hired after September 30, 1996 and before October 1, 1997. An employer must receive written certification of eligibility from the designated local agency on or before the individual is offered work and, within 21 days after the individual begins work, the employer submits the pre-screening notice to the designated agency.

Empowerment Zone Employment Credit

The Departments of Housing and Urban Development and Agriculture have named six cities and three rural areas to be "empowerment zones."

The following areas have already received designation:

Urban areas: Atlanta, Baltimore, Chicago, Detroit, New York City (Boroughs of Bronx and Manhattan), Philadelphia, PA-Camden, NJ.

Rural areas: Kentucky Highlands, KY (Clinton, Jackson and Wayne Counties); Mid-Delta, MS (Bolivar, Sunflower, Leflore, Washington, Humphreys and Holmes Counties); Rio Grande Valley, TX (Starr, Cameron, Hidalgo and Willacy Counties).

Congress is presently considering the addition of many more empowerment zones.

These zones are economically depressed areas identified as needing special government assistance in the form of tax incentives. One of these incentives is an employee tax credit for hiring workers within the zone. If you do business in a designated zone and hire full-time or part-time employees, you may be eligible for a credit. The workers must substantially perform all of their employment services within the zone. The credit is 20% of the first $15,000 of wages and certain related costs (training and education benefits). The top credit is $3,000 per employee each year. There is no limit on the number of employees for which you claim the credit.

Indian Employment Credit

Like the empowerment zone credit, this credit is designed to encourage employment on an Indian reservation. Individuals who are enrolled members of an Indian tribe or spouses of enrolled members are eligible employees in this program provided that they receive more than 50% of their wages from services performed on the reservation. Also, the employees must live on or near the reservation on which the services are performed. The credit is 20% of the first $20,000 of "excess" wages and health insurance costs. Excess wages and health insurance costs are costs over and above amounts paid during 1993 (the measuring year).

IDEA 61: Hire Consultants

If there are aspects of running the business that are beyond your expertise but do not require the services of a permanent employee, consider hiring a consultant. A consultant is an independent contractor in business for him/herself. You pay the contracted amount—a fixed rate for a project, an hourly fee. You are not liable for employment taxes on payments to the consultant. You do not have to pay FICA or FUTA taxes. You also do not have to pay state unemployment insurance or maintain workers' compensation coverage. The payroll tax savings can be substantial!

Warning

The question of whether a consultant is an independent contractor or your employee may be a tricky one, and one that has severe consequences. The IRS and state unemployment offices are constantly on the lookout for employers who treat workers as independent contractors when they should have treated them as employees. An employer can owe back employment taxes for several years. With penalties (for failure to make timely tax deposits; intentional misclassification of employees; failure to file information returns and other penalties) and interest on top of back taxes, misclassification can bankrupt a company!

To make sure that your contractual arrangement with a consultant will stand up to IRS scrutiny, you must understand what the government looks for in making an employee/independent contractor determination. The key issue is a question of control. Who calls the shots? Who is at risk? Did you have a right to control the details and means by which the work was to be accomplished? Do you have a right to fire the worker? Do you furnish the tools and a place to work? If you answered yes to these three questions, then the worker is probably your employee, and you would have trouble sustaining an independent contractor argument.

There are three key aspects to determining control: behavioral control, financial control and the relationship of the parties. Within each of these areas, there are several factors that can be used to assess the degree of control. The following factors (based on an IRS ruling and a training manual for IRS auditors) can be used to make an employee/independent contractor determination:

1. *Instructions.* When a worker is required to comply with instructions given by the party for whom the services are performed, he/she is an employee.

2. *Training.* Requiring training of a worker (working by the side of a trained employee, attending meetings) indicates that the worker is an employee.

3. *Integration.* When the services of a worker were integrally connected with the success of the business, this indicates that the worker is an employee.

4. *Services rendered personally.* When a worker must perform the task him/herself, this indicates that the worker is an employee. When the worker can hire others to perform the work, this could indicate an independent contractor.

5. *Hiring, supervising and paying assistants.* If the person contracting for the work can hire assistants, supervise and pay them, this indicates an independent contractor.

6. *Continuing relationship.* When the relationship between the worker is ongoing, this indicates an employee; when the relationship is of limited duration, this indicates an independent contractor (but a short-term arrangement can be an employer/employee relationship too).

7. *Set hours of work.* In the past, when a worker was required to perform duties within a required time frame, this indicated an employee; if a worker could set his/her own hours, he/she was an independent contractor. However, in today's world, use of flex-time or allowing workers to set their own hours does not preclude employee status.

8. *Full-time required.* When a worker is required to devote full-time to the person for whom services are contracted, this is an employee; when a worker performs only part-time work for one party, and also works for others, this indicates an independent contractor. However, short or temporary work is not determinative; someone who performs one-time services can still be considered an employee based on other "control" factors.

9. *Doing work on employer's premises.* If the work must be performed on the premises of the party for whom the services are contracted, this indicates an employee; when the work can be performed off-site (e.g., at the worker's office), this indicates an independent contractor. However, doing work off-site does not necessarily mean a worker is an independent contractor. Today, there are many "telecommuters" who are employed, but perform the work in their own homes.

10. *Order or sequence set.* When the work must be performed in a set order or sequence as established by the party for whom the services are contracted, this indicates an employee; when the worker can set his/her own work schedule, this indicates an independent contractor. However, with skilled professionals, employers need not necessarily be required to or even able to tell a worker how to perform a certain task. This does not automatically mean that the worker is an independent contractor. In this case, financial control factors may become more significant. For example, a radiologist who reads X-rays for a clinic may be considered an employee even though he/she is not told how to read the X-rays. If the radiologist lacks a financial investment in the business, he/she may be an employee of the clinic.

11. *Oral or written reports.* When a worker is required to submit regular reports, this indicates an employee.

12. *Payment by the hour, week or month.* When payment is fixed on an hourly, weekly or monthly basis, this indicates an employee; where payment is fixed according to the entire job to be done (e.g., a lump sum), this indicates an independent contractor.

13. *Payment of business and/or traveling expenses.* If the person for whom the services are contracted pays business expenses (including travel expenses), this indicates an employee; where the worker must bear the cost of business expenses, this indicates an independent contractor.

14. *Furnishing tools and materials.* If the person for whom the services are contracted provides the tools and materials to do the job, this indicates an employee; when the worker must use his/her own tools and materials, this indicates an independent contractor.

15. *Significant investment.* When the worker has no investment in the business, this indicates an employee; when the worker has invested in the facilities used in performing services which are not typically maintained by employees, this indicates an independent contractor. Having a home office and even a computer is not viewed as a significant investment; renting office space would be a significant investment.

16. *Realization of profit or loss.* When the worker has no stake in whether the business is profitable or not (other than the hopes of salary raises and other fringe benefits), this indicates an employee; when the worker has a real risk of economic loss due to significant investment or a bona fide liability for expenses, this indicates an independent contractor.

17. *Working for more than one firm at a time.* When a worker is required to work solely for one party, this indicates an employee; when a worker performs services for multiple parties, this indicates an independent contractor. However, it is still possible for the worker to be treated as an employee of each party.

18. *Making services available to the general public.* When a worker's services are limited to one party, this indicates an employee; when a worker advertises his/her services to the general public, this indicates an independent contractor.

19. *Right to discharge.* When the threat of dismissal exists for the failure to follow an employer's instructions, this indicates an employee; when the termination of services is governed by contract specifications, this indicates an independent contractor.

20. *Right to terminate.* When a worker can end the working relationship at any time without any liability, this indicates an employee; when termination of the relationship would result in contractual penalties, this indicates an independent contractor.

Protection for Employers

What can you, as an employer, do to avoid having the consultants you hire be reclassified as your employees? Be clear on the arrangement between you and the consultant. Have a written consulting agreement. Spell out the terms and obligations of each party to support the independent contractor arrangement.

Warning

Having a consulting agreement is no guarantee that the IRS will not reclassify the consultant as an employee.

Rely on a safe harbor in the tax law

For federal employment tax purposes, the law allows employers to claim relief under a safe harbor and avoid penalties. There are two requirements for this relief:

1. You must have a reasonable basis for the treatment. A reasonable basis is a case or ruling in which similar consultants were classified as independent contractors. Another reasonable basis is a longstanding industry practice of treating similarly situated consultants as independent contractors. A third reasonable basis is having had a prior audit involving employment issues in which consultants you treated as independent contractors were not reclassified as employees.

2. You must have used consistent treatment. This means always having treated consultants performing the same type of work as independent contractors. You must have issued Form 1099 to report payments to them.

If you have any questions about how to classify a consultant, it may be better to err on the side of safety by treating him/her as an employee. This will cost you more in payroll taxes and, perhaps, benefits, but you avoid exposure for even greater costs later on should you be audited and the consultant is reclassified as an employee.

IDEA 62: Deposit Taxes Promptly to Avoid Penalties

Paying interest and penalties to the IRS is a needless expense, one that many businesses can ill afford. The extent of the possible penalties is explained later. To avoid this unnecessary cost, understand deposit obligations and meet them. First and foremost, you need an employer identification number. Getting an employer identification number was explained in Chapter 3.

Income Tax Withholding and FICA

At the beginning of this Chapter, you learned about income tax withholding and FICA. As an employer, how do you know how much income tax to withhold from an employee's wages? As mentioned earlier, you figure this amount using IRS Circular E. The computation is based on an employee's marital status and withholding allowances. An employee tells an employer how many withholding allowances to take into account by completing IRS Form W-4. This form is generally not filed with the IRS. It is simply filled out by the employee and given to the employer.

As a general rule, employment taxes (income tax withholding and FICA) are not paid directly to the IRS. Instead, they are deposited with an authorized financial institution or Federal Reserve

Figure 6-2

Form W-4 (1995)

Want More Money In Your Paycheck?
If you expect to be able to take the earned income credit for 1995 and a child lives with you, you may be able to have part of the credit added to your take-home pay. For details, get Form W-5 from your employer.

Purpose. Complete Form W-4 so that your employer can withhold the correct amount of Federal income tax from your pay.

Exemption From Withholding. Read line 7 of the certificate below to see if you can claim exempt status. *If exempt, complete line 7; but do not complete lines 5 and 6.* No Federal income tax will be withheld from your pay. Your exemption is good for 1 year only. It expires February 15, 1996.

Note: *You cannot claim exemption from withholding if (1) your income exceeds $650 and includes unearned income (e.g., interest*

and dividends) and (2) another person can claim you as a dependent on their tax return.

Basic Instructions. Employees who are not exempt should complete the Personal Allowances Worksheet. Additional worksheets are provided on page 2 for employees to adjust their withholding allowances based on itemized deductions, adjustments to income, or two-earner/two-job situations. Complete all worksheets that apply to your situation. The worksheets will help you figure the number of withholding allowances you are entitled to claim. However, you may claim fewer allowances than this.

Head of Household. Generally, you may claim head of household filing status on your tax return only if you are unmarried and pay more than 50% of the costs of keeping up a home for yourself and your dependent(s) or other qualifying individuals.

Nonwage Income. If you have a large amount of nonwage income, such as interest or dividends, you should consider making

estimated tax payments using Form 1040-ES. Otherwise, you may find that you owe additional tax at the end of the year.

Two Earners/Two Jobs. If you have a working spouse or more than one job, figure the total number of allowances you are entitled to claim on all jobs using worksheets from only one Form W-4. This total should be divided among all jobs. Your withholding will usually be most accurate when all allowances are claimed on the W-4 filed for the highest paying job and zero allowances are claimed for the others.

Check Your Withholding. After your W-4 takes effect, you can use **Pub. 919,** Is My Withholding Correct for 1995?, to see how the dollar amount you are having withheld compares to your estimated total annual tax. We recommend you get Pub. 919 especially if you used the Two Earner/Two Job Worksheet and your earnings exceed $150,000 (Single) or $200,000 (Married). Call 1-800-829-3676 to order Pub. 919. Check your telephone directory for the IRS assistance number for further help.

Personal Allowances Worksheet

A   Enter "1" for **yourself** if no one else can claim you as a dependent . . . .   **A** _____

B   Enter "1" if:
- You are single and have only one job; or
- You are married, have only one job, and your spouse does not work; or
- Your wages from a second job or your spouse's wages (or the total of both) are $1,000 or less.   **B** _____

C   Enter "1" for your **spouse.** But, you may choose to enter -0- if you are married and have either a working spouse or more than one job (this may help you avoid having too little tax withheld) . . . . . .   **C** _____

D   Enter number of **dependents** (other than your spouse or yourself) you will claim on your tax return . . . . .   **D** _____

E   Enter "1" if you will file as **head of household** on your tax return (see conditions under **Head of Household** above) .   **E** _____

F   Enter "1" if you have at least $1,500 of **child or dependent care expenses** for which you plan to claim a credit . .   **F** _____

G   Add lines A through F and enter total here. **Note:** This amount may be different from the number of exemptions you claim on your return ▶   **G** _____

For accuracy, do all worksheets that apply.
- If you plan to **itemize or claim adjustments to income** and want to reduce your withholding, see the Deductions and Adjustments Worksheet on page 2.
- If you are **single** and have **more than one job** and your combined earnings from all jobs exceed $30,000 OR if you are **married** and have a **working spouse or more than one job,** and the combined earnings from all jobs exceed $50,000, see the Two-Earner/Two-Job Worksheet on page 2 if you want to avoid having too little tax withheld.
- If **neither** of the above situations applies, **stop here** and enter the number from line G on line 5 of Form W-4 below.

- - - - - - - - - - - - - - - - - **Cut here and give the certificate to your employer. Keep the top portion for your records.** - - - - - - - - - - - - - - - - -

| Form **W-4**
Department of the Treasury
Internal Revenue Service | **Employee's Withholding Allowance Certificate**
▶ **For Privacy Act and Paperwork Reduction Act Notice, see reverse.** | OMB No. 1545-0010
1995 |

| 1   Type or print your first name and middle initial   Last name | 2   Your social security number |

| Home address (number and street or rural route) | 3   ☐ Single ☐ Married ☐ Married, but withhold at higher Single rate.
Note: *If married, but legally separated, or spouse is a nonresident alien, check the Single box.* |
| City or town, state, and ZIP code | 4   If your last name differs from that on your social security card, check here and call 1-800-772-1213 for a new card . . . . . . ▶ ☐ |

5   Total number of allowances you are claiming (from line G above or from the worksheets on page 2 if they apply) .   **5** _____

6   Additional amount, if any, you want withheld from each paycheck . . . .   **6** $ _____

7   I claim exemption from withholding for 1995 and I certify that I meet **BOTH** of the following conditions for exemption:
- Last year I had a right to a refund of **ALL** Federal income tax withheld because I had **NO** tax liability; **AND**
- This year I expect a refund of **ALL** Federal income tax withheld because I expect to have **NO** tax liability.
If you meet both conditions, enter "EXEMPT" here . . . . ▶ **7** _____

Under penalties of perjury, I certify that I am entitled to the number of withholding allowances claimed on this certificate or entitled to claim exempt status.

Employee's signature ▶   Date ▶   , 19_____

| 8   Employer's name and address (Employer: Complete 8 and 10 only if sending to the IRS) | 9   Office code (optional) | 10   Employer identification number |

Cat. No. 10220Q

bank. This simply means that you must give a check (by delivery or mail) to an authorized bank by the due date for the deposit. The deposit is accompanied by a deposit slip called IRS Form 8109. New employers will automatically receive deposit slips from the IRS in a coupon book about five to six weeks after an employer identification number has been assigned.

Make the check payable to the depository where you make the deposit. Include on the check your employer identification number, the type of tax (such as Form 941 for income tax withholding and FICA) and the period to which the deposit relates (such as "December 1996").

Before you make a deposit at your local bank, check to see that it is an authorized depository. Deposits made at unauthorized financial institutions can result in penalties. Second, assuming the bank is authorized, if you use a check drawn on an institution other than the one you are using as a depository, make sure that it is willing to accept the other check.

Large corporations are required to make deposits via electronic fund transfers (EFT). Smaller businesses will not be required to make deposits via EFTs for some time. For example, employers who deposited more than $50,000 in 1995 will begin making deposits via electronic transfer on July 1, 1997. However, any business can voluntarily make deposits by EFT, which is governed by an IRS program called TAXLINK. For more information about TAXLINK, call the TAXLINK HELPLINE at (800) 829-5469.

If total tax liability for income tax withholding and FICA is less than $500 per quarter, then payment can be made directly to the IRS along with the quarterly tax return reporting these taxes. However, if you think you will only have a small liability but it then turns out that liability exceeds $500, you can be subject to penalty for not making a timely deposit. Therefore, except in limited cases, most employers must deposit taxes.

When to Deposit Taxes

Except for those permitted to pay liability with their quarterly return as discussed above, your deposit deadline is governed by the amount of your liability during a "lookback period." The lookback period is the four quarters from July 1 through June 30 beginning 18 months prior to the start of the year. Thus, for example, the look-back period for 1996 is based on liability during the period from July 1, 1994 through June 30, 1995. As a practical matter, however, you probably do not have to figure this out. The IRS does it for you. The IRS then notifies employers each November of their schedule for the coming year.

There are two deposit schedules: a monthly schedule and a semi-weekly schedule. This schedule has nothing to do with when an employer pays employee compensation and withholds income taxes and FICA (weekly; monthly). The schedule only refers to when an employer is required to deposit income tax withholding and FICA. The monthly schedule applies to employers whose liability during the lookback period was $50,000 or less. New employers are automatically placed on a monthly schedule for their first year (unless they are eligible for direct payment to the IRS because liability is less than $500). Deposits under the monthly schedule must be made no later than the 15th day of the month following the month to which the tax liability relates. Thus, withholding and FICA for January must be deposited by February 15th.

For employers with larger payrolls, deposit requirements get more complex. Under the semi-weekly schedule, which applies to those whose liability during the lookback period exceeded $50,000, deposits are made as follows:

Payment days/deposit periods	*Deposit by:*
Wednesday, Thursday and/or Friday	Following Wednesday
Saturday, Sunday, Monday and/or Tuesday	Following Friday

If the depository is closed on the day the deposit is required (e.g., it is a weekend or a holiday), then the deposit is made on the next business day.

FUTA taxes

A different deposit rule applies to FUTA taxes. FUTA deposits for all businesses, regardless of the size of the liability, must be deposited by the last day of the first month following the close of the quarter to which the FUTA taxes relate.

Quarter	*Due date*
January, February and March	April 30
April, May and June	July 31
July, August and September	October 31
October, November and December	January 31

Penalties

There are several penalties that can apply to late or misdirected deposits. Penalties for late deposits vary with the degree of lateness:

Penalty Rate	*Degree of Lateness*
2%	Deposits made 1 to 5 days late
5%	Deposits made 6 to 15 days late
10%	Deposits made 16 days or more late (and amounts paid to the IRS within 10 days of the first IRS notice asking for payment)
15%	Amounts unpaid more than 10 days after the first IRS notice asking for tax due or the day on which notice and demand for immediate payment is received, whichever is earlier

No penalty is imposed if there is reasonable cause for the lateness.

Deposit requirements are treated as made on time if they are reasonably close to the day they were due. This means that at least 98% of the actual liability must be deposited on time and any shortfall must be deposited by a makeup deadline. For monthly depositors (explained below) the makeup deadline is the quarterly return for the period of the shortfall. For semi-weekly depositors (explained below) the makeup deadline is the first Wednesday or Friday (whichever is earlier) falling on or after the 15th day of the month following the month in which the shortfall occurred.

Other penalties can be imposed if deposits are made to the wrong place (directly to the IRS, along with a tax return or to a financial institution that is not an authorized depository).

The most severe penalty that can be imposed is the failure to deposit (at all) required "trust fund" amounts. When an employer withholds income taxes and the employee's share of FICA, he/she stands in a position of trust. The funds do not belong to the employer; the employer is acting as an intermediary between the employee and the government. The failure to deposit these trust funds can result in a 100% penalty being imposed on anyone responsible for collecting, accounting for and paying these taxes. A responsible person is an officer or employee of the corporation, partner or employee of a partnership, member or employee of a limited liability company, a sole proprietor or employee of a sole proprietor, or an accountant—anyone who has authority for writing checks and directing how the business spends its funds.

Warning

The penalty applies even though a business may be organized to provide limited personal liability. Thus, for example, a shareholder can be personally on the hook for 100% of outstanding trust fund liability even though he or she otherwise enjoys limited personal liability.

The 100% trust fund penalty only applies if the action not to pay is considered willful. But the term "willful" is loosely interpreted for this purpose. It means that if an owner or employee knows of the obligation to deposit trust funds but fails to meet it (e.g., knows these taxes have not yet been deposited but instead pays a supplier), the action is considered willful.

IDEA 63: File Employment Tax Forms on Time to Avoid Penalties

Collecting and depositing tax forms on time is only the first step in a cumbersome process of reporting to the IRS and the state. As an employer, you are required to file certain returns with the IRS and your state. Avoiding penalties for late filing and non-filing is an important cost-saving measure for every business.

Here is a partial listing of your federal filing requirements.

Deadline	Form	Description
January 31	Form W-2	Compensation statement furnished to employees
	Form 1099	Information return furnished to independent contractors
	Form 940 or 940-EZ	Unemployment return (annual) filed with IRS
	Form 941	Social Security and income tax withholding return (4th quarter of prior year) filed with IRS
February 10	Form 940 or 940-EZ	Unemployment return filed with IRS if tax deposited in full and on time
	Form 941	Social Security and income tax withholding return (4th quarter of prior year) filed with IRS if tax deposited in full and on time
February 28	Form W-2	Copy A (along with transmittal Form W-3) filed with SSA
	Form 1099	Information return filed with IRS
April 30	Form 941	Social Security and income tax withholding return (1st quarter) filed with IRS
May 10	Form 941	Social Security and income tax withholding return (1st quarter) filed with IRS if tax deposited in full and on time
July 31	Form 941	Social Security and income tax withholding return (2nd quarter) filed with IRS
August 10	Form 941	Social Security and income tax withholding return (2nd quarter) filed with IRS if tax deposited in full and on time
October 31	Form 941	Social Security and income tax withholding return (3rd quarter) filed with IRS
November 10	Form 941	Social Security and income tax withholding return (3rd quarter) filed with IRS if tax deposited in full and on time

If any of the filing deadlines falls on a Saturday, Sunday, or legal holiday, the filing deadline becomes the next business day. For example, if October 31, the deadline for filing Form 941 for the third quarter, falls on a Saturday, the filing deadline becomes November 2 (November 1 would be a Sunday).

Warning

Check with your state Employment Tax Department for its own filing requirements.

A sample IRS Form W-2 and IRS Form 1099 are re-printed in fig. 6-3 and 6-4. You cannot reproduce these forms for your own use. The actual forms that must be used have several layers (with either carbons or self-duplicating paper). For example, a Form W-2 has six layers so that a copy of the form can be sent as required to the Social Security Administration, four copies are given to the employee (for filing with a federal, state, and/or local income tax return and one additional copy for the employee's records) and the last copy for the employer's records. The Form 1099 has three layers: one for the IRS, one for the worker and one for the employer.

All forms are available from the IRS by calling (800) 829-1040. You can also purchase W-2s and 1099s from your local office supply or stationery store.

Relief for small business

The SBA, IRS and Treasury Department are developing a one-page quarterly reporting system for small employers (for those with 10 or fewer employees). A pilot program is scheduled for late 1996 in locations as yet to be determined. While it is too early to say whether this proposed simplified reporting system will be beneficial to small businesses, it is important to keep an eye on this new program in the works.

Figure 6-3

a Control number			
		OMB No. 1545-0008	

b Employer's identification number	1 Wages, tips, other compensation	2 Federal income tax withheld

c Employer's name, address, and ZIP code	3 Social security wages	4 Social security tax withheld
	5 Medicare wages and tips	6 Medicare tax withheld
	7 Social security tips	8 Allocated tips

d Employee's social security number	9 Advance EIC payment	10 Dependent care benefits

e Employee's name, address, and ZIP code	11 Nonqualified plans	12 Benefits included in box 1
	13	14 Other

15 Statutory employee	Deceased	Pension plan	Legal rep.	Hshld. emp.	Subtotal	Deferred compensation

16 State	Employer's state I.D. No.	17 State wages, tips, etc.	18 State income tax	19 Locality name	20 Local wages, tips, etc.	21 Local income tax

(O)

Department of the Treasury—Internal Revenue Service

Form **W-2** Wage and Tax Statement **1996**

Copy 1 For State, City, or Local Tax Department

5 WA

---

a Control number			
		OMB No. 1545-0008	

b Employer's identification number	1 Wages, tips, other compensation	2 Federal income tax withheld

c Employer's name, address, and ZIP code	3 Social security wages	4 Social security tax withheld
	5 Medicare wages and tips	6 Medicare tax withheld
	7 Social security tips	8 Allocated tips

d Employee's social security number	9 Advance EIC payment	10 Dependent care benefits

e Employee's name, address, and ZIP code	11 Nonqualified plans	12 Benefits included in box 1
	13	14 Other

15 Statutory employee	Deceased	Pension plan	Legal rep.	Hshld. emp.	Subtotal	Deferred compensation

16 State	Employer's state I.D. No.	17 State wages, tips, etc.	18 State income tax	19 Locality name	20 Local wages, tips, etc.	21 Local income tax

(O)

Department of the Treasury—Internal Revenue Service

Form **W-2** Wage and Tax Statement **1996**

Copy 1 For State, City, or Local Tax Department

5 WA

Figure 6-4

9595	☐ VOID	☐ CORRECTED	

PAYER'S name, street address, city, state, and ZIP code	**1** Rents $	OMB No. 1545-0115	**Miscellaneous Income**
	2 Royalties $	**19 96**	
	3 Other income $	Form **1099-MISC**	
PAYER'S Federal identification number	RECIPIENT'S identification number	**4** Federal income tax withheld $	**5** Fishing boat proceeds $	**Copy A**
RECIPIENT'S name		**6** Medical and health care payments $	**7** Nonemployee compensation $	**For Internal Revenue Service Center**
Street address (including apt. no.)		**8** Substitute payments in lieu of dividends or interest $	**9** Payer made direct sales of $5,000 or more of consumer products to a buyer (recipient) for resale ▶ ☐	**File with Form 1096.**
City, state, and ZIP code		**10** Crop insurance proceeds $	**11** State income tax withheld $	For Paperwork Reduction Act Notice and instructions for completing this form, see **Instructions for Forms 1099, 1098, 5498, and W-2G.**
Account number (optional)	2nd TIN Not. ☐	**12** State/Payer's state number		

Form **1099-MISC**   Cat. No. 14425J   Department of the Treasury - Internal Revenue Service

Do NOT Cut or Separate Forms on This Page

7

CHAPTER

Keeping Down the Cost of Equipment, Space and Intangibles

Whatever type of business you are starting or running, you need equipment, a place to operate, and certain intangibles—a company name, a product name. These assets— personal property, real property and intangibles—are a significant part of any business. Reducing the cost of acquiring and carrying these assets can mean signifi-cant dollar savings to your business.

   In this chapter you will learn various strategies for reducing the cost of acquiring and using equipment, realty and intangibles.

Idea 64: Identify Your Asset Needs

Knowing the assets you have or need as a business is an important part of the cost of starting your business venture.

Equipment

Obviously, the nature of the business dictates exactly what equipment is needed. If you are in a service business, your equipment needs may be limited to a telephone, a computer, a fax machine, a copier and, perhaps, a pager. If you are in retail, you may need cash registers and display cases in addition to office equipment. If you are in manufacturing, you will need machinery to produce your product. If you are a craftsperson, you need specialized tools.

For cash-poor businesses, big ticket equipment needs present a real problem. Heavy machinery aside, most businesses today cannot get by without a computer. It has been estimated that the cost of a pentium computer, necessary software, a modem and a laser printer can run between $3,500 and $8,500! What happens if you lack the finances to buy the equipment needed to run the business? Do not be discouraged. You may be surprised to find out that you can afford to have the equipment you need. First of all, you do not necessarily have to buy the equipment; leasing may be a good alternative. Second, if you do buy the equipment, there may be significant tax incentives that serve to offset the cost of the equipment. In effect, Uncle Sam is shouldering a portion of your purchase costs. And there are many ways to cut equipment costs.

Realty

Again, the nature of your business dictates your realty needs. If you manufacture products, you need a plant; if you are in the consulting business, an office—even one in your home—is all that you require. Whatever your needs, there are several ways in which you can cut your monthly bills for this asset.

Intangibles

All businesses have some intangibles, whether they know it or not. Intangibles are a class of assets that cannot be touched or seen but have value to the business. Many intangibles fall into a category called intellectual property (such as patents, copyrights, and trade secrets). All businesses, for example, have one type of intangible: a unique name that is worth protecting. Many companies also have another type of intangible—special product names ("trademarks"). Some trademarks have become so popular that they have become generic names for the product. For example Aspirin used to be Bayer's name for its pain remedy; now it simply means a pain reliever with acetaminophen as one of its ingredients. Scotch tape, tissues, ketchup and jello are but a few examples of company product names that have become generic. Another intangible common to all businesses is called "good will." It is that special quality—name, reputation—that a business builds up. Good will has value that can be bought or sold.

IDEA 65: Start with Equipment You Already Own

When starting a business, equipment needs may represent a significant portion of start up costs. You need the equipment to get going, but getting the equipment is another matter. When cash is short, it may be better to use whatever equipment you already own personally rather than buying duplicate equipment for the company. For example, if you already have a home computer that is adequate for your initial business needs, simply contribute the computer to the business. (It is an investment in the business the same as if you put in cash.) The same is true for other equipment—power tools contributed to your contracting business, office furniture to your service business.

Tax Consequences

Businesses can recover the cost of equipment purchases by depreciating them over set periods of time. (Depreciation is explained in greater detail later in this chapter.) This means deducting a portion of the cost of the equipment each year. Theoretically, when the cost of the equipment has been fully depreciated, the equipment will no longer have any value to the business. For example, if you purchase equipment that the tax laws say has a seven-year life, at the end of seven years, presumably, the equipment will have been used up or obsolete and it will be time to replace it with new equipment. When you contribute property to a business (rather than having the business buy new equipment), the business essentially steps in your shoes for purposes of depreciating the contributed property. Thus, if you paid $1,000, it is this figure (called "basis") that the business will use for depreciation.

The basis of equipment is reduced each year by depreciation deductions. If equipment starts with a basis of $1,000 and depreciation for the first year is $200, then the basis of the equipment at the end of the first year is $800 ($1,000 – $200).

The same rules apply for purposes of determining gain or loss if the equipment is sold or exchanged (rather than simply used up and junked). Thus, if you paid $1,000 for equipment you contribute to the business, then for purposes of determining gain or loss on a sale or exchange of this equipment, the $1,000 is treated as the equipment's basis. Thus, if it sells for $1,200, the business has a gain; if it sells for $800, the business has a loss.

There is a potential downside to contributing your personal property to the business. If you still need to use the equipment (such as a computer) for personal purposes, you may jeopardize tax write-offs for the business. The problems of mixed use property (business and personal use) are discussed in greater detail later in this chapter.

IDEA 66: Lease Rather than Buy Equipment

Where dollars count and cash flow is tight, it may be better for you to lease equipment rather than buy it. Leasing is readily available for cars, computers, faxes, telephone systems and other equipment. Leasing requires less money up-front and smaller payments over the term of the lease (when compared with financing an equipment purchase).

> **Example:** The business needs $5,000 of computer equipment. You do not have the funds to buy it outright. To finance the purchase of the computer equipment, you are paying for the entire cost of the computer equipment over time, plus interest. To lease the equipment, you are only paying for a portion of the cost of the equipment over the term of the lease, plus interest. Of course, if you buy the equipment, you will own something once the loan term is complete; with a lease, you do not own anything at the end of the lease term. You may, however, have the option of purchasing the equipment at its residual value (specified in the lease), such as 10% of the purchase price.

Leasing may allow you to enjoy the use of more expensive equipment for the same monthly cost of buying it because you are only paying the leasing company for a portion of the cost of the item (the leasing company retains the equipment at the end of the lease). Leasing can also let you use the latest technology. Instead of buying a computer that will be outdated within 18 months to 30 months, consider leasing one for a limited time (e.g., 18 months). You pay only for your use of the computer for that period; you do not have to pay for the entire computer. At the end of the lease term, you can lease a new computer containing the latest technology.

Automobiles

One of the key decisions that many businesses must make is whether to buy or lease a car. The same considerations used to decide whether to buy or lease a computer also affect the decision on the car:

- *Up-front costs and termination fees.* What does it cost to activate the lease? To terminate it? Check all fees carefully. Ads claiming low monthly costs may be based on the fact that you are required to pay a sizable amount up-front. Also, find out if there are special up-front costs sometimes called "acquisition fees" which can be several hundred dollars. Find out about termination fees, sometimes called disposition fees. These fees, which can also be several hundred dollars, are payable simply because the lease is up (the leasing company claims the fee is used to process the car on termination).

- *Monthly carrying costs.* What is the monthly payment?

- *What is left at the end?* Both a computer and a car are assets that decline in value over time, rather than appreciate. Therefore, you must decide whether it is advisable to buy an entire asset that will certainly be worth less when you are done paying for it. Other assets may, however, appreciate over time and make them more valuable to own rather than lease.

- *Consider limitations on a lease.* It may not make sense to lease if these limitations wind up costing you more than simply buying. For example, car leases typically have a limit on the number of miles that can be driven each year; mileage over the limit is costly (10 cents to 15 cents per mile). The least expensive lease may have a 12,000 mile annual limit; a more costly lease may permit 15,000 miles per year. If you expect to use the car for 20,000 miles a year, then you know at the outset that the there will be an additional cost to the lease for the excess mileage.

- *Tax considerations of buying versus leasing.* If you buy the car, you can depreciate its cost. However, dollar limits severely limit annual write-offs (discussed later in this chapter). In lieu of claiming depreciation, business use of a car can be deducted by using a standard mileage allowance based on cents-per-mile (31 cents per business mile in 1996). On the other hand, if you lease, you cannot claim any depreciation. You can deduct your lease payments. However, if the car is considered a "luxury car," (the dollar amount is re-defined each year), then you may be required to include in income a certain amount designed to equate the lease deduction with what would have been claimed for depreciation had the car be purchased.

Warning

Regardless of whether you decide to buy or lease, be sure to check the insurance costs of the model you are considering. Insurance costs vary considerably from car to car.

Getting the Best Lease Terms

Whether you buy or lease equipment, payments over a period of time reflect an interest rate. When taking a lease, be sure to find out what interest rate you are paying. If the charge is high, you may be able to negotiate a lower one. Or you may just find that it is cheaper to buy the equipment rather than lease it.

Find out what it will cost if you want to get out of the lease. What if your business goes under before the end of the lease term? Will you be personally on the hook for the balance? What if you need a newer model before the end of the lease term? Will you have to make a large payment to prematurely terminate the lease? Look for hidden costs. What, for example, are the charges you must pay when the lease is up? There may be "handling charges," "service charges" or other costs.

Establish the buyout cost at the end of the lease. If you want to buy the equipment when the lease is up, what will it cost you?

IDEA 67: Make Equipment Last Longer

The longer you can use what you already own, the greater your savings in the long run.

Buy Better to Save in the Long Run

Look at the item that you need to buy. Can you get by with a lower-priced model, perhaps last year's model? Do you need to have the most recent and most expensive version of the item? If you are pressed for funds, you may tend to look at lower-priced models as a way to economize. What may seem like a bargain to begin with may wind up costing you more over the long term.

For example, buying a slow modem because it has a lower ticket price than a faster one will certainly cost the business more over time. The difference between a modem that runs at 14,400 bauds versus one that runs at 28,800 bauds may be a few hundred dollars. However, the slower modem will need more time to transfer data over the telephone lines, costing more in telephone charges. What is more, if the business uses on-line providers to the Internet that charge by the hour, then the lower modems will also run up higher monthly on-line provider charges. Finally, your time is money. The slower modems will make you waste your time (and cause frustration) waiting for responses; time that could have been used to greater advantage.

The same reasoning applies to the purchase of a computer. Buy one that runs as fast as current technology allows. Again, the up-front cost may be greater than buying a more modest machine. In the long run, however, buying for speed will save money because of the time it saves you and your business. When buying a computer, review the software you plan to run. Then make sure that the hardware will be sufficient. For example, if you will be doing a lot of number crunching, you need a machine that is fast. Otherwise, you will waste your time just sitting in front of the monitor waiting for tasks to be completed.

For some types of equipment, "better" means heavy-duty. Such upgraded equipment may prove more cost effective over time.

Buy the best you can afford for the money you have. You will save in the long run by avoiding costly repairs and the need for early replacement.

Keep What You Have in Good Repair

Today we have become conditioned to the expendable economy—when it breaks, replace it. This thinking may cost you unnecessary dollars in the long run.

Preventative maintenance

Take care of what you already own. Do annual or other periodic servicing on equipment to keep it in a state of good repair. Keep track of maintenance schedules in a log book or other recordkeeper to ensure regularity. Simple steps, like oiling and cleaning, can help machines last years longer.

Repairs

Get broken equipment repaired. While the cost of some servicing is high, if the equipment is still up-to-date, it may be advisable to get it repaired rather than junking it when broken. With this in mind, you may want to buy service contracts for certain equipment. For example, you may want to take an on-site service contract for your computer if your business cannot function without it. The use of the service contract may more than offset the charges for service. And you can ensure prompt repair of a vital piece of equipment.

$$Extra Savings

Keeping equipment in good repair can save not only on replacement costs but can also avoid costly employee accidents or even fines imposed by OSHA.

IDEA 68: Shop Mail Order

The mail-order business allows you to find just abut anything you require for your business without leaving your office. Today, most products—office supplies, computers, tools and other equipment—are found in catalogs. There are several cost-saving advantages to shopping through catalogs.

First, the cost of mail-order goods generally is lower than what can be found in retail stores. Of course, you have to know what you are buying to be savvy about the price. Check about return policies so that you will not lose anything if you are dissatisfied with the product in any way.

Second, if you buy your equipment through the mail from an out-of-state supplier, you will save on sales tax (different states have different rules regarding sales tax on out-of-state sales). While there are shipping costs to consider, the savings on sales tax more than offsets these costs. (Some mail order companies even absorb delivery costs for orders over a certain dollar amount.)

Third, you save the time and travel expenses of not having to go to the stores to shop for the items you need.

While the dollar and time savings of catalog shopping may be significant, there are a couple of important drawbacks to consider:

- Catalog shopping may be helpful for some of your needs but not for others. Some businesses, for example, may like to order supplies from a catalog because they are familiar with the brands and little can go wrong. On the other hand, ordering a computer through the mail may not be for everyone. Some prefer the ability to go into a store to check things out and bring back faulty items.

- You may not find what you need. Sometimes what you are looking for can only be found in a specialty store or through special order. For example, a catalog may offer a standard size of a particular item. If you need a different size, you may not be able to get it through the catalog.

IDEA 69: Buy Secondhand

While new equipment may be needed for some aspects of your business, you may be able to keep costs down by buying some items secondhand. In today's parlance, secondhand equipment is referred to as "pre-owned." There are, for example, companies that recondition the more recent models of computers and re-sell them. The cost of these reconditioned computers: About 40% of the retail price, a substantial savings. What is more, these reconditioned machines even come with warranties!

Did You Know. . .

According to one study, more than 10 million personal computers are junked each year.

Will secondhand do? It depends on what the item will be used for. If, for example, you are a craftsperson, the tools of your trade should be top of the line and pre-owned tools may not suffice. But you may be able to get away with using a slower computer model to do your billing and recordkeeping. This is where you can save money. For example, if you can get by with an older operating system (for use as word processors, form generators or other simple functions), a refurbished 386 or 486 machine with a black-and-white monitor can be bought for as little as $500 as compared with a pentium system (and color monitor) of $2,500 or more!

Office furniture is an area where many small businesses can save money by getting pre-owned goods. Back offices need not be furnished with new desks and chairs. But if your office is host to clients and customers, slightly worn may give a poor impression. In this case, only new will do.

Only you know your business and its needs. If you think that used equipment will meet your requirements, then look through your local newspapers for businesses that are going under and try to acquire some of their equipment. For example, if you are planning to set up a retail store, you might want to buy some items (such as a cash register, display cabinets, or office safe) from a store that is going out of business and liquidating its assets.

Forced liquidations by companies in bankruptcy or sheriff's sales are other ways to buy used goods at reduced costs. Check your local newspapers for listings of bankruptcy or sheriff's sales.

Here are some places to look for second hand equipment:

Type of property	*Where to look*
Forfeited property (seized by U.S. Customs Service)	EG&G Dynatrend, PAL Customers Service Support 23000 Clarendon Blvd., Suite 705 Arlington, VA 22201 Phone (703) 351-7887
Computers	Computer Renaissance (85 franchised stores nationwide) Phone (612) 520-8500 to locate a convenient store
Computers	Chicago Computer Exchange 5225 South Harper Chicago, IL 60610 (312) 667-5221
Displays for trade show exhibits (tabletops, portables, modulars and custom)	Second-Life Exhibits Inc. 100 Justin Drive Chelsea, MA 02150
Furniture (cannot ship used furniture) and some office equipment (may be able to ship)	Aaron Rents & Sells 5720 General Washington Drive Alexandria, VA 22312 Phone (703) 750-0787
Government surplus	General Services Administration Properties, Consumer Information Center Department 514A Pueblo, CO 81009 Phone (800) 472-1313

To locate other suppliers in your area, call the International Facility Management Association (713) 623-4362 or the National Office Products Association (703) 549-9040.

Warning

In buying secondhand, be sure to inquire about warranties. Make sure there is some warranty. For example, on pre-owned computers, the warranty varies from between 60 days and 90 days (parts and labor).

IDEA 70: Time Equipment Purchases to Maximize Depreciation Deductions

Depreciation is a deduction for a portion of the cost of business equipment over the life of the property. The life of the property is generally determined by recovery periods set by the IRS (listed below). Depreciation may be accelerated during the early years of ownership, meaning that a greater portion of the cost of the equipment can be deducted in the first several years. Since deductions serve to offset revenue, it reduces business profits subject to tax, resulting in tax savings.

The depreciation system that is currently in use is called MACRS and applies to tangible property placed in service after 1986. There are two subcategories to this system: the basic system, General Depreciation System (GDS) and an alternate system, the Alternative Depreciation System (ADS). The systems differ in two ways: the recovery period over which depreciation is claimed and the method for figuring depreciation. The basic system is used unless the alternate system is elected or is required to be used. Neither system can be used for certain property, such as intangibles (patents, copyrights, etc.), motion picture films or videotapes, sound recordings and certain other property.

To figure depreciation, you need to know the following five things:

1. *The equipment's recovery period.* There are a number of classes to which various types of property are assigned. The term of the class (e.g., five-year property) is the recovery period—the time over which the property is depreciated (subject to adjustment for conventions). The recovery periods include:

   - 3-year property (taxis, tractor units for use on the road, certain handling devices for manufacturing food and beverages, special tools for manufacturing rubber products and certain animals)

   - 5-year property (cars, buses, trucks, airplanes, trailers and trailer containers, computers, peripheral equipment, office machinery, property used in construction, logging equipment, property used to manufacture organic and inorganic chemicals, property used in research and experimentation and certain breeding and dairy cattle and goat)

- 7-year property (office furniture and fixtures, property used in printing, recreational assets, property used to produce jewelry, musical instruments, toys, sporting goods and motion picture and television films and tapes, as well as breeding and horses and any property not assigned to another class)

- 10-year property (barges, tugs, vessels and similar water transportation, single purpose agricultural or horticultural structures placed in service after 1988 and trees or vines bearing fruits or nuts)

- 15-year property (depreciable improvements to land, such as bridges, fences, roads and shrubbery)

- 20-year property (farm buildings other than single purpose agricultural or horticultural structures and municipal sewers.

2. *The basis of the property for depreciation.* This is generally the cost of the property (including sales tax). If property is acquired any way other than purchase (e.g., you convert property you own personally to business use or contribute your property to your corporation), then the new owner of the property (the business) steps into your shoes, taking over your basis. For example, on January 1, 1997 you form a corporation and transfer to it your computer (valued at $3,500 just a month before) in exchange for stock in the corporation. The corporation's basis in the computer for depreciation purposes is $3,500. However, when using the carryover basis, the basis used by the business cannot be greater than the value of the property at the time of conversion. For example, if the computer cost $3,500 but was only worth $3,000 on the day it was transferred to the corporation, the corporation's basis would have been limited to $3,000.

3. *The date the property was placed in service.* Depreciation begins on the date on which property is "placed in service." This is not necessarily the same date as the date on which the property is purchased. The property must be ready and available for its specified use. Thus, if you order and pay for a computer on September 1 which is not delivered to your business until October 1, the date the property is placed in service is October 1, not September 1.

4. *The applicable convention.* You buy five-year equipment for your business. You can depreciate it over five years. Right? Wrong! Certain conventions apply that effectively spread out the period over which the property is depreciated. These conventions include:

- The half-year convention assumes that property was placed in service in the middle of the year regardless of the actual date on which the property was placed in service. As such, you can only claim one-half of the otherwise allowable depreciation for the first year. Thus, for example, for five-year property, one-half of the first year's depreciation is claimed in year one; depreciation will be claimed over a six-year period to permit a full write-off of cost. Under the half-year convention, property is treated as disposed of in the middle of the year, regardless of the actual date of disposition.

- The mid-quarter convention supersedes the half-year convention if more than 40% of the cost of all property placed in service during the year is placed in service during the last quarter of the year. Under this convention, all property placed in service (or disposed of) during the year is treated as placed in service (or disposed of) in the middle of the applicable quarter.

    Example: In 1997, a business places in service two items: a machine (number 1) costing $2,500 and a machine (number 2) costing $10,000. Assume that machine number 1 is placed in service in February and machine number 2 is placed in service in December. In this case, the mid-quarter convention applies since more than 40% of all property ($12,500) placed in service during 1997 was placed in service in the last quarter of the year ($10,000). (Actually, 80% of all property was placed in service in the last quarter of 1997.)

    However, suppose machine 2 was placed in service in February and machine number 1 was placed in service in December. In this case, the mid-quarter convention does not apply (and the half-year convention applies). This is because only 20% of the cost of all property placed in service during the year was placed in service during the last quarter of 1997.

    The fact that the business is subject to the mid-quarter convention in one year does not influence whether it is subject to that convention in a subsequent year. It merely determines how the equipment subject to the mid-quarter convention will be depreciated over its entire recovery period. Thus, for example, equipment placed in service in 1997 which is subject to the mid-quarter convention continues to be depreciated accordingly for the remainder of its recovery period. But if that same company places equipment in service in 1998 and the mid-quarter convention does not apply for that year, then that equipment is never subject to the mid-quarter convention.

5. *The depreciation method.* Depreciation method is the manner in which depreciation is claimed over the recovery period of the property. Some methods are considered accelerated depreciation because they permit a greater write-off in the earlier years of ownership. Accelerated depreciation methods include a 200% declining balance rate, a 150% declining balance rate and the 150% election. Another method is called straight line depreciation. This method spreads the write-offs evenly over the recovery period of the property. The straight line rate is used when an election is made to use it or when ADS applies.

As a practical matter, you do not have to compute the rate under the applicable convention. The rates have already been worked out for you by the IRS. You simply apply the applicable rate to the basis of the property to arrive at the annual depreciation deduction for that property. The rates for depreciation of equipment are as follows:

MACRS Rates—Half-Year Convention

Year	3-year property	5-year property	7-year property
1	33.33%	20.00%	14.29%
2	44.45%	32.00%	24.49%
3	14.81%	19.20%	17.49%
4	7.81%	11.52%	12.49%
5		11.52%	8.93%
6		5.76%	8.92%
7			8.93%
8			4.46%

MACRS Rates-Mid-Quarter Convention—200% Rate
Three-Year Property

Year	1st quarter	2nd quarter	3rd quarter	4th quarter
1	58.33%	41.67%	25.00%	8.33%
2	27.78%	38.89%	50.00%	61.11%
3	12.35%	14.14%	16.677%	20.37%
4	1.54%	5.30%	8.33%	10.19%

Five-Year Property

Year	1st quarter	2nd quarter	3rd quarter	4th quarter
1	35.00%	25.00%	15.00%	5.00%
2	26.00%	30.00%	34.00%	38.00%
3	15.60%	18.00%	20.40%	22.80%
4	11.01%	11.37%	12.24%	13.68%
5	11.01%	11.37%	11.30%	10.94%
6	1.38%	4.26%	7.06%	9.58%

Seven-Year Property

Year	1st quarter	2nd quarter	3rd quarter	4th quarter
1	25.00%	17.85%	10.71%	3.57%
2	21.43%	23.47%	25.51%	27.55%
3	15.31%	16.76%	18.22%	19.68%
4	10.93%	11.97%	13.02%	14.06%
5	8.75%	8.87%	9.30%	10.04%
6	8.74%	8.87%	8.85%	8.73%
7	8.75%	8.87%	8.86%	8.73%
8	1.09%	3.33%	5.53%	7.64%

$$Extra Savings

If the 200% declining balance rate is used, you can switch to the straight line when it provides a deduction of equal or greater value than the accelerated rate.

The following table shows you when it becomes advantageous to use the straight line rate.

When to Change to Straight Line Method

Class	Changeover Year
3-year property	3rd
5-year property	4th
7-year property	5th
10-year property	7th
15-year property	7th
20-year property	9th

The 150% rate is used for 15-year and 20-year property over the GDS recovery period. Again, the half-year or mid-quarter convention must be applied. You can change over to the straight line method in the year in which it gives you the greater write-off (as noted in the table below).

The ADS must be used for the following property:

- Listed property not used more than 50% for business. Listed property includes cars and other transportation vehicles, computers and peripherals (unless used only at a regular business establishment), and cellular telephones.

- Tangible property used predominantly outside the U.S.

- Tax-exempt property.

- Tax-exempt bond-financed property.

- Imported property covered by an executive order of the President of the U.S.

- Property used predominantly in farming and placed in service during any year in which you elect not to apply the uniform capitalization rules to certain farming costs.

The alternate depreciation system requires depreciation to be figured using the straight line method. This is figured by dividing the cost of the property by the alternate recovery period. In some cases, the recovery period is the same as for the basic system. In some cases it is longer.

Recovery Periods Under ADS	
Cars, computers, light duty trucks	5 years
Furniture and fixtures	10 years
Personal property with no class life	12 years
Nonresidential/residential real estate	40 years

You can elect to use the alternate system for other property in order to claim more gradual depreciation. The election applies to all property within the same class placed in service during the year (other than real estate).

Now that you know the basics of depreciation, consider how to maximize your deductions.

- Time equipment purchases during the year to ensure that the mid-quarter convention does not apply (or that it does apply if it would be more advantageous). The only way to know for sure which is more advantageous is to run the numbers. This requires you to plan equipment purchases in advance. Establish new equipment needs at the start of the year, then time purchases to accommodate cash flow availability and depreciation objectives.

- Elect to use the ADS if the business cannot benefit from accelerated depreciation. An election to use the alternate system may be helpful when, for example, the business is first starting out and does not have sufficient income to offset large depreciation deductions. Use of the alternate system can also help to avoid alternative minimum tax and the special depreciation computations required for alternative minimum tax. A note of caution: make the ADS election carefully since you cannot change your mind once the election has been made.

- Switch to the straight line method when it results in a greater annual depreciation deduction than is allowable under an accelerated depreciation method. There is no real downside to this election. The business must simply be tuned in to this opportunity.

For tax purposes as well as good business practice you should keep a record of the equipment to purchase and other relevant information for depreciation. The following IRS worksheet can help you in this recordkeeping task:

Warning

There is a dollar limit on the amount of depreciation that can be claimed on cars and light trucks (6,000 pounds or less, without passengers). The dollar limit depends on when they are placed in service. For example, a car placed in service in 1996 is subject to a first-year limit of $3,060. The depreciation limit for the second year (the amount deducted in 1997) is limited to $4,900. The third year limit is $2,950 and the limit for each year thereafter is $1,775.

IDEA 71: Use a Tax Break to Defray Equipment Costs

If you buy equipment and your business is profitable, you may shift some of the cost of the equipment to Uncle Sam. You may elect to "expense" the cost of equipment in full in the year of purchase instead of writing it off over time using depreciation. This is called "first-year expensing" or the Section 179 deduction.

Basics of Expensing

For 1996, you can elect to deduct up to $17,500 of the cost of tangible property used in your business. The dollar limit increases as follows: $18,000 in 1997, $18,500 in 1988, $19,000 in 1999, $20,000 in 2000, $24,000 in 2001 and $25,000 in 2003.

Warning

The property must be acquired by purchase. Thus, you cannot expense equipment that you contribute to the business; the business must go out and buy it. If property is acquired in whole or in part by means of a trade (you trade in one machine for another), you cannot use expensing for the portion of the property acquired by trade.

Figure 7-1

Depreciation Worksheet

Description of Property	Date Placed in Service	Cost or Other Basis	Business/ Investment Use %	Section 179 Deduction	Depreciation Prior Years	Basis for Depreciation	Method/ Convention	Recovery Period	Rate or Table %	Depreciation Deduction

Printed on recycled paper

Generally, expensing does not apply to equipment you lease to others. This restriction on leased property does not apply to equipment leased by corporations. However, expensing is allowed for equipment leased to non-corporate businesses if you manufactured the property and leased it for a term which is less than half of the property's class life and, for the first 12 months the equipment is transferred to the lessee, the total business deductions for the equipment are more than 15% of the rental income for the leased property.

There are a number of limits on expensing equipment.

Dollar limit

No more than the dollar limit can be deducted in any one year. (There is an additional dollar limit for certain equipment placed in service in an empowerment zone designated by the Department of Housing and Urban Development (HUD) or the Department of Agriculture or on an Indian reservation.) The dollar limit applies on a per-taxpayer basis. If you own more than one business, you must aggregate your allocable share of expensing deductions and then deduct no more than the dollar limit on your individual return.

> **Example:** In 1997, you have a sole proprietorship that purchased a $10,000 machine. You are also a 50% partner in a partnership that purchased a $30,000 machine. Your aggregate expensing deductions are $25,000 ($10,000 from the sole proprietorship and 50% of the $30,000 from the partnership). You can deduct only $18,000, the dollar limit for 1997. The balance of the deduction, $7,000 ($25,000 – $18,000) is wasted and will never be taken.

Husbands and wives are treated as one taxpayer for purposes of this dollar limit. Thus, in 1997 a couple can claim only one $18,000 deduction on a joint tax return. It does not matter which spouse had the property interest. Filing separately will not entitle each to a full deduction since the dollar limit on a separate return by a married person is $9,000 (one half of $18,000).

Warning

Despite the dollar limit for expensing in general, cars are subject to a lower dollar limit as explained earlier in this chapter.

Investment limit

The expensing deduction is designed to encourage small businesses to make equipment purchases. Larger businesses cannot take advantage of the deduction opportunity because every dollar of investment in equipment over $200,000 reduces the dollar limit. In 1997, if a business buys equipment costing more than $218,000, no expensing deduction can be claimed since the dollar limit has been reduced to zero ($218,000 − $200,000 = $18,000 excess investment which fully offsets the $17,500 expensing limit).

Taxable income limit

The business must be profitable to enjoy the expensing limit because a taxable income limit applies. Expensing deductions cannot exceed taxable income from the active conduct of a business. (Active conduct means that you participate in the business in a meaningful way, such as in the management or operations of the business.) Taxable income for purposes of this limit has a special meaning. It means taxable income from the business without the expensing deduction, the deduction for one-half of self-employment tax (applicable to sole proprietors, partners and members in limited liability companies), and net operating loss carrybacks and carryforwards. If this taxable income limit operates to limit your current expensing deduction, any unused deduction can be carried forward and used in a future year.

> **Example:** Your taxable income limit (which does not reflect the current expensing deduction) is $10,000. In 1997, you place in service a machine costing $15,000. Your expensing deduction for 1997 is limited to $10,000, your taxable income. You can carry forward the unused $5,000 to be used in a future year when there is sufficient taxable income from your business activities to offset it.

Limits for pass-through entities

In the case of S corporations, partnerships and limited liability companies (treated as partnerships for federal income tax purposes), the dollar limit, investment limit and taxable income limit apply at both the owner and entity levels. For example, each partner must apply the dollar limit, investment limit and taxable income limit on his/her individual return; the partnership must also apply these limits.

Warning

If the equipment is sold, otherwise disposed of, or ceases to be used in the business, there may be "recapture" of the deduction. This means that a portion of the deduction must be included as an item of income. The amount of recapture depends upon how long the equipment was used in the business. The longer the period of use, the smaller the amount of recapture. If the equipment is sold at a gain, recapture is not additional income but only a reclassification of that income from capital gain to ordinary income.

Recapture is figured by comparing the expensing deduction with the ordinary depreciation deductions that would have been claimed if expensing had not been elected. Thus, if equipment is not disposed of until the end of the period for which depreciation would have been taken (such as seven years for most equipment), then there is no recapture to be concerned about.

IDEA 72: Nail Down Maximum Depreciation Deductions for "Listed Property"

Certain property is called "listed property" and is subject to special depreciation limits. Listed property is:

- Cars

- Other transportation vehicles (including boats)

- Computers and peripherals, unless used only at a regular business establishment owned or leased by the person operating the establishment. A home office that satisfies the tax law requirements (discussed later in this Chapter) is treated as a business establishment.

- Cellular telephones (or similar telecommunication equipment)

These are the only items of listed property because they have been specified as such in the tax law. For example, fax machines, non-cellular telephones and beepers are not treated as listed property because the tax law has not included them in the category of listed property.

If business use of listed property is not more than 50% for business during the year, then the basic depreciation system (explained earlier) cannot be used. Under the basic system, accelerated depreciation can be claimed. Where business use of listed property is not more than 50% for business during the year, you must use the alternate depreciation system. Under this system, depreciation can be figured only with the straight line method. Divide the cost of the property by the alternative recovery period. For cars, computers and other listed property, the alternative recovery period happens to be the same as the basic recovery period—5 years.

Use of the alternate depreciation system means that instead of accelerating depreciation deductions to the earlier years of ownership of the property, depreciation deductions will be spread evenly over the recovery period of the property.

When is it desirable to claim accelerated depreciation in order to maximize write offs, and be sure that business use exceeds the 50% threshold? How do you prove business use? This can be problematic. It is helpful to keep a log book in which business use can be recorded. For example, in the case of a car, the tax law requires that you have written proof of business use in the form of a log book, diary or other written material. Use of a car is based on the percentage of mileage (and not the amount of time). The following sample log can be used to record car mileage that will satisfy tax law requirements for claiming accelerated depreciation for a car (assuming business use exceeds 50%).

Sample Log for Car Use

Date	Purpose of trip	Odometer	Breakdown of miles driven					
				Start	End	Business	Investment	Personal

For a computer, a cellular phone or other listed property, again, use of a log book or diary is advisable. The law is not entirely clear on "use" in the case of a cellular phone. Is it the time spent on the phone? Is it the cost of the calls? Keep a good record in any event to support your claim.

IDEA 73: Share Office Space

If your office space requirements are modest, you can save on rent by sharing space and other facilities. Some offices allow you to rent your office, while sharing secretarial help, photocopying and, perhaps, library access. Since you do not have to rent out your own space for these additional functions, you can save on rent. Also, since you are only paying for a fraction of the use of these functions, you save additional amounts.

To find out about local shared office space, look at trade association and professional organization newspapers and magazines. These often carry ads for available space.

IDEA 74: Use "Incubators" for Business Start Ups

Depending on the nature of your business and where you are located, you may be able to find low-cost space to start or run your business in a special environment called an "incubator." This is a special space designed to encourage small business to grow. In addition to the low-cost space (free or substantially less than other commercial space), you may also find support services (secretarial services and meeting rooms), shared office equipment (copier, fax machine) use of technical equipment (such as computers—sometimes free; sometimes a small charge), financial help and technical assistance. What is more, you will be in an environment with other small businesses with whom you can share information and ideas.

Did You Know. . .

Today, there are more than 530 incubators nationwide. They boast an impressive success rate for start ups. Originally, incubators were started to encourage technology and science-related businesses, but today about a quarter of participants are service businesses.

If you are starting a technology or scientific business, you may be able to find free or inexpensive space for starting up in a university-supported "incubator." A number of schools across the country encourage start ups by offering not only space but also technical and support assistance. Or you may be able to find an incubator that is supported by a local economic development agency.

For more information about incubators in general, or to locate one near you, contact the National Business Incubation Association (NBIA) at (614) 593-4331 or look at its web page (http://www.nbia.org).

IDEA 75: Use a Home Office

Where you start or run your business can have an important impact on your bottom line because the cost of space in commercial buildings may be high. Even if it can be acquired at reasonable rates (especially with today's abundant supply of commercial space in many localities), why spend the money when you do not have to? If your business is the type that can function from a home office environment and you have the extra space to devote to business use, then consider setting up head-quarters from home.

There are several money-saving reasons to use a home office:

- *You save on rent or mortgage payments that would have been spent on outside space.* Lowering your monthly business overhead can alleviate considerable pressure, especially in the start up phase of your business.

- *You save on commuting expenses.* You do not have to spend on gasoline or other transportation costs to get from your home to an outside business location. And the time you save in not having to commute to an outside office can be put to more productive use.

- *There are tax incentives to a home office.* A portion of your otherwise personal expenses (a share of your rent or mortgage interest and related expenses) becomes a deductible business expense. Travel costs from your home to clients, customers or other business contacts and back again are also deductible.

These costs savings may help to explain why nearly 85% of all home businesses were still in operation three years after starting up. The number of home businesses that close up each year is just 5%. In other words, home is a good place to start a business.

The term "home office" connotes an office environment. It can mean much more. It is not limited to a den used as office space, complete with telephone and computer. It can also include a garage or basement space used for manufacturing, research and development or creative endeavors. In fact, home offices have been the starting locations for many of today's most successful and diverse U.S. companies: Ford Motor Company, Microsoft and Walt Disney Company to name just a few. These companies grew beyond the confines of a home and moved on to larger quarters. Still, a home office can remain the focal point of a business.

Here are some more reasons to base your businesses at home:

- Today, about 25 million Americans operate a business in a home (this figure does not include those who are employed outside the home but do some work, or telecommute, from a home office).

- The majority of home businesses are owned by men who are age 40 or older.

- Most home-based businesses are run by professionals and are information-related (using a computer, a modem and other technology).

- The average income from a home business is around $58,000, 20% earn more than $75,000 and 1.7 million earn six figures or more!

- Home-based businesses enjoy greater productivity (perhaps as much as 25% more).

Zoning

Zoning laws in most localities have not kept pace with the boom in home-based businesses. The laws were originally written to keep out certain types of businesses; neighbors did not want automotive shops or kennels being run next door. The laws did not anticipate the current boom in home offices facilitated by the computer and other technological changes. You may find that the law in your area prohibits all home-based businesses except one-person operations with no employees which do not have any visits by clients or customers or certain traditional home-based businesses (music lessons, tutoring, doctors, dentist, attorneys). However, things are changing. Pressure is being brought to bear by home-based business owners and by the Home Office Association of America (HOAA) (800-8009-4622) and the American Association of Home Based Businesses (800-447-9710). Some localities have even seen the home office as a revenue-raising opportunity, with Chicago, for example, charging $150 for an annual license to run a business from home.

Warning

If you want to set a business from your home (or are already doing so) check with your city or town government (zoning board, planning board, building department) to determine current zoning rules and whether you fit within them. If you do not, you may be able to ask for a variance. Get a permit if you are required to have one. Avoid substantial penalties that may be imposed if you operate a home-based business in violation of the zoning laws.

Solutions to Image Problems

Some people may be afraid to run a business from home because of image—the address may not have enough cache; the interior may not be suitable for hosting clients and customers. You can run a business from home to save money while still solving image problems in an inexpensive way.

Use an outside address

You do not have to pay rent for an outside office for the purpose of obtaining a prestigious address. You can use a "front" for this purpose. *Mail Boxes Inc.* (800-789-4MBE) and other similar enterprises allow a home-based business to use an address that indicates a well-situated office location. You pay only for the box rental (even though the address need not include the box number). This address can also be used to receive certain freight deliveries (check with the box company on their per-parcel limits).

Meet at outside locations

If you do not want to host clients or customers in your home (perhaps your access is limited) you can arrange to meet in outside locations: at the client/customer/supplier's location, at a restaurant or at any other convenient location that is conducive to business.

Tax Write-offs For Home Offices

Just because you run a business from your home does not automatically mean that you can deduct a portion of your rent or depreciation on the home you own as a business expense. At the current time, the tax law severely limits which home offices are eligible for deduction. To deduct expenses related to a home office, two separate tests must be met.

Test 1

The home office must be one of the following three:

1. Your principal place of business. Your home office is treated as your principal place of business if it is the place where you conduct your business. It may be your prime activity or a sideline business. As long as it is the main location for the particular activity, it is your principal place of business.

   If you conduct the activities of one business in more than one location, you must determine whether the home office is the principal place of business. This determination is based on all the facts and circumstances. Two primary factors used to make this determination are the relative importance of the activities performed at each business location and the amount of time spent in each location. The "relative importance test" is considered first. Only if it is inconclusive do you then look at the relative amount of time spent in each location. According to the IRS, it may be possible that after you examine both primary factors you will reach the conclusion that there is no principal place of business (and no home office deductions can be claimed).

If the essence of your business is to meet with people at their locations, or to deliver goods or services at other locations, great weight is given to where the contact occurs. The performance of necessary or essential activities (such as planning, practicing, and doing the administrative tasks of billing, collecting and maintaining records) in a home office does not automatically mean that the home office is your principal place of business. Thus, under this criteria, an interior decorator or a plumber whose business is focused on services performed outside the home could not deduct home office expenses.

If you run more than one business from a home office, each business must meet the home office requirements in order to deduct any home office expenses.

2. A place to meet or deal with patients, clients or customers in the normal course of your business. If you meet with patients, clients or customers in a home office, you can deduct home office expenses. The home office need not be your principal place of business. You can conduct business at another location. Your home office can be a satellite office. However, if you use your home office only to make or receive phone calls with patients, clients and customers, you do not meet this test. While making or receiving phone calls can arguably be viewed as "dealing" with patients, clients or customers, the IRS will not view it as such.

This test generally allows professionals—attorneys, doctors, accountants, architects and others—to deduct home office expenses. Even though they have another office, they can still use a home office and deduct related expenses as long as the meeting or dealing with clients is more than occasional; it must be on a "regular" basis. Also, the home office must be used exclusively for business. You cannot use the home office for personal activities during the time when it is not used for business.

3. A separate structure (that is not attached to your house or residence) which is used in connection with your business. If you have a separate freestanding structure on your property, you can treat it as a home office if you use it exclusively and regularly for your home office activity. A separate structure may be a garage, a studio, a greenhouse or even a barn. Check your local law. If it treats a structure as an "appurtenance," then it is not a separate structure. Assume you do have a valid separate structure. It need not be an office in order for expenses to be deducted as home office expenses. The separate structure need not be the principal place of your business activity. It need not be a place to meet or deal with patients, clients or customers in the normal course of your business. It simply must be used in connection with your business.

Example: You own a flower shop in town. You have a greenhouse on your property in which you grow orchids. You can deduct the home office expenses of the greenhouse.

Test 2

The home office must used exclusively and regularly for business. Exclusive use of a home office means that it is used solely for your business activities and not for personal purposes, including investment activities. If you have a spare bedroom or a den that you have equipped with a computer, telephone and perhaps a fax/modem, you cannot meet the exclusive use test for a home office if you also use that room as a guest room or family den.

The exclusive use test does not require you to set aside an entire room for business purposes. You can meet the exclusive use test if you merely clearly delineate a portion of a room for business. It must be a separately identifiable space. However, you need not mark off this separate area by a permanent partition to satisfy the separately identifiable space requirement.

There are two important exceptions to the exclusive use requirement: day-care facilities and storage space (storage of inventory and samples on a regular basis for a retail or wholesale business run from the home). If a portion of your home is used for either of these purposes, then deductions are allowed even though the exclusive use test is not satisfied.

Assume that your business use of your home satisfies the requirements for being classified as a home office for tax purposes. What expenses does this status entitled you to deduct? You need to distinguish between direct expenses (which are fully deductible) and indirect expenses (which are deductible only to the extent they relate to the home office). Direct expenses relate solely to the home office (e.g., painting the office); indirect expenses relate to the entire home (e.g., rent). Here is a list of some indirect expenses:

- Deductible mortgage interest
- Real estate taxes
- Depreciation
- Rent
- Utilities
- Insurance
- General repairs to the home (such as servicing the heating system)
- Security systems
- Snow removal
- Cleaning

Only the portion of indirect expenses related to the business use of your home is deductible. How do you make an allocation of expenses? An allocation can be made on any reasonable basis. You can do it on a square footage basis. Divide the square footage of your home office by the square footage of your entire home to arrive at the percentage of business use.

Example: Your home is 1,800 square feet. Your home office is 12' × 15', or 180 square feet. Therefore, your home office use is 10% (180 divided by 1,800). Alternatively, if the rooms in your home are relatively equal in size, then you can allocate on the basis of room. So if you have five rooms and use one for business. You can allocate $1/5$ of expenses, or 20%, for business.

Once you have determined your business percentage, you apply this percentage against each indirect expense. For example, if your business percentage is 20% and your total real estate taxes for the year are $5,000, you may treat $1,000 ($5,000 × 20%) as part of your home office deduction. The balance of your real estate taxes continues to be deductible as an itemized deduction on Schedule A.

Casualty losses may be either an indirect or direct expense, depending upon the property affected by the casualty. If, for example, your home office is damaged in a storm and you are not fully compensated by insurance, you claim your loss as a direct expense. If, however, the damage is to your entire home (such as a roof leak), you treat the loss as an indirect expense.

If you rent your home, you can deduct the business portion of rent as an indirect expense. If you own your home, you cannot deduct the fair rental value of your home office but you can claim depreciation on your home office. In figuring depreciation, the deduction is based on the lower of the fair market value of the home at the time you converted it to business use, or the cost of the home.

Generally, utility expenses—for electricity, gas, oil, trash removal and cleaning services—are treated as indirect expenses. The business portion is part of your home office deduction; the non-business portion is not deductible. However, in some instances, you may be able to deduct a greater portion of a utility expense. For example, if you can show that electrical use for your home office is greater than the allocable percentage of the whole bill, you can claim that additional amount as a direct expense.

The business portion of a homeowner's insurance policy is part of your home office deduction. It is an indirect expense. If you also pay additional coverage directly related to your home office, then treat the additional coverage as a direct expense. You may, for example, carry special coverage for your home office equipment (computer, library, etc.) or a personal liability rider for on-premises injury to patients, clients or customers.

Repairs may be direct or indirect expenses, depending on their nature. A repair to a furnace is an indirect expense; a repair to a window in the home office itself is a direct expense.

A home security system for your entire home can give rise to two types of write-offs. First, the business portion of your monthly monitoring fees are indirect expenses. Second, the business portion of the cost of the system itself may be depreciated. This depreciation also becomes part of your indirect expenses.

Telephone expenses are not part of your home office deduction. They are separately deductible. However, if you maintain a home office, there is a special rule that limits a deduction for a telephone line. You may not deduct the basic monthly service charge for the first telephone line to your home as a business expense. You can, however, deduct business-related charges, such as long-distance calls for business, or for call answering, call waiting and call forwarding. You can also deduct the entire phone bill of a second phone line used exclusively for business. You can deduct any additional lines used for business, such as dedicated fax lines. If you need to keep costs down by using only one phone line, consider using a simple device that lets you direct calls not only to your phone for regular calls but also to your fax, answering machine or modem.

Warning

Not every home-related expense can be treated as a home office deduction. The cost of landscaping and lawn care cannot be treated as a home office expense.

Deduction Limits

Home office deductions cannot exceed your gross income from the home office activity. For those who conduct their primary business from home, the gross income limit may not pose any problem. As long as the business is profitable, deductions will be allowed. However, in the start up phase of your business or in bad years when revenues are low, your home office deductions may be limited. If your gross income from your home office business activity is less than your total business expenses, your home office deduction is limited. Your deduction for otherwise nondeductible expenses (such as utilities, depreciation) cannot exceed gross income from the business activity, reduced by the business portion of otherwise deductible expenses (such as home mortgage interest, real estate taxes) and business expenses not attributable to business use of the home (such as salaries or supplies). This sounds rather complicated, but the IRS has made it somewhat easier. Form 8829, Expenses for Business Use of Your Home, which is used by sole proprietors to figure their home office deduction, incorporates this limitation. Simply follow the line-by-line instructions to figure your allocations.

If, after applying this ordering of deductions, you still have unused home office deductions, you can carry forward the unused portion. The carryforward can be deducted in a future year when there is gross income from the same home office activity to offset it. There is no time limit on the carryforward. You can claim the carryforward even though you no longer live in the home in which the deduction arose as long as there is gross income from the same activity to offset the deduction. Be sure to keep adequate records to support your carryforward deduction.

> **Warning**
>
> If your home-based business is incorporated and you lease a portion of your home to the business, the business can deduct the cost of the lease. You, however, cannot deduct any expenses related to the home office (other than typical homeowner expenses deductible as itemized deductions, including mortgage interest and real estate taxes).

IDEA 76: Offsetting Business Start Up and Organizational Expenses with Tax Deductions

When you start your business, regardless of the formal arrangement you wind up using, you will undoubtedly incur certain expenses. These are called business start up costs and organizational expenses. These costs require you to lay out money for certain services and other expenditures. However, to the extent that you can deduct them, you help defray the cost. In a sense, the government becomes your partner, sharing in the expense of starting up your business. Since a deduction reduces the amount of income otherwise subject to tax, the tax not paid by virtue of the deduction is the government's contribution to your effort.

Generally, start up expenses are viewed in the tax law as capital expenditures that are not currently deductible. They are expenses incurred to acquire a capital asset, namely your business. However, under a special rule you can elect to amortize these costs (deduct a ratable portion of expenses) over a period of not less than 60 months. If you should sell your business before you have fully deducted these costs, you can claim a deduction for the unamortized portion on the final return for the business.

Start Up Costs

Expenses you pay to investigate the purchase or start up of a business as well as expenses to get the business going are treated as start up costs. These include:

- A survey of potential markets
- Analysis of available facilities, labor and supplies
- Advertising for the opening of the business
- Travel and other expenses incurred to line up prospective distributors, suppliers or customers

- Salaries and fees for consultants

- Fees for professional services

- Other expenses which would have been deductible if they had been incurred to operate a going business but were actually paid or incurred prior to the commencement of business operations.

Special rules for partnerships

If you set up a partnership, certain expenses unique to this form of business organization can be amortized. These amortizable costs for organizing a partnership include costs incident to the creation of the partnership that are chargeable to the capital account and would have been amortized over the life of the partnership if the partnership had a fixed life.

Presumably, limited liability companies that are taxed as partnerships for federal income tax purposes can amortize their organizational expenses in the same way as partnerships.

Large partnerships whose interests are sold to the public may incur nondeductible syndication costs. These nonamortizable costs include commissions, professional fees, and printing costs related to the issuing and marketing of partnership interests. A more complete discussion of expenses related to publicly traded partnerships is beyond the scope of this book.

Special rules for corporations

If you set up a corporation, either a C or S corporation, certain expenses unique to this form of business can be amortized. These amortizable costs for organizing a corporation include:

- Temporary directors

- Organizational meetings

- State incorporation fees

- Accounting services for setting up the corporation (e.g., costs of setting up the corporation's books and records; making and filing an S election)

- Legal services to draft the charter, by laws, terms of the original stock certificates, and minutes of organizational meetings

- Other expenses incident to the creation of the corporation that would be chargeable to the capital account and that could be amortized over the life of the corporation if the corporation had a fixed life

You cannot amortize certain organizational expenses related to selling stock. Nonamortizable expenses of selling stock include commissions, professional fees and printing costs.

IDEA 77: Protecting Intellectual Property on a Tight Budget

There is a special category of intangibles that deals with the creative aspects of a business. These are referred to collectively as intellectual property. It include patents, trademarks, tradenames, customer lists, processes, copyrights and more. Treated similarly to intellectual property under the tax law is a franchise right.

Patents

Say you come up with a new idea for a product or process. Can you protect it? The answer is a qualified yes. You may be able to get a patent which gives you the exclusive right to use your idea for a limited period of time. It is a property right that is granted by the federal government. Patent protection lasts for 17 years (14 years for design patents). During this period, you can use your idea exclusively or license its use to others. After 17 years (or 14 years), the idea is part of the public domain and anyone can use it without payment to you.

There are three types of patents: (1) utility patents for a new or useful process, machine, manufacture, or composition of matter or any new or useful improvement to an existing one; (2) design patents for a new, original or ornamental design for an article of manufacture (appearance of the article); and (3) plan patents for the invention, discovery or asexual reproduction of distinct or new plants.

Getting a patent is a legal process that can be timely and costly. First decide whether you want patent protection. Then decide how much of the process you can do yourself (to save money) and when you need to call in an expert (which can be costly).

A patent gives you an exclusive right, but only for a limited period of time. Another way of protecting an idea is to treat it as a trade secret or process. This type of asset is only as protected as you can make it—there is no way to file for protection. To obtain a patent, you must show the U.S. Patent and Trademark Office that your idea is unique (has not been patented before). To protect a trade secret or process, you must simply try to keep it from the public. For example, let's say you develop a special skin cream. You might want to patent it to keep others from copying your formula (if it is the kind that can be discovered through a chemical analysis or other method). But even if you can obtain a patent, your protection expires at the end of 17 years and then anyone can make and market the cream. Alternatively, if you believe that no one can figure out the precise formula that makes your cream unique, you may just want to keep the formula a secret. This kind of protection can last as long as you can keep it a secret. This is how Coca Cola has retained its unique flavor all these years.

Assume you have a machine or item that you developed and plan to market but need patent protection to keep others from selling your exact product. Take some simple steps to protect your idea.

- *Document your idea.* Until such time as you formally file for a patent, take various steps to protect your idea should competing claims ever arise.

- *Keep a notebook as you develop each step of your idea.* Be sure to date each page.

- *Write a description of your idea, sign it before a public notary, seal the signed statement in an envelope and mail it to yourself using registered mail.* Do not open it (until it should become necessary to do so in a court proceeding). Keep it in a safe place.

- *Use a disclosure document from the U.S. Patent and Trademark Office (Washington, DC 20231).* This is a form filed with the U.S. Patent and Trademark Office along with two photocopies (or photographs) of the idea or drawing. The filing fee is $10. The disclosure document is evidence of the dates of conception of an invention but it does not provide any patent protection. The USPTO keeps a disclosure document active for two years; presumably the patent process will be started within this period. Use of a disclosure document is particularly advisable if you want to raise money. It shows potential lenders or investors that you have taken preliminary steps to protect your invention.

- *Get a patent.* Once it has been determined that patent protection is advisable, seek out a qualified patent expert (a patent attorney or patent agent). The process can take some time (from preliminary searches through the granting of a patent). The U.S. Patent and Trademark Office itself is barred from assisting in the preparation of a patent application. Expect to pay several thousand dollars for expert assistance. In addition, filing fees and other costs payable to the U.S. Patent and Trademark Office can run several hundred dollars.

For general patent protection information, see the Patent and Trademark Office's web site at http://www.uspto.gov.

Warning

Do not think you can protect yourself simply by labeling your product "patent pending" or "patent applied for." It is unlawful to do this unless the patent process has actually begun and you may be subject to penalties for falsely labeling your product.

Copyrights

Statutory protection can be obtained for methods of expression, namely creative works—books, songs, wallpaper and fabric designs, games, even computer software. Protection gives the creator the exclusive right to market the work for the work for the life of the author plus 50 years. (For works done "for hire" and for anonymous and pseudonymous work, protection is for the shorter of

75 years from publication or 100 years from creation.) Registration entitles the creator to use the symbol "©" to denote the copyright.

You can file for protection yourself with the Register of Copyrights, Copyright Office, Library of Congress, Washington, DC 20559; (202) 707-3000. The cost of registering a copyright is $20 (although additional fees may apply).

$$Extra Savings

You can obtain free information booklets ("Copyright Basics" and "Publications on Copyrights") by contacting the Copyright Office.

Trademarks

Let's say you come up with a unique name for a protect. Can you ensure that no one else will use that name? The answer is yes. There are several ways to handle trademark protection. Trademark protection applies to a word, phrase, symbol or design, or a combination of words, phrases, symbols or designs which identify or distinguish the source of goods or services. (A service mark is the same as a trademark except it serves to distinguish a service rather than a product. However, the generic term "trademark" is commonly used to cover both categories.)

Common law protection

Common law recognizes that a mark used for goods and services belongs to the one who created it. However, it is often difficult to protect a mark from being used by someone else without some statutory protection. You can show the public that you consider the mark to be yours by designating it with a "™" for a trademark or "sm" for a service mark. The mark need not be registered in order to use these symbols. In fact, they need not even be under application for registration. Of course, use of the symbol does not guarantee that the mark is valid.

State trademark laws

States have their own laws establishing protection for marks used on goods and services. However, these laws do not provide as broad protection as federal laws.

Federal trademark law

This law provides protection to a trademark nationwide (and can even be registered in some foreign countries). Federal protection lasts for 10 years, with 10-year renewal periods. After the fifth year of the original registration, the owner must file an affidavit with certain information in order to keep the trademark alive (and the option for renewals open). Federal registration entitles the owner to use the symbol "℗ and prevents others from using the mark.

To get federal trademark protection, you must have a trademark in use in interstate commerce ("first use"). This simply means that you have affixed a mark to your product and shipped it to a customer in another state. Keep records on when the mark was first put in use (as shown on the product itself, invoices, bills of lading, letters from customers requesting the product with reference to the trademark). Then you need to do a trademark search to ensure that it has not been used before. Finally, you can apply for trademark registration from the U.S. Patent and Trademark Office (the address is listed above). File the application (PTO Form 1478), supporting documentation and the filing fee.

Understand that not all trademarks can be registered. For example, a state flag cannot become your company's unique (and registered) trademark. If you do not yet have a trademark, you might consult a marketing/advertising expert to develop one.

Ideas and Secrets

If you have an idea or trade secret that you want to protect for your commercial use, what can you do? First decide whether it is patentable or copyrightable. A concept, for example, cannot be copyrighted but it may be worthy nonetheless of some protection. A trade secret is any formula, pattern, device or compilation of information that can give you a competitive edge. How can you protect an idea or trade secret? Guard it as you would any secret. Keep the idea in a safe place. Mark any correspondence or other written material that mentions the idea "Confidential" or "Secret." Teach employees to guard the idea and treat it as a secret. When hiring new employees, have them sign a nondisclosure agreement (see sample below). If you fail to treat it as a secret and it becomes public, you will have no legal recourse.

$$Extra Savings

You can deduct the cost of obtaining protection for intellectual property. If you go through the time and expense of getting a patent or copyright, you can depreciate your costs over the life of the protection. What costs are included? The cost of drawings or photographs, models or prototypes, supplies, travel costs; attorney's fees and government registration fees. Let's say you do get a patent or copyright but it turns out to be worthless. You can then deduct your remaining costs in the year in which it becomes worthless.

If you buy a patent or copyright for use in your business, you can simply write off your cost over the remaining life of the protection. If you pay for a patent in annual installments figures as a percentage of revenues, then your write-off for the patent is the amount of the royalty you pay each year. But if you acquire a patent or copyright when you buy a business, then you can write off the portion of the cost of the business allocable to the patent or copyright over a period of 15 years.

SAMPLE EMPLOYEE NONDISCLOSURE AGREEMENT

Agreement entered into on the date entered below between (INSERT EMPLOYEE'S NAME), ("the Employee"), and (INSERT YOUR COMPANY'S NAME), ("the Company").

WITNESSETH:

WHEREAS the Company has trade secrets and proprietary information that it wishes to keep secret, said trade secrets or proprietary information consisting of (but is not limited to) technical information, inventions, processes, machinery, computer software, research, techniques, formulas, pricing, customer lists, supply sources, financial data and other confidential information; and

WHEREAS the Employee desires to have employment with the Company.

NOW, THEREFORE, the parties mutually agree that:

1. In consideration of the Employee's employment by the Company, the Employer agrees that he/she not use for him/herself or disclose to others during the course of employment or at any time after the termination of employment with the Company any trade secrets or confidential information in violation of this Agreement.

2. Upon termination of the Employee's employment with the Company he/she will return to it all property (including originals, copies, notes or abstracts) pertaining to the Company's business.

3. The Company shall be entitled to full injunctive relief for any breach.

4. This Agreement shall be binding upon the parties, their personal representatives, successors in interest and assigns.

IN WITNESS THEREOF, the parties have executed this agreement on this......day of......................199___.

_____

Company

_____

Employee

IDEA 78: Planning for Intangibles When You Buy a Business

If you buy an existing business, part of what you pay for includes intangibles: the name of the business, perhaps customer lists, copyrights or patents, a covenant not to compete and good will. In Chapter 1, you learned about allocating the purchase price of a business to its various assets, including intangibles.

Intangibles acquired with the purchase of a business are called Section 197 intangibles (named after a section in the Internal Revenue Code). The portion of the cost of the business allocated to these assets can be amortized over a period of 15 years starting with the month in which the business was acquired.

Section 197 intangibles include:

- Goodwill

- Going concern value

- Workforce in place

- Patents, copyrights, formulas, processes, designed, patterns, and know-how

- Customer-based intangibles

- Supplier-based intangibles

- Licenses, permits and other rights granted by a governmental unit or agency

- Covenants not to compete

- Franchises (other than a sports franchise), trademarks or tradenames

Warning

Section 197 intangibles do not include interests in a corporation, partnership, trust or estate, a sports franchise, interests in land, certain computer software and certain other excluded items.

8

Reducing Travel and Entertainment Expenses

Travel and entertainment are generally components of any business. Some types of businesses depend upon travel. Some use entertainment occasionally to solicit business.

Travel costs include airfare, trainfare, cars and car rentals, taxis, hotel rooms, meals and even incidental expenses (such as laundry while away on business, room charges for faxing and other business services). Entertainment costs include business meals and tickets for the theater or sporting events. However, there are stringent tax rules on deducting travel and entertainment expenses, including special recordkeeping requirements.

In this chapter, you will learn about a number of ways you can reduce the costs of travel and entertainment.

IDEA 79: Nail Down Deductions for Travel and Entertainment

For some businesses, travel and entertainment is an integral part of business operations. The costs of travel and entertainment may be significant, but unavoidable. To the extent that the business can deduct these costs, taxes are reduced and are important savings to you. The key to deducting travel and entertainment expenses is understanding the tax rules. These rules detail what you can deduct. Different rules apply to different types of expenses. The rules also contain special recordkeeping requirements. The failure to satisfy these requirements can cost you otherwise valid deductions. Be forewarned that the rules are complex, but ignorance in this area can cost you precious tax write-offs.

Basics for Deducting Travel Expenses

Do you travel throughout your city to visit suppliers? Do you travel across the country to see one customer? Can you deduct the costs of these trips? The answer depends on a number of different factors.

Local transportation costs

Local transportation costs include the cost of work-related travel within the area of your "tax home." Your tax home is the entire city or general area of your regular place of business. If you have more than one business interest, then it is the location of your main business and is based on the comparative time spent in each location and the income derived from each business interest. If you do not have a regular place of business, then you are considered an itinerant without any tax home.

As a general rule, the costs of commuting between your home and work place are not deductible because they are considered personal expenses. This rule does not change merely because the commute is unusually long or because you do work on the way (for example, you read reports on the train; you talk to clients on your car phone; you display advertising on your car).

There are a few exceptions that make certain commuting expenses deductible.

1. If you have a regular place of business but work at temporary locations on a short-term or irregular basis (such as a few days or weeks at a time), then you can deduct the cost of travel between your home and the temporary work site. Thus, for example, if you have an office downtown for your interior design business, you can deduct the cost of travel from your home to clients' homes or offices (and the cost of travel from their homes or offices back to your home). But if you do not have a regular place of business and always work at temporary work sites in the metropolitan area (city and surrounding suburbs) of your home, the IRS says that you cannot deduct your transportation costs. However, the Tax Court has allowed a deduction for transportation costs despite IRS objections, so the issue is not yet settled. Of course, if you travel outside your metropolitan area, both the IRS and the courts agree that the costs of traveling between your home and a temporary work site outside your area are deductible.

2. If you have a home office that is the principal place of business for the activity conducted there, then the cost of traveling from your home to your clients or customers or to other business locations is deductible. For example, if you run an insurance business from a home

office, occasionally going to clients' homes to explain insurance options or to get policies signed, you can deduct the cost of traveling between your home and the clients' homes and back again.

3. If you must haul tools or equipment to your job site and you use a trailer or have to make other special arrangements, then the additional cost of commuting with the tools is deductible. The basic transportation costs are still treated as nondeductible commuting expenses. For example, if you rent a trailer to haul tools from your home to your business, you may not deduct the expenses of using your car but you can deduct the cost of renting the trailer that you haul with your car.

Out-of-town travel costs

If you travel on business away from home, you can deduct not only the cost of transportation, but also personal costs—food, lodging and incidentals. You must be away from your "tax home" (the area of your business) for more than one day. You are required, because of the distance or the length of the business day, to get sleep or rest away from home in order to meet the demands of your work. This is called the "sleep or rest" rule. And your travel away from home must be considered "temporary." The travel must be expected to last no more than one year and, in fact, does not last longer than one year.

> **Warning**
>
> Special rules limit the deduction for airfare when travel is both for business and personal purposes which can reduce or eliminate deductions completely. Different limits apply to domestic and foreign travel. The cost of bringing a spouse along on business is not deductible unless the spouse also works for the company and is required to be present for business reasons.

Deductible travel costs include (1) transportation costs, (2) lodging, (3) meals and (4) other related expenses.

1. *Transportation costs:* The cost of a ticket to travel by air, train or bus between your home and a business destination is deductible. However if you receive the fare for free because of "frequent flyer" miles or otherwise, then the cost is not deductible. The cost of travel by ship may not be fully deductible. Transportation costs also include local costs once you arrive at your business destination (for example, car rental fees and gas as well as taxi fare between the airport and your hotel are deductible, as is travel between the hotel and the location of clients and customers). Of course transportation costs for personal travel (sightseeing, visiting relatives, shopping and other non-business activities) are not deductible.

2. *Lodging costs:* The cost of hotel, motel or other accommodations is deductible if the nature of the business trip requires an overnight stay in order for you to sleep or properly perform your job.

3. *Meals:* The cost of your meals on a trip away from home is partially deductible. This is because deductible business meals, whether near your office or on out-of-town travel, are subject to a 50% limit. The cost of meals includes food, beverages, taxes and tips. However, if the meals are considered to be lavish or extravagant, then the deductible portion is limited to the amount that is reasonable. What is considered reasonable is based on the facts and circumstances of the situation. Just because the meal is eaten in deluxe hotels, restaurants, night clubs or resorts does not automatically make costs lavish or extravagant.

When deducting meal costs, there is a choice in what can be deducted: (1) Keep track of all costs and deduct these actual costs or (2) use a standard meal allowance set by the IRS (a rate that varies with the location of your travel).

4. *Other deductible travel costs:* While you are away from home on business, you may incur a number of miscellaneous or incidental travel expenses. These expenses are deductible in full. They include, for example, the reasonable cost of cleaning and laundering your clothes. They also include tips you pay for services rendered in connection with any deductible expenses (such as a meal, a taxi ride, a bellhop). You may also incur any number of miscellaneous expenses that are deductible (for example, telephone charges to talk to your office or send a business fax, computer rental fees, public stenographer's fees).

Warning

The standard meal allowance is primarily for your employees. It cannot be used by someone who is just related to the employer. You are considered related if your employer is your brother, sister (half or whole), spouse, parent, grandparent, child, or grandchild. You are also considered related if you own, directly or indirectly, more than 10% of the value of your employer's stock. Indirect ownership arises when you have an interest in a corporation, partnership, trust or estate that owns stock in your employer's corporation or if family members own stock in your employer's corporation. Note, however, that using the standard meal allowance does not eliminate the need for other recordkeeping, as explained later in this idea. Also, the standard meal allowance is still subject to the same 50% limit as actual meal expenses.

Basic Rules for Deducting Meals and Entertainment Expenses

In order to be deductible as a meal and entertainment expense, an expense must be an ordinary and necessary business expense (common and accepted, helpful and appropriate to your business), and meet either (1) the directly-related test, or (2) the associated test.

Directly-related test

The directly-related test is met if you can show that the main purpose of the business/entertainment activity was the active conduct of business and that you did, in fact, engage in business during the entertainment period. You must have more than a general expectation of getting income or some other business benefit at some future time. You need not devote more time to business than entertainment in order to satisfy this test. You simply have to demonstrate that all the facts, including the nature of the business transacted and the reasons for conducting business during some form of entertainment, support a business purpose. You need not show that business income or some other business benefit actually resulted from a specific entertainment event. You will be presumed to pass the directly-related test if the entertainment is in a clear business setting (a hospitality room or suite at a convention). You are presumed to fail the directly-related test if you are on a hunting, skiing or fishing trip, on yachts or other pleasure boats, nightclubs, golf courses, theaters and sporting events unless you can show otherwise. You must show that you engaged in a substantial business discussion (explained under the "associated test" below) during the entertainment at these locations or events, despite the obvious distractions.

Associated test

If you cannot meet the higher standard of "directly-related," you may still be able to show that the entertainment was associated with the conduct of your business. This test requires showing that the expense directly precedes or follows a substantial business discussion as well as that it is associated with your business. You must have a clear business purpose for having the entertainment expense. This includes entertainment to get new business or encourage continued business with existing clients or customers.

There is no quantitative way to show to show that a business discussion is "substantial." There is no prescribed amount of time you must meet or discuss business. You do not have to devote more time to business than entertainment. You do not even have to discuss business during the entertainment itself. Whether the entertainment meets the associated test depends on the facts and circumstances of the situation. You must be able to show that you actually held a business discussion with the intent to get income or other business benefit in the future. Goodwill entertainment is considered to satisfy the associated test.

Other requirements

In addition to meeting the directly-related or associated test, you must show that the cost of the entertainment was not "lavish or extravagant." There are no dollar amounts that equate to lavish or extravagant; a determination is based on the facts and circumstances. However, no deduction is allowed for fees paid to scalpers, ticket agents or ticket brokers for tickets to theater, sporting or other events above the face amount of the tickets. Also the cost of skyboxes and other private luxury boxes at a sports arena is limited. These boxes are generally rented for a season or a series of events, such as playoff games or a world series. When the cost covers more than one event, you cannot deduct more than the total of the face value of non-luxury box seats times the number of seats in the box. In this case, the 50% limit applies (see below.)

Home entertainment

If you entertain business associates, customers or employees at your home, can you deduct your expenses? The answer depends on whether you discuss specific business during the course of the dinner or other entertainment event. Business dinners may be conducive to business discussions. Other types of social gatherings, such as pool parties, may not be as conducive to business discussions and may raise questions with the IRS. To bolster deductions, keep the guest list small (no more than 12) in order to be able to hold discussions with all guests; a larger group may make it difficult to show that you had business discussions with each guest.

When entertaining at home, do not mix the guest list. The presence of non-business guests may support the conclusion that the gathering was not for business reasons and that business was not discussed. Taxpayers have not fared well in proving that parties for personal events—a child's wedding, birthday or bar mitzvah—were held for business even though business guests attended. (They could not even deduct the costs allocated to the business guests.)

50% limit

Even if your meal and entertainment costs are legitimate, they are only partially deductible. Meals and entertainment expenses are deductible only to the limit of 50% of cost. This means that even if you are entitled to claim a deduction, you can only write off half of the cost; the other half remains nondeductible. The 50% limit applies to meals eaten while traveling away from home even if they are paid with a per diem reimbursement rate.

The 50% limit does not necessarily apply to all business meals or entertainment. There are some important exceptions:

- Promotional activities (meals given to customers who sit through presentations).

- Meals paid for recreational, social, or similar activities primarily for the benefit of employees (food at a company picnic).

- Food and beverages provided to employees as a tax-free fringe benefit (on-premises free coffee machines, donuts and such).

There is no total dollar limit on what you can spend for meal and entertainment expenses. Cost, however, cannot be "lavish or extravagant."

Club dues

The cost of dues, including initiation fees, to clubs organized for pleasure, recreation or other social purposes is not deductible. But dues to business (business leagues, trade associations, chambers of commerce, boards of trade, real estate boards and business lunch clubs), professional (bar associations and medical associations) and civic organizations (Kiwanis, Lions, Rotary, and Civitan) are deductible.

$$Extra Savings

Nondeductible club dues (such as country club dues) for an employee (including yourself if your business is incorporated) can be turned into a deductible expense by treating the payment of club dues on behalf of an employee as additional compensation. In this way, the business can claim a deduction for club dues as compensation, not as travel and entertainment costs. This option applies only to club dues that would otherwise be deductible were it not for a specific prohibition against these dues. Thus, it applies only if the club is used for business (not for personal purposes). The election to treat club dues as additional compensation can be made on an employee-by-employee basis.

Spouses' expenses

If you take your spouse or a friend with you on business entertainment or you take a client's or a customer's spouse along, are the spouse's expenses deductible? In general, the answer is no. However, if you can show that the purpose for including the spouse was clearly for business and not some social or personal purpose, then the spouse's costs are deductible. Thus, for example, if you are entertaining an out-of-town client who brings his/her spouse, then the costs for both the client's spouse and your spouse are deductible.

Recordkeeping

Business expense deductions can be disallowed unless there is adequate substantiation to back up the expenses. For travel and entertainment expenses, there are two main ways to prove costs: Actual substantiation or reliance on a per diem rate. First look at actual substantiation; then consider how recordkeeping can be simplified with the use of per diem rates.

There are a number of elements to substantiate for each business expense: the amount, the time, the place, the business purpose for the travel or the business relationship with the person or persons you entertain or provide gifts to, and, in some cases, a description of the item. The exact type of substantiation required depends on the item of business expense.

Travel

Show the amount of each separate expense for travel, lodging, meals and incidental expenses. Total these items in any reasonable category. For example, you can simply keep track of meals in a category called "daily meals." Also note the date you left for the trip and the date you returned as well as the days spent on the trip for business purposes. List the name of the city or other designation of the place of travel as well as the reason for the travel or the business benefit gained or expected to be gained from the travel. While this may sound like a great deal of recordkeeping, as a practical matter, hotel receipts may provide you with much of the information necessary since they typically show the dates you arrived and departed, the name and location of the hotel and separate charges for lodging, meals, telephone calls and other items. You need not get documentary evidence if the item (other than lodging) is less than $75 or, in the case of transportation costs, if a receipt is not readily available. Thus, if a cab ride is $9 and the driver does not provide you with a receipt, you are not required to show documentary evidence of this expense.

Meals and entertainment

List expenses separately. Incidental expenses (e.g., telephone) may be totaled on a daily basis. List the date of the meal or entertainment. For meals or entertainment directly before or after a business discussion, list the date and duration of the business discussion. Include the name and address or location of the place for the entertainment and the type of entertainment if it is not apparent from the name of the place. Also list the place where a business discussion was held if entertainment is directly before or after the discussion. Again, state the business reason or the business benefit gained or expected to be gained and the nature of the business discussion. Include the names of the persons entertained, including their occupations or other information to identify them, and who took part in the business discussion. If the deduction is for a business meal, show who was present at the meal. Restaurant receipts typically supply much of the information required (the name and location of the restaurant, the number of people served and the date and amount of the expense). Jot down the business aspect of the meal or entertainment (a request for a business referral, an attempt to sell your services).

A canceled check, along with a bill, generally establishes the cost of a business item. A canceled check alone does not prove a business expense without other evidence to show its business purpose.

Missing, lost or inadequate records

What if you lose your records or have not kept good ones? If records are inadequate, an item may still be deductible if you can prove by your own statement or other supporting evidence an element of substantiation. Of course, you may be forced to undergo administrative appeals or even go to court to prove your case. A court may, for example, allow an estimation of expenses under certain circumstances. Where receipts are destroyed, you may be able to reconstruct your expenses. You must show how the records were destroyed (fire, storm, flood). The IRS may require additional information to prove the accuracy or reliability of the information contained in your records.

Per diem rates

If the company reimburses travel and meal expenses using per diem rates, then you need not retain documentary evidence of the amount of an expense. The per diem rate is deemed to satisfy the proof of the amount of the expense. However, use of the per diem rate does not prove any of the other elements of substantiation. For example, if an employee is reimbursed for business travel using per diem rates under what is called the "high-low method," the employee must still show the time, place and business purpose for travel.

Audits

The area of travel and entertainment expenses attracts a great deal of scrutiny from the IRS and often gives rise to audits. However, this should not be cause for alarm. As long as your deductions are legitimate and you have records to back them up, then IRS questions about them should not cause any problems to you.

For further information about travel and entertainment costs, see IRS Publication 463, Travel, Entertainment and Gift Expenses. For a listing of per diem rates see IRS Publication 1542. To receive these publications free of charge, call (800) 829-1040.

IDEA 80: Teleconference to Save on Travel Expenses

Meeting with clients, suppliers and customers outside your business can be costly, especially when out-of-town travel is required. Today's technology provides a simple and inexpensive alternative—teleconferencing. Use your telephone or other technology to meet and discuss business. Here are your teleconferencing choices:

- *Conference* **calls.** These can be used to bring together parties at more than two locations. Most office-type telephone equipment readily permits this type of calling.

- *Speaker phones.* Telephone audio permits a number of people to listen and converse at the same time.

- *Picture phones.* A relatively new technology permits parties speaking to each other to see each other at the same time. To use this technology, you must own the equipment that can provide it. Today, such equipment is quite costly, but watch for costs to come down as the technology becomes more popular.

- *Videoconferencing.* This is the same principal as picture phones, but it permits a large group of people to view and hear a speaker at the same time. One-way videoconferencing allows only one end to see and hear the other; two-way videoconferencing allows each end to interact. Videoconferencing is not cheap and, of course, two-way videoconferencing is more expensive than one-way videoconferencing. However, costs seem to be coming down. For example, Kinko's offers two-way videoconferencing throughout the country at a cost of $150 per site per hour (which means at least $300 per hour since at least two sites are involved). The sites can be any of Kinko's locations or it can arrange hookups at other convenient locations in cooperation with Sprint. (call Kinko's Videoconferencing: 800-78-KINKOS). In assessing the cost of videoconferencing in comparison with travel, take into account that when several employees are involved, the travel costs almost certainly exceed that of videoconferencing. What is more, multiple locations (e.g., New York, Chicago and Los Angeles) can be in on the same videoconference—a substantial savings over the cost of travel to those locations.

- *Computer conferencing.* This form of conferencing allows various parties to communicate without actually speaking or seeing each other. Messages are inputed and others can receive them immediately or at their convenience. Conversations can be developed through a return of messages.

$$Extra Savings

There is an added bonus to teleconferencing (besides saving on travel expenses): a savings on travel time. The time not spent on travel can be used more productively for other purposes.

IDEA 81: Implement Cost-Saving Measures

If you cannot avoid travel (teleconferencing or other long distance communications just won't do), then look into ways to reduce your travel and entertainment budget. Keep in mind that no matter how well you keep records and how legitimate your expenses may be, only one half of the cost of business meals and entertainment is deductible. Therefore, it behooves you to try to keep expenses as low as possible. Here are some miscellaneous ideas the can help you reduce your outlays for travel and entertainment:

Air Travel

There are several strategies for reducing the cost of air travel:

- *Shop around for the best ticket prices.* They vary considerably from one airline to another. Also, if you have the flexibility of traveling into or out of different airports, you may be able to get a better fare even though your distance to another airport is insignificant. For example, in the New York City area, there are three airports: La Guardia, Kennedy and Newark. Fares into or out of these airports can differ considerably, so choose the one that will result in the lowest fare.

- *Schedule travel to include a Saturday stayover.* Air travel tickets cost less if they include a Saturday. (The IRS even allows a deduction for a room and meals required because of a Saturday stayover, even if you spend your day sightseeing or on other personal activities.)

- *Schedule travel well in advance.* Last minute booking results in the highest airfare. Plan your travel so that tickets can be purchased in advance.

- *Use connecting flights where the connection entitles you to a lower fare.* When flying long distances, certain connections may reduce the total airfare. While this may require additional travel time (and the inconvenience of making connections), you may want to do it for the cost savings.

Using a travel agent versus do-it-yourself

Do you save money by using a travel agent? Perhaps. But more important, the travel agent should be able to guide you on decisions of where to stay (and where to stay away from).

You can do some booking on your own. There is a wealth of travel information on the Internet. But there is still concern about giving out your financial information (your credit card number) on the Internet. It may be advisable to book the old-fashioned way—via the telephone.

Car Rentals

Use trade associations or other group member discounts to get the lowest rental charges. Compare costs between the different rental companies; there may be a surprising difference. The so-called budget rentals may not cost less than the leading national rental companies.

Remember to waive the additional charge for collision and other insurance if you put your rental on a credit card that guarantees this coverage or if your personal automobile policy provides the coverage.

Meals

Schedule meals to reduce overall costs. For example, instead of business dinners, meet clients, customers or suppliers for lunch. Lunch costs are generally much lower than dinner bills.

By the same token, hold "power breakfasts" instead of business lunches. Again, the costs will be much less.

IDEA 82: Use Discounts and Rebates

There are many travel and entertainment related discounts and rebates that can be used to substantially reduce your costs for these expenditures. Here are some strategies you can use to reduce costs:

Air Travel

If you travel on business more than occasionally, it will pay to enroll in a frequent flyer program. Mileage accumulated under the program can be used for free air travel (or ticket upgrades).

Warning

The IRS has ruled that if employees fail to return frequent flyer miles to an employer (they use the miles for their personal travel), this can cause tax problems. The IRS received a lot of criticism for this ruling and its position on the issue is not clear at this time.

If you are enrolled in a frequent flyer program, look for ways to maximize your frequent flyer miles. For example, United Airlines offered 500 frequent flyer miles for roundtrip fares booked electronically during 1996. American Airlines gives frequent flyer miles to MCI customers (2,000 extra miles to enroll, plus 5 miles for every one minute of long-distance service). There are even special MasterCard or VISA credit cards that give frequent flyer miles with respect to all purchases by charge.

Lodging

Hotels generally give discounts for business travelers but you have to ask for them. Discounts are not automatic.

Use a "reselling consolidator" to book your lodging. Since the reselling consolidator does quantity booking, it can command a better room price. There is no additional cost to you for using the reselling consolidator's service. Just call and book the rooms through the consolidator if you are traveling to a city that it services.

Reselling Consolidator	*Telephone Number*
Accommodations Express (Atlantic City, Boston, Chicago, Fort Lauderdale, Las Vegas, New Orleans, New York, Orlando, Philadelphia and Washington DC)	(800) 307-8680
Central Reservations Service (Miami, Orlando, New York, San Francisco)	(800) 950-0232
Hotel Reservations Network (Boston, Chicago, New Orleans, New York, Orlando, San Francisco, Washington DC)	(800) 964-6835
Quickbook (New York and some other cities)	(800) 789-9887
RCM Travel Center (cities nationwide)	(800) 245-5738
Room Exchange (cities in the U.S., Caribbean, Europe and Asia)	(800) 846-7000

Warning

There may be a cancellation fee if the room is not used as booked. In some cases, you may even lose the cost of the room.

Car Rentals

If you rent a car when you travel to another city, you may be able to reduce your costs. National car rental companies are always offering special deals—weekly rates, weekend rates or some other rental arrangement—that will qualify for lower rates. Ask what deals are currently being offered.

Check whether you are eligible for discounts. Members of various professional and trade associations as well as AARP members usually qualify for a small percentage off the total rental price. Ask for a group member discount.

Meals

Use discount cards or meal discount clubs to buy business meals. Discount cards take a percentage (such as 25%) off the bill. Some cards apply the discount even to drinks, tips and tax; some limit the discount to the base cost of the meal. The card looks like any other credit card; some discount clubs even let you simply charge to your credit card and they then apply the discount on your total monthly meal charges. In looking into discount cards or meal discount clubs, be sure to check for limitations: Are they good only at certain restaurants? (Would this be convenient for you?) Are there blackout periods (such as Saturday night or holidays) during which no discounts will be granted? Are there special membership costs to use the discount program?

CHAPTER 9

Handling Advertising, Marketing and Promotion

You may have a great product or service, but if the public does not know about it, or about your company, you may have a difficult time ringing up sales or fees. This is where advertising, marketing and promotion come in. Today, there are an increasing number of forums in which to advertise or promote your product or service. Some of these forums include:

- *Signs and billboards*
- *Direct mail*
- *Telemarketing*
- *Internet opportunities (web pages)*
- *Print advertising (classified, magazine and newspaper ads)*
- *Radio, television (network and cable)*
- *Promotional contests and prizes*
- *Sponsorship (e.g., little league teams)*
- *Trade shows*
- *Yellow pages*

Knowing how to use these forums most effectively while keeping costs low can make a big difference to the success of your business. Some of the above advertising choices are either low-cost or free. Others may involve significant costs. Make sure that you investigate the options so that you can choose wisely.

In this Chapter, you will learn about a number of free promotion alternatives. You will also find out how to minimize your advertising costs. You may even learn about some ways to market your company that you may not have considered before.

IDEA 83: Seek Referrals

The best way to generate business is word-of-mouth. Why is it the best? There are two good reasons: It need not cost you anything and the clients and customers that come your way are already sold on you. Knowing how to generate referrals is an important part of running your business.

- *Ask for referrals.* It may seem simplistic, but to get referrals from existing clients and customers, you should ask for them. For example, if you provide a service, ask your existing clients/customers whether they know of anyone else who might want/need your assistance.

- *Offer "rewards" for referrals.* Give discounts, "free" products/services to anyone who steers new clients/customers your way. Be clear about what you are offering. (For example, make the offer for a limited time if you do not want it to come back to haunt you months or years down the road.)

- *Thank those who referred clients/customers to you.* Again, it may seem too obvious, but be sure to thank anyone who has sent you a new client or customer (a note or a phone call). Simple courtesies go a long way; they may bring additional referrals in the future.

- *Network for referrals.* Networking is designed to bring in business by way of personal referrals. Network groups may meet before the business day (such as at 7:00AM for breakfast), during lunchtime or during the evening hours. There may be little or no fee (other than the cost of the meal) to participate.

- *Join networking groups* that can offer you an "exclusive" on your product or service.

Warning

It is generally not advisable to join a networking group that already has, for example, three travel agents if you are seeking referrals to your travel business. Before joining a group, ask what controls are used to limit the number of people in competing businesses.

IDEA 84: Use the Media for Free

The best kind of marketing for your business does not cost you any money. It is free! It falls under the banner of "news" that can be carried by newspapers, magazines, radio and television. When your company has something that is newsworthy, let the media know about it. To your delight, you may find that the company will enjoy positive coverage at no charge.

Write a News Release

The best way to see that your company's "news" gets picked up by the local media is to write a press release. This accomplishes two important things. It ensures that the information you want to convey (the name of a new product, the name of a person just promoted, the opening of new offices) will be reported correctly. The names will be spelled right; the dates will be exact. The second advantage to writing a press release is that it relieves those in the media from having to do the work themselves—added incentive for using your piece.

The sample news releases on the following page can be used to notify newspapers of some important change or event at your company. The first is appropriate for announcing a promotion or a new employee; the second is for announcing a new product, a new office, a joint venture with another company or any other interesting development.

Remember, these are only samples provided for the purpose of giving you some idea of what a press release looks like. You can readily adapt them to best convey your company's story. For example, instead of "FOR IMMEDIATE RELEASE," you can give a release in advance of a story with the future release date.

In preparing press releases, use standard $8^1/_2 \times 11$ paper or your company letterhead. Be sure to include the "slug marks" (or "End") at the end of the story to indicate the end. If a press release continues for more than one page, be sure to include "MORE" at the bottom of the first page to indicate additional material to follow on the next page.

You can dress up your press release with a photo—a picture of a person, your storefront, your product. In submitting a photo, it need not be black and white; color may even be appreciated. However, a newspaper can only use high contrast photos since low contrast photos do not reproduce well.

$$Extra Savings

You can reduce the cost of submitting photos by using slides instead of prints.

Find out about media deadlines. If your local newspaper closes its stories for the following day at 6:00PM, be sure to submit material that has "FOR IMMEDIATE RELEASE" prior to that

SAMPLE PRESS RELEASES

Sample 1 for announcing a new/promoted employee:

FOR IMMEDIATE RELEASE

(DATE OF PRESS RELEASE)

Contact: (YOUR NAME)

(YOUR COMPANY NAME)

(TELEPHONE/FAX NUMBER)

(NAME OF YOUR COMPANY), based in (NAME OF CITY/TOWN MAIN OFFICE/ STORE) today named (NAME OF EMPLOYEE) to the position of (TITLE). He/she will be responsible for (DESCRIBE AN ASPECT OF THE JOB). (NAME OF EMPLOYEE) joins (NAME OF COMPANY) from (NAME OF PRIOR EMPLOYER).

####

Sample 2 for announcing a new product:

FOR IMMEDIATE RELEASE

(DATE OF PRESS RELEASE)

Contact: (YOUR NAME)

(YOUR COMPANY NAME)

(TELEPHONE/FAX NUMBER)

(NAME OF YOUR COMPANY) today announced that it will begin to sell (NAME OF PRODUCT), (DESCRIPTION OF PRODUCT) in (TYPES OF STORES, e.g., supermarkets, pharmacies, office supply companies, etc.). (GIVE BRIEF STORY OR BACKGROUND, e.g., period of testing; reason for new product, etc.)

####

deadline in order to make the next paper. Otherwise, a day is lost and the story grows stale. To find out about submission requirements, ask your local papers for their media kits (which are free).

Call the Media

If some unique event is transpiring at your company, you may want to alert the media. A simple phone call may draw the attention of newspapers, radio or even television if something important or unusual is happening. For example, if you are opening a factory and hiring a significant number of workers in an otherwise depressed area, the media may consider this newsworthy.

Did You Know. . .

When Aaron Feurstein's factory burned down in Lawrence, Massachusetts in late 1995 and operations were shut down, it was ordinary news. But when he announced that he was continuing everyone's salary and benefits for a month (a cost of more than $1 million!) it was big news. He made national headlines, was featured in *People* magazine and was even invited to attend President Clinton's State of the Union Address. He could not have bought this kind of publicity, yet he got it for no additional cost!

Create Your Own "News"

Do not wait for something to happen that you can then report to the media. Make it happen. Here are some ideas you may be able to use:

- Give an employee award for service in your business or to the community, something that would be of interest to the general public.

- Celebrate something—your grand opening, your first anniversary in business or the first year that a product has been on the market.

- Sponsor an event that the media may want to cover; for instance, a seminar (discussed later in this chapter).

- Hold a contest. Let the media know about the contest so they can follow it. Then announce the winners.

- Conduct your own survey. You may find that nine out of ten people prefer your product/ service over that of a competitor, or that while using your product/service, a certain percentage of people experienced positive results.

Be creative and you will find that free publicity will easily come your way.

IDEA 85: Give Seminars

Depending on the nature of your business, you may be able to promote it to the public by giving seminars. These can be held at your facility, a local hotel, a community center or even the local library. The cost of hosting seminars can be modest—perhaps a small fee for the use of a room at a hotel, the cost of some refreshments and the cost of advertising the seminar or specifically inviting guests to attend.

You can offer the seminars free of charge to attendees. Alternatively, you can charge a small admission. This will cover your out-of-pocket costs for hosting the seminar. You may even make some profit if turnout is better than expected!

You can use the seminars to inform attendees about your product or service. You can also use the seminars to sell your product or service. Get attendees to buy on the spot or sign up for your services.

Publicizing Your Seminar

There are a number of approaches you can use to bring in attendees. First, you can contact existing clients and customers with personal invitations (by phone or through a written invitation). Using a formal invitation can be costly if you figure in printing the invitation and postage costs. But if the business that can be generated from the seminar will offset this cost, personal invitations may be worthwhile.

Use mailing lists to invite prospective clients and customers. Mailing lists can be pricey (discussed later in this Chapter) but may still be a good way to reach new leads.

You may be able to get free advertising on radio or in the local newspapers under "public service announcements." To receive this free advertising, your seminar generally must be cast as one of interest to the general public rather than as a sales pitch by you. As such, refrain from direct selling at the seminar; you can contact interested attendees following the seminar.

As a minimum, be sure to get all the mileage you can out of your attendees. Take down names and addresses. (Have a sign-in sheet or provide cards to be completed by attendees.) Add these names to your mailing list. While the attendees may not buy your product or service on the spot, you can approach them later because you will know where to reach them.

IDEA 86: Keep Mailing Costs Down

Direct mail is no longer the "junk mail" of yesterday. It is now an important advertising alternative for many companies. Direct mail allows you to offer special come-ons, such as coupons, reply envelops, or stickers. What is more, you can tailor your direct mail campaign to selected households.

Did You Know. . .

Today, bulk mail exceeds $20 billion annually.

There are generally three cost components to consider in direct mail campaigns: the mailing list, the print and the postage costs.

Mailing lists. Mailing lists can be bought from list brokers or list managers who compile the list and can tell you what type of person or household is on the list. For example, certain publishers sell mailing lists of their subscribers. (In reality, you are merely "renting" the list. You do not have exclusive rights to it but only the right to use it for a set time.) By knowing the average household income of the subscribers, you can determine whether this list is suitable for your product or service.

Print. What will you include in your mailing? A coupon for a discount on your product or service? A price list? You can have your mailings prepared professionally. However, you can save significantly on printing costs (with almost equal results) if you have a computer and a good printer. A color laser printer can produce quality mailings at a surprisingly reasonable cost.

Postage. If you do a great deal of advertising and promotion via the mail, the ever-increasing cost of postage is of considerable concern. You can use a professional mailer (a mailing house) to handle your mailings. The cost generally runs about 52¢ per piece, which covers both postage and the envelopes. A mailing house can offer this price through its bulk-mail permit. If your annual mailings are significant enough, it may even pay for you to get a bulk-mail permit (currently $85 per year). This lowers your postage costs to 22.6¢ per piece.

U.S. Postal Services

The Post Office is a good place to start for advertising and promotion. It provides a number of special services for small business. The Post Office can help your business put a mailing list on disk and add the extra four digits to zip codes to facilitate bulk mailings. It can also provide your company with a report on undeliverable mail to help you continually update your mailing lists. The Post Office gives seminars for business owners about how to use the mail effectively (such as using nine digit zip codes). Anyone in business, whether incorporated or not, can set up a "corporate account" to enable Express Mail to be billed and paid for on a monthly basis. Free post office supplies—mailing envelopes, Express Mail labels—can be sent directly to your business with just a phone call. For more information about the various services available to small business owners, call the U.S. Postal Service Business Center at (800) 374-8777.

The U.S. Postal Service as well as private overnight and parcel carriers have various programs designed to keep mailing costs down and make life easier for small business owners.

Mailing Newsletters

If you mail a newsletter to clients and customers for promotional purposes, you can do so via first class mail or with bulk mailing. Obviously, there is a big difference in the cost of these mailing alternatives. Choosing the best one for you depends on the size of your mailing list. If you are in the business of selling a newsletter, then be sure to build the cost of postage into your subscription price.

Save on Bulk Mail

The U.S. Postal Service began a pilot program in early 1996 to allow small businesses to better target direct mail in special areas at reduced rates. The program is called "Neighborhood Mail" and it saves a business money in several ways. First, the cost of mailing is at third class rates (currently 11.7¢ per item), the same rates usually charged for bulk mailings. But businesses save in two other important ways. There is no need to buy a mailing list because the business's enclosure is sent to all within the "neighborhood." Also, there is no need to address envelopes since the enclosures are automatically delivered to all within the "neighborhood." If and when this program will be available nationwide remains to be seen; ask for it at your local post office.

Co-oping

You can reduce your bulk mailing costs (mailing lists, print and postage) by co-oping. This is advertising with a group. For example, if you were planning to send coupons in a bulk mailing, consider using a group mailer containing coupons from several vendors. The charge for cooperative direct mailings depends on the company you use, the advertising you insert (2-color, 4-color or premium) and the number of addresses you send to. For example, Val-Pak®a national franchise for cooperative direct mail to consumers, charges between $400 and $600 for a one-time, 2-color mailing to 10,000 households. Prices are reduced for those who mail regularly throughout the year (volume discounts). Check your Yellow Pages for a listing of co-op mailing groups.

The e-mail alternative to bulk mailing

With the cost of postage high, a new form of bulk mailing is gaining popularity—bulk e-mailing. Many businesses are turning to the Internet for advertising because the cost of a phone call (particularly in the local area) is typically less than the cost of postage.

Warning

Depending on your on-line service and your telephone service, e-mailing may cost more than standard mail service.

E-mailing is a good way to get your company's name before the public and promote your product or service. Full service providers (CompuServe, America Online and Prodigy) can help a business automate this process and make it most effective. Be sure to used a "closed list." (A closed list limits to whom the message is sent.)

Other tips for making your e-mailing most effective:

- Use a short message to make sure that it will be read (and to keep telephone charges down).

- Include the company's address and regular telephone number.

- Ask for feedback from readers to help you hone your e-mailing program.

IDEA 87: Book "Air Time" Most Effectively

Radio and television advertising may be necessary or helpful to make your business grow. Perhaps you have been put off from using this avenue of advertising because of the fear of high costs. In reality, costs may be more affordable than you think; your fear may be unjustified. Today, radio advertising is highly effective and surprisingly inexpensive. Television advertising in this age of cable T.V. and local access can also be surprisingly affordable. What is more, these modes of advertising are proven winners for promoting businesses and selling products and services.

To keep costs down, it may not be advisable to attempt to "do it yourself." Sure, you can call up a station and it will be glad to book your advertisement. But how do you know which station to use? How often should you run your ads for optimum return? And are you getting the best price? The answer to all of these questions should lead you to the conclusion that an expert is required in this area.

Use a Media Buyer

A media buyer is someone who knows the radio and television advertising business. A media buyer can design an advertising campaign that will maximize exposure while working within your budget. He or she will help you select the appropriate programs on which to run your ads. This decision is based on marketing information available from the stations such as the demographics of listeners (on radio) or watchers (on television). More specifically, a media buyer will use some type of system or formula to plan a media campaign. For example, the Optimum Effective Schedule (one type of system for scheduling radio spots) uses a mathematical formula to estimate how many listeners are being reached by radio spots. By using this information, you will be able to work out how often the ads need to run. A one-shot exposure may be a waste of money; similarly, excessive exposure may also be a waste of money. Finally, since a media buyer is buying air time for more than one client, he/she can command better rates from the stations than you can as a single advertiser.

Finding a media buyer

How do you find a media buyer? Try the Yellow Pages. Alternatively, you can consider contacting an existing advertiser that impresses you. Ask which media buyer the advertiser uses. Referrals from satisfied customers are the best sources to find what you want.

If you decide to act as your own media buyer, be sure to request a media kit from your local television and radio stations. This will tell you about the demographics (what audiences are being reached by what programs) and about costs.

IDEA 88: Set Up a Web Page

With the information age upon us, you cannot ignore the opportunity to participate in the technology.

Did You Know. . .

It is estimated that there are currently about 200,000 web sites and nearly 20 million people who "surf the web" (browse the Internet).

The web can be used to provide information (enhance your company image) or specifically to sell your products and services. Consider setting up a web page for your business that can be accessed from the world wide web.

Did You Know. . .

One large mutual fund family spent an estimated $3.4 million setting up its web site!

In getting a web page, there are three different costs to consider:

- *Design.* What will your page look like? What other information will it be linked to? These are questions that are answered in the design phase of getting your company on the web.

Design is critical because good design ensures that a web page will be found frequently by key words when users search the web. You can design your own page, using one of a number of software programs for this purpose. In fact, Windows 95 enables the user to set up a simple web page. Similarly, the on-line providers (Prodigy, America Online and CompuServe) allow you to set up a simple web page.

If you are not up to the task or want something more complicated than the type of page the existing commercial software programs can offer, then go to experts. In this case be prepared to pay several hundred dollars (or even a thousand dollars) for design services.

The fee you pay for expert assistance in setting up your web site should include design, development and installation. In working with an expert, find out how many images or graphics will be included. Also find out how many pages of text can be accommodated on the web page. Finally, find out how many links (which are essentially like automatic cross references to other pages) will be included.

- *Hook-up fee.* Typically, there is a one-time connection fee to a storage service (the location that mans the web page. This fee is usually modest (around $100). Simple web sites go through existing on-line services like America Online, CompuServe or Prodigy.

- *Monthly storage fee.* Since web pages must be available for access from other computers on the Internet, they are maintained at a central computer site that can be accessed by users. The monthly charge for this storage can be as little as $100 but also can be more, depending on several factors (whether it is manned round-the-clock, how busy the site is and more).

Before jumping into using a web page, make sure it will be cost-effective. If you are only providing a local service, it may not make sense to use a web page that provides national exposure. If, however, you are selling a product that could be ordered from anywhere, a web page may be an excellent vehicle for getting out the name of your company and product.

If you decide to use a web page, make sure it has the capability of showing you how many "hits" you've received (how often people have looked at your web page) to see if the costs continue to be justified.

If your business is entirely local and your clients or customers are not the type to surf the net, then it may be a needless expense to set up and run a web page. You will probably not generate sufficient business from it to justify its costs.

IDEA 89: Write Your Own Print Ads

Today, the computer has made it easy for just about anyone to turn out professional print ads without having to use outside professionals. The cost savings are tremendous, but you must know how to do it or your efforts will be wasted.

Copy and Artwork

There are usually two parts of an ad—what you say and any pictures or diagrams you include. In writing copy (the words), keep it simple. In advertising, less is usually better than more. Just make sure to include all essential facts: the name, address and telephone number of your company, price and model number information and any other facts to allow the reader to know what you are selling and what the terms of sale are. For example, if you are running a particular sale, be sure to include the last day you will honor the sale price. Be certain that what you say in the ad is legal (see Avoiding Costly Mistakes later in this chapter). Check the ad carefully for grammatical errors and typing mistakes.

The ad should be laid out in such a way that the reader will be drawn to it and can easily grasp what you are trying to say. Layout—how the print is arranged on the page and what artwork is included—is critical. Try different arrangements. (On a computer, it is easy to move things around until you are satisfied with the results.)

What kind of artwork will you include? Your company logo? Pictures? There are easy and relatively inexpensive ways to import pictures or other artwork into your ad. Computer "clip art"—premade pictures and shapes—can be used. Some software programs contain a limited number of clip art objects. Separate clip art software can be purchased for a very modest cost. Alternatively, a scanner can bring more sophisticated artwork into your ad. Scanners can be relatively inexpensive, but the better ones (with higher resolution) are several hundred dollars or more. For some companies, it may not make sense to purchase a scanner if it will only be used to write occasional ads. Of course, only you can decide whether the purchase of a scanner is needed and, if so, whether it is cost effective.

Business Cards

Some ads can be handled simply by using a pre-printed business card. For example, a newspaper spot may replicate your business card. This eliminates the need to write any special copy. It also means that your logo will be represented in the ad if you already include it on your business card.

IDEA 90: Avoiding Costly Advertising Mistakes

There is a myriad of advertising choices. The best choice for you depends on the nature of your business (what you are trying to sell) and your available funds. Obviously, you want to keep costs down as much as possible and avoid waste.

Choose the Best Media Format for Your Business

Several media choices have already been covered earlier in this chapter. How do you know which type is best for you? One criteria is to get the biggest bang for your buck. You want your advertising dollars to go as far as possible. One way to accomplish this is to compare the cost of print media (magazine or newspaper advertising) with the cost of broadcast media (radio). This requires an analysis of how many people you are reaching with your ads. To do this, use the following formulas to figure a "cost per thousand ratio" (CPT ratio).

Print media CPT $=$ Cost of an ad $\times$ 1,000 Circulation

Broadcast CPT $= \dfrac{\text{Cost of unit of time} \times 1,000}{\text{Households reached at set time}}$

This helps you to arrive at a dollar amount for each person/household you reach. For example, if you spend $500 on an ad in a magazine with a circulation of 100,000 readers, the cost per reader is $5. Now let's see what the CPT would be for that same $500 advertising expenditure in broadcast media. For example, say the cost of a radio spot (a 30-second ad) is $500 and the station estimates that household listening at the time of that spot is 100,000, then the cost of the ad per-household is $5. In this example, you've reached about the same audience with the same dollars. But if the circulation of the magazine had been only 50,000, it would have raised the cost-per-reader to $10, which is double the cost of the radio spot.

However, cost alone may not be a good basis for making advertising placement. Consider other factors. For example, broadcast media is more flexible than print media. The ads can be changed virtually within hours of airtime; print media has a considerable time delay. Also consider frequency. Frequency is a captive of cost. The more you can afford to run an ad, whether in broadcast or print, the more frequently it will appear. But you may get greater repeat viewing with print media than you might otherwise expect. An ad in a magazine may be viewed over and over again by the same person who repeatedly scans the magazine. A radio spot is only heard again if it is rebroadcast, at additional cost.

Avoid Lawsuits, Fines and Penalties

Your main goal in advertising is to sell your product or service. But you do not want to engage in false or deceptive ads that could lead to costly lawsuits, fines and penalties. What you don't know can hurt you.

Did You Know. . .

The regulation of advertising is governed primarily by the Federal Trade Commission (FTC). It has the power to prevent and correct false advertising. For example, you cannot make false claims about your product, nor about another company's product.

The FTC has issued various guidelines (rules, guides, opinions, policy statements) designed to help businesses ensure that their advertising is lawful. A comprehensive source of guidance on lawful advertising is the Guides on Advertising Allowances and Other Merchandising Payments and Services (commonly referred to as the "Fred Meyer Guides"). The Guides cover, for example, discriminatory promotional payments. These would include promotional allowances given to some but not all customers. Such advertising is illegal.

IDEA 91: Use an Ad Agency

A local mom and pop store may be able to handle its own advertising; a company that wants to market a product nationwide may need professional assistance. Here is where the use of an advertising agency comes in. But how do you know which agency to use? There is no single answer. What might be a good selection for one type of company may not serve the interests of another. Get several different agencies to make presentations to you. This will help you to determine how much they want your business and how in tune they are with your company.

Factors in Choosing an Agency

There are several factors you can use to select an advertising agency. These include:

- *Size of the agency.* Do you want to work with a large or a small agency? The answer may be dependent more on the size of your advertising budget than on your personal preference. You might want a large agency but it might not want your company as a client, given the size of your company's advertising budget. Of course, the agency must be large enough to be able to handle all your advertising needs.

- *Reputation of the agency.* Obviously, you want an agency that enjoys a solid reputation for its effectiveness.

- *Knowledge of your industry.* You want an agency that knows your industry. This will help it to design the ad program that is most effective for your product or service. However, the fact that the agency knows the industry may mean that they service a competing company. This is something you do not want. If they do not currently have a competing client and you want to make sure that they do not later take one on, be sure to include this provision in your contract.

- *Account executive.* Do you know which account executive you will be working with? This is key. The account executive is the person who quarterbacks your advertising. This is the person you will be working with. Make sure you know not only the reputation of the agency but also the reputation of the account executive that will be assigned to you. Also make sure you can work comfortably with the account executive.

The following is a checklist that can be used to assess the agencies that you approach.

Checklist for Choosing an Agency

Factors	Yes	No	Unsure
I prefer a small agency	____	____	____
The agency enjoys a solid reputation	____	____	____
The agency knows my industry	____	____	____
I have confidence in/can work with the account executive	____	____	____

Making a Contract With an Advertising Agency

Be sure you understand what you are committing to. Make sure that the contract spells out all of the terms you deem important.

Until you are comfortable with the working arrangement (how the agency will be responsive to your views and how successful its ad campaign will be), try to keep the contractual arrangement as short as possible. The agency may require a certain time commitment from your company—three months, six months, a year. Seek to limit the period, provided there are options to renew.

Make sure that the financial arrangements are clear. What are the fees? Reimbursements for expenses? Obligation for liability insurance to cover defamation or other actions arising out of the advertising? For example, are fees set as a fixed percentage? Increasingly popular are performance-based fees. Agencies are paid according to how much sales increase (which assumes that the increase is due to advertising efforts). Some advertising agencies may not charge for anything except for their creative efforts. The reason: They receive a percentage of the ad placement. For example, suppose the agency commands a 15% discount for ad placement. You pay the full amount; the agency keeps the 15% discount.

Spell out the services to be rendered by the agency. Will it conduct marketing surveys? Conduct research? Do public relations work? Do media placement only?

Understand how your company will work with the agency. How will ad approvals be obtained? Be sure to reserve the right to have ads reviewed by your legal counsel to see that they comport with FTC standards and restrictions. Will your company own the rights in the creative materials developed by the agency?

10

Improving Your Cash Flow with Smart Credit and Collection Policies

Paying your bills in an effective manner and getting paid for your goods or services in a similarly effective manner may be the key to your business success—or failure. According to the SBA, the failure to properly plan cash flow is one of the leading causes for small business failures.

You need to understand how cash flow works and how it affects your business. To do this, you need to have a basic understanding of general accounting principles and certain terminology. Cash flow should be viewed in accordance with the operating cycle. The operating cycle is simply the period beginning with the acquisition of inventory and ending with collection of payment for sales. During this period, cash flows in and out of a business. The first phase of the business cycle eats into your cash; the last phase replenishes it. To be able to meet all of your business obligations—payroll, rent, taxes, and other expenses that arise throughout the operating cycle—you need to know how to effectively handle all aspects of cash flow: your payments and your collections. You need to know how to keep costs down and collections up.

Payments and collections involve two important terms: accounts receivable and accounts payable.

- *Accounts receivable.* This is a term used to describe amounts you owe for products and services you purchase. It is important for businesses to pay promptly in order to establish good credit because good credit can lead to favorable payment terms.
- *Accounts payable.* This is a term used to describe amounts owed to you for products or services you have provided to others. With sufficient cash flow being a problem for many small businesses, prompt receipt of payment becomes critical. Sometimes it can even mean the difference between a company surviving or going under. There are several ways in which you can speed up collections and ensure payment.

This chapter focuses on the beginning and ending phases of the business cycle. In this chapter, you will learn about ways to improve your cash flow with smart credit and collection policies. Some ideas may be modest, resulting in only small savings. Still, every dollar saved is important because the dollars add up.

IDEA 92: Establish and Protect Good Credit

Good credit will save you money in the long run. Your cost for borrowing money will be lower and your need to borrow money may be reduced. But how do you ensure that your credit rating remains high when you are starting out with limited funds? There are several strategies to follow.

- *Be sure to pay on time.* If you have a bill that is due in 30 days, you need not pay before the due date. However, if you are in a position to pay early, you can accomplish two things. You can show the vendor or supplier your creditworthiness. You may also be able to command a discount off your bill. Ask the creditor whether immediate payment entitles you to a reduction.
- *Monitor your cash flow to protect your paying ability.* Anticipate your expenses, many of which are fixed, and see that there will be sufficient funds to meet these expenses. Cash flow planning is discussed later in this Chapter.
- *Don't let a cash crunch prevent you from trying to work things out.* If you have regularly paid on time but find yourself in a temporarily difficult cash crunch, a vendor or supplier may extend your payment deadline interest free. For example, if you have a net 30 day deadline, ask for a grace period of 45 days or even 60 days. This additional payment period may allow you to receive payment on your goods or services . . . payment that can then be used to pay the vendor or supplier.

IDEA 93: Plan for Cash Flow

A business simply will not succeed if cash flow is left to chance. You cannot be casual about it. You cannot merely use what is available to pay existing bills as you might with your personal finances.

In business, you need to plan ahead to ensure that there is enough cash on hand each month to pay your expenses (payroll, suppliers, debt service, rent, etc.).

Make Monthly Cash Flow Projections

When you start up a business, it is common to make cash flow projections to see what is needed to carry the business forward until revenues make it self-sustaining (see Chapter 1). However, just because you are up and running does not mean you can ignore this practice of making cash flow projections. This practice continues to be a vital part of running a business. If projections show that cash will be short, then you need to adjust operations accordingly. Maybe you need to cut back on certain purchases. Maybe you need to trim salaries or staff positions. By the same token, if your projections show that you are fortunate to have more than enough cash (in fact "excess" cash), then you also need to make changes. Excess cash means that you may be borrowing too much (incurring needless interest costs) or not putting your cash in needed places (such as toward expansion).

In making projections be sure to take into account all expenses, including legal fees and capital expenditures that may be nonrecurring (only occur once). Also, when making projections, be real-istic about collections. Do not assume that all accounts receivable will be paid within 30 days. In your cash flow projection, make an allowance for late and even unpaid receivables.

If possible, it may also be a good idea to build a cushion into your cash flow that can be used to avoid bank service fees for insufficient balances. Check with your bank about the minimum cash balance your account must maintain in order to avoid additional banking fees.

The following worksheet can be used to make cash flow projections.

Worksheet for One-Year Estimated Cash Flow

	Jan.	*Feb.*	*Mar.*	*Apr.*	*May*	*Jun.*
Cash in*						
Cash in bank						
Petty cash						
Cash sales						
Receivables						
Total cash in**						
Disbursements***						
Cash balance ****						

continues

Worksheet for One-Year Estimated Cash Flow (continued)

	Jul.	*Aug.*	*Sep.*	*Oct.*	*Nov.*	*Dec.*	*Total*
Cash in*							
Cash in bank							
Petty cash							
Cash sales							
Receivables							
Total cash in**							
Disbursements***							
Cash balance ****							

*Amount on hand at the first of each month

**Total of cash in, cash sales and accounts receivable

***Payments for rents, wages, utilities and other expenses

****Difference between total cash in, etc., and disbursements as of the end of each month

Review cash flow projections

Your initial projections should be adjusted periodically (monthly, quarterly). Any time you get a new client or customer (or lose one) or undertake additional costs (hire new workers, move to more expensive quarters, buy new equipment), you may need to make adjustments. Even as your business grows, do not ignore the importance of regularly reviewing cash flow projections.

Use computer software to forecast cash flow

In an effort not to be caught short, consider using a software program designed specifically for tracking cash flow. There are stand-alone cash flow programs that exist solely for this purpose. Or use the cash flow portion of a general office management program to track cash flow.

In forecasting, it is up to you to set your parameters. Decide on the time you want to forecast—a month, six months, a year. During your start up phase, you need to keep a very close eye on cash so a monthly forecast is advisable. As your business matures, you can take a longer view.

Obtain a line of credit

To gain a cushion against unexpected cash needs, apply to a bank for a line of credit. This is a loan that is used only when and to the extent that you need it. You pay interest only on the amount you actually borrow, not for the entire credit line.

But understand that a line of credit will generally be granted only when the business is in good shape, cash flow-wise. A lender naturally wants to be sure that it will be repaid (and good cash flow is the best demonstration of this ability). Thus, apply for a line of credit in good times. Then it will be there for you should you need it in a crunch.

Strategies For Improving Cash Flow

If you find that projected cash flow will not meet anticipated obligations, you need to take steps to increase your cash position. Consider the following strategies:

- *Improve collection of receivables.* Adopt smart invoicing practices (discussed later in this chapter). Become more aggressive on collection of delinquent accounts.

- *Tighten up on extending credit.* Instead of allowing customers to buy on credit, require immediate payment. If you feel you must extend credit, be more limited in what can be bought on credit (such as over a set dollar amount).

- *Increase sales.* Take steps to boost sales. Increase advertising and marketing efforts. This may require you to make additional cash outlays, but may prove cost-effective in the long run. Try innovative sales techniques to increase receivables.

- *Delay paying bills.* Wait as long as possible to pay outstanding payables (for example, pay a net 30 day sale on the 27th day, not on the day the bill is received). But do not wait so long that you incur unnecessary interest costs or lose your good credit standing with vendors, suppliers or lenders.

- *Change pricing.* You may have to raise the price of your goods and services. However, be aware that a price increase can depress sales, (especially in a highly competitive market-place), resulting in lower receivables.

Did You Know. . .

According to the U.S. Labor Department, it is harder to raise prices in the 90's than ever before. Therefore, a price increase should be a last resort for improving cash flow.

IDEA 94: Adopt Smart Invoicing Practices

If your business is the type that invoices goods or services (rather than requiring immediate payment at the time the goods and services are provided), then it is advisable to set up invoicing policies that will help you collect your payment as promptly as possible. Here are some suggestions.

- *Invoice immediately.* Instead of waiting until the end of the month to invoice all outstanding amounts, invoice at the time the product is sold or the service is provided (within two days). This can lead to quicker payment. Why? Many clients and customers may pay according to their own billing cycle. The faster you send your invoice, the better your chances of catching their billing cycle. For example, under a customer's billing cycle, all invoices received before the 1st of the month are paid on the 10th of each month. Suppose you sell your product to this customer on the April 20th. If you wait until the end of the month to send your invoice, it will not be received until some time in May. This means that it will not get paid until June. If the invoice had been sent on April 20th, it would have been received before May 1st and would have been paid on May 10th—a full month sooner. Another reason for prompt billing is that delayed billing communicates to the customer that it is acceptable to be late; if you are prompt in billing, then payment should also be prompt.

- *Offer discounts for immediate payment.* Consider a 1% or 2% discount if the bill is paid in full upon receipt. The discount that you give away may be more than offset by having the balance of the funds in hand and available to meet your business needs.

- *Use pre-numbered inventory receipts.* This will allow you to track payments more easily. For example, if you use consecutive numbering for your invoices and your invoice receipts show that you have received #0107 and #0109, you can immediately see that an invoice which should have been paid (#0108) has not yet been received. This, in turn, will allow you to stay on top of collections.

IDEA 95: Use Cash Back Credit Cards

If you regularly charge certain business expenses—gasoline for your car, the purchase of incidental supplies, entertainment costs for clients and customers—consider using cash-back credit cards. These are regular credit cards that operate like any other bank credit card, but they give you a bonus. You may be rewarded with 1% of the total charges. Thus, for example, if you charge $10,000 per year, you would receive $100 at the end of the year. While this savings is not significant, there is no real downside.

The only warning I have applies if you do not expect to pay the balance in full each month and will be carrying a balance. In this case, the interest rate charged on the balance may be higher than the rate charged by credit cards that do not offer cash back.

IDEA 96: Understand the Ups and Downs of Checks versus Charges

There are three methods of payment, called the Three C's, that you can receive for the products or services you provide: cash, check or charge. Obviously, cash is the best method since cash in hand is final payment to you. With check or charge, there are both positives and negatives to consider.

Check

In some businesses, this is the typical form of payment. If you provide services to a client under contract, you will receive payment by check. There is no alternative. A check becomes cash to you when it clears. This depends on where the check is drawn and on your state banking rules. For example, local checks clear faster than out-of-state checks.

If you are in the retail business, your customers may not have the cash nor the credit card to pay for your goods. Bank check may be their only means of payment. From a merchant's perspective, if the check is good, then this is a satisfactory method of payment because the merchant receives 100% on the dollar (in comparison with payments under a credit card as explained below). Unfortunately, despite receipt of a check, you may ultimately not receive payment for the goods you've sold because the check may not be good. How can you minimize the odds of receiving a bad check?

- *Get the check writer's telephone number.* Many honest people have bank problems. Checks they thought had cleared and against which they wrote checks to others (including your company) may simply not have cleared. As a result, the check given to you bounces. You can redeposit the check for collection. Many times this is all that is required to ensure collection. However, sometimes there are additional problems. A telephone call to the customer may bring the desired results: payment in the form of another check (one drawn on another account) or cash.

- *Get the check writer's driver's license number.* Sometimes customers may not be honest people. In this case, you want to preserve your legal rights to seek redress, including pressing criminal charges. To do this, be sure to write down the number of his/her driver's license on the check. If the check is bad, this number will help the police locate the check writer. Understand, however, that pressing legal charges may not ensure that you will receive payment.

- *Use a service to check out the check writer.* Available in some locations, there is a service (similar to the service that verifies a credit card's remaining purchasing power) that will do a quick credit check on the check writer. Essentially it looks to see if there are funds available to cover the check. In the event the information proves to be wrong, the merchant still receives payment, not from the customer but from the service that did the check.

Credit Cards

"Plastic" is a common form of payment today. With many people worried about carrying around cash, shoppers may be more inclined to pay by credit card. Also, many need to make purchases in excess of their cash (they carry balances on their charge from month to month). As a merchant, you are virtually required to accept a credit card as a form of payment.

Other businesses as well as retailers may need or want to accept credit card charges as payment (mail-order catalogues, restaurants). Today, even service providers are increasingly accepting credit cards.

When choosing a bank to serve as a collection processing point for your credit sales, make sure to shop around. Banks charge different fees for this service. Try to negotiate lower fees.

Special concerns for home-based businesses

Some banks or other credit card services simply will not handle merchant authorization for home-based businesses. If you run a mail order business or other company from your home and want to offer customers the option of charging purchases, you may have difficulty finding a company to allow you this option. Here are a couple of places that will process credit card charges for home based businesses:

- *Card Establishment Services, Inc. (CES),* New York, NY (212-262-5299) offers Visa, MasterCard and American Express card authorization. The company provides necessary equipment ($20–$33 per month). It charges between $1.49 and 3%, depending on the nature of the business (e.g., mail order, retail).

- *EMS (Electronic Merchant Systems),* Beverly Hills, CA, offers Visa, MasterCard, and American Express card authorization. The company will come to your home office to physically inspect it. (The company does not want to approve credit card processing for bogus businesses.) The company supplies software, modem, and other information ($50–$60 month) and charges about 2% cost (the same as other businesses).

Another alternative for home-based businesses looking for merchant authorization is to find merchant authorization through a business organization or trade association. Ask any association of which you are a member (or considering becoming a member) whether they offer this referral service.

Yet another alternative is to go through an independent sales organization (ISO) which acts as an intermediary between your business and a bank. There are, however, a number of fees and charges that make this alternative less attractive than direct authorization. These fees can include nonre-fundable application fees (up to $200); equipment charges (rental of the terminal up to $80 per month); service fees between 2% and 7%, plus a per transaction charge; monthly fees (statement fee, usage fee) and more.

IDEA 97: Use Credit Reports to Avoid Collection Problems

In the rush to sell products or services, you may be too eager for a sale. True, you may ring up that sale, but will you collect on it? You need to know whether the client or customer will pay for the product or services you have supplied.

One way to make an educated guess on a client or customer's ability to pay is to see whether that party has a good paying history. While past performance is no guarantee of future payment, it can allow you to decide whether to furnish the goods or services to that party. By using credit reports, you can hopefully reduce your risk by ensuring payment and avoiding the need for costly collection procedures. You can get credit information from a credit service. Obviously, a retailer is not going to run a credit check on every person who walks through the door. But if you have big ticket items or large contracts, a credit check is in your best interest.

Dun & Bradstreet

One of the best known credit services for businesses is D&B. It can provide you with credit information about a prospective or existing client or customer. All you have to do is call a toll-free number with information about the client or customer. Alternatively, information can be fed to D&B via modem from your computer. Verbal information is generally available within a few hours; a written report can be sent or faxed later.

There are different payment plans offered by D&B. You can pay on a per-credit report basis. If you deal with only a few major clients or customers each year, you may only need a couple of reports and the per-report charges may make sense. Alternatively, you can contract for unlimited reports for less than $1,000 per year. This may be an extremely high charge for a start up or small business to handle. However, D&B provides more than just credit reports for this fee: It claims that its additional services will more than offset the fees by the additional business you can generate. These additional services include:

- *Marketing information.* D&B can help your business identify potential customers, vendors and suppliers.

- *Monitor accounts.* D&B can alert you to changes occurring in your existing customers' businesses that may affect collections. For example, if one of your existing customers is experiencing severe financial difficulties (e.g., lawsuits, liens, bankruptcy, or other public filings), D&B can warn you about the situation. This will allow you decide whether to continue providing goods or services to the customer.

- *Third party collections.* D&B can lend its name to your collection efforts. Hopefully, this will serve as leverage to impress tardy clients and customers into paying.

For more information about D&B services and costs, call (800) 234-3867. You will be given a local telephone number for the sales office nearest you.

IDEA 98: Use a Collection Agency

When your in-house efforts to receive payment for goods or services you provided have failed, you may want to consider outside assistance like a collection agency to recover payment. Waiting beyond 60 or 90 days to seek collection may mean that you have not only lost the time value of the money (you may have had to incur greater borrowing because of the delinquent collection), but your chances of a full recovery are also greatly diminished.

A collection agency is an independent third party that works in several ways. You can use a collection agency simply to send out reminder letters in the hopes of bringing in past due fees. For this type of service, the collection agency may charge a flat fee. For example, for a flat fee of $20 per account, a collection agency may send out up to five reminders, including an attorney's letter. Alternatively, you can use the agency's more aggressive services to collect, allowing the agency to use the full force of the law (including litigation). In this case, collection agencies typically receive one-quarter to one-half of the amount collected (depending on what they usually charge and on what you can negotiate with them as a percentage arrangement). Remember that the amount collected may not necessarily be the full amount you billed.

> **Example:** Assume that you performed services for a customer and billed him or her $2,000. After failing to collect payment for three months, you turned collection over to an agency that charges one-half of the amount recovered. The agency takes legal action and recovers $1,200. You receive $600 of your initial $2,000 bill (one-half of the $1,200 recovered). Still, $600 may be better than no recovery and you did not have to waste your time and efforts on this recovery. (You may have been able to recover the same amount recovered by the agency if you had litigated as explained later in this chapter, but this would have required your own time and effort.)

In dealing with collection agencies, understand that some states license them while others do not. In states that do not require collection agencies to be licensed, find out whether the agency has posted a bond for the protection of the companies that it services. This will give you some recourse in case of problems with the agency paying you for amounts it has recovered on your behalf.

IDEA 99: Sue to Recover Unpaid Bills

If you fail to receive payment for goods or services you have provided to others, you may feel wronged—and rightly so. But should you sue to recover your loss? Suppose you have already tried to collect but your best efforts have failed. You might want to sue, but lawsuits usually require the services of an attorney. This can be a significant expense, one that is not justified in view of what you hope to recover. Still, you might want to pursue legal action on your own, without the assistance of an attorney. If the claim is small enough, you can represent yourself in small-claims court.

Small-Claims Court

Most states have set up special courts, called small-claims courts to handle smaller actions in an expeditious manner. Procedures are generally informal. Best of all, claims can usually be heard quite promptly; usually within one to two months.

Many of the rules for small-claims court differ greatly from state to state. In deciding whether to go forward with this course of action, be sure to understand whether you can legally use this type of forum, whether it is available in your locality and what you can expect. Here are some of the questions you might want answered before going forward with your case in small-claims court.

- Can you recover more than just the amount of the bill in the form of punitive damages or some specially crafted relief (for example, an order to the defendant to return the property to you)?

- If you sue, can be you subject to a counterclaim?

- What is a dollar limit on the amount you can hope to recover?

- Does your form of business organization prevent you from using small-claims court. Some states allow corporations to sue in small claims court; others do not.

- Can you be represented by an attorney? Some courts allow you to be represented by an attorney if you choose; other do not.

- What are the filing fees?

Here is a state-by-state rundown on some of the key factors in deciding whether to bring your case to small-claims court.

State	*Factor*
ALABAMA	
Maximum claim	$1,500
Attorneys	Allowed (required for collection agencies)
Other considerations	Equitable relief permitted
ALASKA	
Maximum claim	$5,000
Filing fee	$15
Attorneys	Allowed (required for collection agencies)
ARIZONA	
Maximum claim	$1,500 (excluding interest and costs)
Attorneys	Allowed if both parties agree in writing
Other considerations	Equitable relief permitted
	Collection agencies not permitted
ARKANSAS	
Maximum claim	$3,000
Attorneys	Not allowed
Other considerations	Corporation with no more than 3 stockholders can sue or be sued in this court
	Collection agencies not permitted
CALIFORNIA	
Maximum claim	$5,000 (with exceptions)
Attorneys	Not allowed (corporation can appear only through an employee, officer or director)
Other considerations	Equitable relief permitted
	Collection agencies not permitted
	Legal advisors will help free of charge
COLORADO	
Maximum claim	$3,500
Filing fee	Claims up to $500: $8 for plaintiff; $4 for defendant; $501 to $2,000: $16 for plaintiff; $11 for defendant; over $2,000: $25 for plaintiff; $21 for defendant
Attorneys	Not allowed
CONNECTICUT	
Maximum claim	$2,000
Filing fee	$20
Other considerations	Parties can agree to submit case to a commissioner for a speedy hearing and not be bound by the rules of evidence

State	Factor
DISTRICT OF COLUMBIA	
Maximum claim	$2,000
DELAWARE	
No Small Claims Court	
FLORIDA	
Maximum claim	$2,500 (excluding interest, costs, and attorney's fees)
Attorneys	Allowed
GEORGIA	
Small Claims Court	Only in certain counties; other courts may use small claims procedures
Maximum claim	$5,000 (but not uniform in all counties)
Attorneys	May be allowed
HAWAII	
Maximum claim	$2,500
Attorneys	Allowed
Other considerations	Award of costs in court's discretion
IDAHO	
Maximum claim	$3,000
Filing fee	$18
Attorneys	Not allowed
Other considerations	Collection agencies not allowed
ILLINOIS	
Maximum claim	$2,500 (excluding interest and costs)
Attorneys	Allowed
Other considerations	Judgment debtor may be ordered to pay in installments if unpaid past 3 years
INDIANA	
Maximum claim	$3,000; $6,000 in Marion County (excluding interest and attorney's fees)
Attorneys	Allowed
IOWA	
Maximum claim	$3,000
KANSAS	
Maximum claim	$1,800 (limit on 10 claims per year)
Filing fee	$16.50 for claims of $500 or less; $36.50 for claims over $500
Attorneys	Not allowed until judgment

continues

State	Factor
KENTUCKY	
Maximum claim	$1,500 (excluding interest and costs); 25 claims per business location per year
Attorneys	Allowed
Other considerations	Collection agencies/collectors not allowed
LOUISIANA	
Maximum claim	$2,000
MAINE	
Maximum claim	$3,000 (excluding interest and costs)
Attorneys	Allowed
Other considerations	Debtor can be ordered to return, refund, repair or rescind
Monthly installments	($15 minimum) can be ordered for non-indigents
MARYLAND	
Maximum claim	$2,500 (excluding attorney's fees)
Attorneys	Allowed
MASSACHUSETTS	
Maximum claim	$1,500
Filing fee	$10 for claims of $500 or less; $15 for claims over $500
Attorneys	Allowed
Other considerations	Equitable relief permitted
	Mediation available
	Payment in installments can be ordered
MICHIGAN	
Maximum claim	$1,750 (no more than 5 claims in 1 week)
Attorneys	Not allowed (corporations appear by an employee who is not a full-time attorney)
MINNESOTA	
Maximum claim	$7,500
Attorneys	Not customary
MISSISSIPPI	
Maximum claim	$1,000
Attorneys	Allowed
Other considerations	Debtor can be ordered to return property
	Court provides collection assistance

State	*Factor*
MISSOURI	
Maximum claim	$1,500 ($2,500 in certain counties) (excluding interest and costs)
Filing fee	$5 for claims under $100; $10 for all other claims
Attorneys	Allowed
MONTANA	
Maximum claim	$3,000 (excluding costs)
NEBRASKA	
Maximum claim	$1,500 (10 claims per year)
Filing fee	$9
Attorneys	Not allowed
NEVADA	
Maximum claim	$3,500
Attorneys	Not allowed
NEW HAMPSHIRE	
Maximum claim	$2,500 (excluding interest and costs)
Filing fee	$25
NEW JERSEY	
Maximum claim	$1,000
NEW MEXICO	
No Small Claims Court	
NEW YORK	
Maximum claim	$2,000
Filing fee	$2 ($3 in some cases)
Attorneys	Allowed
Other considerations	Collection agencies not allowed
	Corporations and partnerships cannot sue in Small Claims Court
	Arbitration available
New York City Commercial Small Claims Court	Corporations and partnerships can sue in amounts up to $2,000 (5 claims per month)
NORTH CAROLINA	
Maximum claim	$2,000
Attorneys	Allowed
Other considerations	Recovery of property permitted

continues

State	Factor
NORTH DAKOTA	
Maximum claim	$2,000
OHIO	
Maximum claim	$1,000
Attorneys	Allowed
OKLAHOMA	
No special court	Special small claims cases can be docketed in district court
Maximum amount	$2,500
Attorneys	Allowed
Other considerations	No collection agencies
OREGON	
Maximum claim	$2,500
Attorneys	Allowed only with judge's consent
PENNSYLVANIA	
Maximum claim	$4,000
RHODE ISLAND	
Maximum claim	$1,500
Filing fee	$5
SOUTH CAROLINA	
Maximum claim	$2,500
Attorneys	Allowed
SOUTH DAKOTA	
Maximum claim	$4,000
Filing fee	Claims up to $100: $4
	Claims up to $1,000: $10
	Claims over $1,000: $20
TENNESSEE	
Maximum claim	$10,000
Other considerations	Note: State does not have small claims court but does have similar procedures
TEXAS	
Maximum claim	$5,000 (excluding costs)
Filing fees	Yes
Other considerations	Collection agencies not permitted

State	Factor
UTAH	
Maximum claim	$5,000
Filing fee	Claims of $2,000 or less: $25
	Claim over $2,000: $60
Attorneys	Allowed
Other considerations	Collection agencies not permitted
VERMONT	
Maximum claim	$3,500
Filing fee	Claims of $500 or less: $25
	Claims over $500: $35
Attorneys	Allowed
Other considerations	Some equitable relief
VIRGINIA	
Maximum claim	$1,000 (excluding interest)
Attorneys	Not permitted
WASHINGTON	
Maximum claim	$2,500
Attorneys	Corporate plaintiff cannot be represented by an attorney or paralegal
WEST VIRGINIA	
Maximum claim	$3,000 (excluding interest and costs)
Filing fee	$3 automation fee; $20 court support resources fee
Other considerations	Credit card payment of costs
WISCONSIN	
Maximum limit	$4,000
Attorneys	Allowed
WYOMING	
Maximum limit	$2,000
Filing fee	$4
Attorneys	Allowed

How to Proceed

Ask your small claims court about its rules (call the clerk of the court in your locality). The court may have a brochure explaining the rules of the court and how to proceed. It can also provide you with the forms needed to commence your claim. You must know whether you can sue the party who has not paid you in the court closest to you. For example, you generally must sue a party in the court presiding over the location in which the act giving rise to the action occurred (or where the other party resides). In the case of a corporation, "residence" is the place where the corporation does business.

You must also know who can serve the complaint upon the other party. For example, you may be able to serve your complaint by certified or registered mail. You may be required to use a sheriff or an adult approved by the court to serve your complaint.

You must know the time-limit for filing an action. This is called the "statute of limitations." You may be required, for example, to start your suit within two years from the date that the claim arose, or you might have four years to bring your suit. Be sure to check that you still have time remaining to start an action. If you do, then be sure to follow through within the time-limit remaining.

You can also find out about default judgments. For example, if the party you are suing does not respond to your complaint within a certain time (set by law), then you win automatically (by default). You can then try to collect on your judgment.

Other Courts

If you cannot use small-claims court (for example, if your claim exceeds the limit allowed for small-claims court in your locality), then consider suing in the appropriate court. Weigh carefully the costs of proceeding with your claim. There may be significant costs involved. Additionally, litigation may require a large time commitment on your part—time that could be spent generating fees or selling products.

Warning

Getting a judgment in your favor is one thing; collecting that judgment is quite another. You may win what turns out to be only a moral victory. Understand that you may have no more chance of collecting your money after a suit than before it.

IDEA 100: Ensure Tax Write-Offs for Bad Debts

Let's assume that you've taken all the precautions you could to collect your payables but have had no success. As a last resort, you can recoup some of your investment in furnishing the goods or services if you are able to deduct your loss as a bad debt.

Business bad debts are fully deductible as ordinary losses. They serve to offset ordinary business income. To be treated as a business bad debt, the debt must be closely related to the activity of the business. There must have been a business reason for entering into the debtor-creditor relationship. Business bad debts typically arise from credit sales to customers. They can also be the result of loans to suppliers, customers, employees or distributors. Credit sales are generally reported on the books of the business as accounts receivable. Loans to suppliers, customers, employees or distributors generally are reported on the books of the business as notes receivable. When accounts receivable or notes receivable become uncollectible, they become business bad debts.

How much is the bad debt worth? Accounts receivable and notes receivable are generally carried on the books at fair market value. Thus, when they are uncollected, they are deductible at fair market value. This is true even when that value is less than the face value of the obligations.

Impact of Loans On Your Business or Associates

If your business is set up as a corporation and you loan money to it that the corporation later defaults, you cannot claim a bad debt deduction unless it was a true loan. If you advanced money to the corporation that was actually a contribution to its capital, then you cannot claim a bad debt deduction when the corporation fails to repay you. If the corporation is "thinly capitalized" (there is little equity compared to the amount of its debt), this indicates that the advance was a capital contribution and not a bona fide loan. But even if the corporation is not thinly capitalized, an advance may be treated as a capital contribution if the corporation fails to treat it as a loan. Be sure to have the loan entered as such on the corporate books. Also see that the corporation makes required payments of interest and principal when due.

Assume that the advance to the corporation is in fact a debt and not a contribution to capital. Then, you must determine whether the bad debt is a business bad debt or a non-business bad debt. If you made the loan to protect your investment in the company, it is viewed as a non-business bad debt (which is treated as a short-term capital loss, but only if it is entirely worthless). If you made the loan to protect your salary from the company, then it is viewed as a business bad debt (deductible as an ordinary loss).

Let's say your business is set up as a partnership and doesn't make it. If you have a partnership that breaks up and the partnership still owes money to suppliers or others, you may be forced to make payments if your partner or partners do not. This payment may be more than your share of the partnership's debts. In this case, you can claim a bad debt deduction if your partner or partners were insolvent and you were required to pay their share.

If you go out of business but still try to collect outstanding amounts owed to you, potential bad debt deductions are not lost. You can still claim them as business bad debts if the debts become worthless after you go out of business.

Warning

A cash basis taxpayer who provides services but fails to receive payment cannot deduct this nonpayment as a bad debt. Since the fees were never reported as income, the failure to receive the fees is not deductible.

Example: You have a consulting business and use the cash basis method to account for your income. You provide consulting services to a client and bill $2,500 for your services. The client pays you $1,000 but goes out of business before paying the balance. You cannot receive any payment in the client's bankruptcy proceeding (because there are simply no assets with which to pay creditors). You cannot deduct the $1,500 ($2,500 fee – $1,000 received) that you never received. This is because you never had to report the $1,500 as income under your method of accounting. True, you are out the time and effort it took to generate the fee. Unfortunately, the tax law does not underwrite this type of loss.

CHAPTER 11

Reducing
Insurance Costs

Insurance costs are a big part of a business's initial and ongoing expenses. For some businesses (especially those that are labor intensive or those manufacturing or selling certain high-risk items), insurance can be one of your biggest single expenditures.

In this chapter you will learn about the kinds of insurance you need and ways in which you can reduce insurance costs or otherwise meet insurance obligations on a tight budget.

IDEA 101: Identify the Kinds of Insurance You Need

There are a number of different kinds of insurance that are applicable to businesses. The following list highlights some of the critical kinds:

- *Accident and health insurance.* This is the cost of medical coverage for yourself, employees, spouses and dependents.

- *Automobile insurance.* Liability and collision coverage for cars used for business.

- *Business interruption insurance.* This provides payment during a period in which the business is forced to close (a natural disaster or a civil riot).

- *Casualty insurance.* Reimbursement for property damage occasioned by floods, fires, storms and other casualty destruction to property.

- *Credit insurance.* This provides coverage for nonpayment of debts owed to the business.

- *Disability insurance.* This provides payment to you and employees who become unable to work due to physical or mental impairment. The injury need not be job-related (as in the case of worker's compensation discussed below). In buying disability insurance, be sure to understand the policy's definition of "disability." Some pay off only if you are totally disabled (unable to perform any kind of work). Better (and more expensive) policies pay off when you are unable to perform the duties of your current job.

- *Key-person life insurance.* This policy protects the business from the loss of an owner or other key employee. The theory behind the insurance is to give the business funds to enable it to look for a replacement as well as cover any losses in the interim.

- *Life insurance.* This type of policy insures the lives of the owners and is often used as a funding mechanism for a buy-sell agreement (which buys out an owner's interest in the event of death, retirement or disability).

- *Overhead insurance.* This policy covers the costs of rent, salaries, and other overhead expenses during periods of illness by an owner.

- *PBGC coverage.* Businesses that maintain defined benefit plans (pension plans that gear contributions on an actuarial basis to provide employees with a certain amount at retirement) are required to pay premiums to this quasi-federal agency. The premiums protect employees in the event that the plan fails.

- *Performance bonds.* Businesses may be required to secure this coverage to ensure the faithful performance of employees and/or the business's performance on a contract.

- *Product liability insurance.* This coverage protects a business from claims that the products you manufacture or sell are defective and have caused injury to the public.

- *Professional liability coverage.* This coverage protects professionals (doctors, lawyers, accountants) in the event of malpractice claims. Even if professionals incorporate, they cannot avoid personal liability for actions in the course of their professional duties.

- *Unemployment coverage.* Unemployment coverage protects employees from involuntary terminations. Coverage is mandated by federal and state law. Federal unemployment coverage is collected as an employment tax. States may also levy unemployment insurance premiums. Self-employed individuals cannot obtain unemployment insurance (even if they would prefer to have the coverage) since they are not employees.

- ***Worker's compensation.*** Businesses are required to provide this coverage for workers who are injured in the course of employment.

Quite of few of these types of insurance are common to all businesses. All businesses should, for example, have casualty insurance to protect business property. Some types of insurance apply only to certain businesses. Only professionals, for example, can maintain malpractice (professional liability) insurance; only businesses with defined benefit plans must pay PBGC premiums. Review the kinds of insurance available and follow up on the types your business requires.

IDEA 102: Cut Insurance Costs . . . General Approaches

In today's economy, you must have adequate insurance to cover a variety of needs. It will not save the business money in the long run to underinsure; your exposure to lawsuits is just too great.

Did You Know. . .

Despite the good reasons for carrying adequate insurance, about 12% of all small businesses (defined here as those with fewer than 10 employees) go "bare" (do not carry any liability insurance).

Make sure that you periodically review your existing coverage to see that it is adequate and that it covers all of your needs. For example, if you lease a business car, make sure that you have "gap insurance" to cover the difference between what is owed on the lease and the car's value should the car be stolen or totaled. Also be sure that insurance with respect to a home office is appropriate (discussed later in this chapter).

Regardless of the type of insurance you buy, there are several general strategies that any type of business can use to reduce premiums. These include:

Shop around for the best insurance coverage

Different insurance carriers may charge different rates for the same protection. Get price quotes from several insurance companies.

In making price comparisons, be sure that you are comparing apples to apples. The coverage may not be identical. Use the following checklist to compare policies being offered to you. In the column under "policy feature" be sure to list such features as the deductible, the elimination (or waiting period), the dollar amount of coverage provided (be it for property, liability or otherwise), discounts, and the insurance company's rating (as determined by checking some established scales such as A.M. Best's).

Policy feature	Policy A	Policy B	Policy C
Price	$	$	$

Get multiple coverage discounts

If you can take different coverage from the same insurance company (liability coverage, automobile insurance, etc.), you may be entitled to a multiple coverage discount. The discount is automatic. But do not go with the same carrier only to receive the discount. If the rates on separate coverage, when added together, are less than the total premiums paid to one carrier (after taking the discount into account), then the discount does not offset the savings from having separate policies from separate insurance companies.

Ask for other discounts

In addition to multiple coverage discounts, you may be entitled to premium discounts for other reasons. For example, property insurance discounts may be given to businesses with security systems, fire detectors or other safety devices.

$$Extra Savings

Businesses can write off the costs of security systems, fire detectors and other safety devices through expensing or depreciation (discussed in Chapter 7). With insurance savings on top of tax write-offs, the cost of this protection may be very modest and well worthwhile.

Car insurance discounts may be given to those who drive more than a certain number of miles per year and to those who complete a driver's safety course. When buying a particular type of coverage, ask what type of discounts are available and whether you qualify. You may be able to make adjustments to take advantage of a discount. For instance, suppose a discount is available if smoke detectors are wired into central alarm companies. (In any event, you may want to take this step as a safety measure.) The cost of the premium discount will only serve to offset a cost (wiring into the central alarm) that you had already wanted to undertake.

Increase the deductible

It is axiomatic that an increase in the deductible on any policy will reduce the premium. The same can be said for an elimination or waiting period (the time before which a policy will begin to pay benefits) which is applicable to some types of insurance (such as disability insurance). Insurance is generally designed to cover losses that are out of the ordinary; not merely ordinary losses. Therefore, take the largest deductible that you think the business can handle.

However, do not reduce the deductible to the point where it is no longer cost-effective. For example, it may be frugal to increase the deductible on car insurance from $250 to $500, or even $1,000. It may not make sense to increase it above $1,000 because it will mean that the business will have to bear the cost of all minor fender-benders (which could be considerably more than the savings on the premiums).

Reduce the need for insurance claims

Insurance costs can rise when you make claims on your policy. Therefore, one of the best ways to keep insurance costs low is to set up business practices that will reduce the risk of loss.

- ***Keep your premises safe to avoid accidents.*** If you have employees, an insurance representative can conduct an inspection of your premises and make recommendations to increase safety.

- ***Use devices or methods to safeguard property.*** For example, use a central alarm station for both fire and burglary. Also, properly store hazardous materials or substances.

- ***Make products that you sell safe and reliable.*** This will avoid product liability claims.

Avoid duplicative coverage

It is a waste of money to buy coverage for a liability that you already have coverage for. If you travel on business, for example, you can avoid the automatic collision insurance charged by rental car companies if you use an American Express card to charge the rental. The green, gold and platinum personal American Express cards, as well as the Corporate Card for Small Business, already provide this coverage. (The Corporate Card for large businesses does not provide automatic collision coverage.)

Switch policies

Do not assume that the policy you initially buy (for whatever type of coverage) is the one you will stay with for years. Every year, it is advisable to review the policies you own. Continue to shop around for better deals.

Also, look to upgrade coverage as your business grows (and your exposure to litigation increases).

Avoid insurance fraud or other problems

If you have any questions or problems with an insurance carrier, be sure to check with your state insurance department.

See appendix A for a listing of the phone numbers of state insurance departments.

IDEA 103: Keep Initial Employee-Related Insurance Costs Low

When you start a business that will have employees, the law requires you to have certain insurance coverage—disability, worker's compensation, unemployment insurance. Costs vary with the nature of your business, whether your workers are male or female (yes, insurance costs differ according to sex), your locality and other factors.

Initial costs for disability (worker's compensation) are based on your projection of the number of employees (the size of your payroll) and the amount of gross receipts you expect to take in during the first year. With this information, the insurance company estimates premium costs. You pay this amount for coverage during the first year. Then, an insurance audit (a check on your actual experience during the year) will determine whether the estimate for first-year coverage was too high or too low. If it was too high (you were too optimistic about how much revenue you expected the business to earn in the first year), then you will receive an insurance credit to be applied against coverage in the second year (or possibly a refund of excess insurance payments). Of course, if you were too conservative in your estimate, you will owe additional premiums to make up the shortfall for the first year.

Since you supply the information upon which the premiums are based, you can control insurance costs for the first year. It may be better to err on the side of being too conservative (rather than too optimistic) in order to avoid large premiums in the first year. Of course, your estimates must be realistic. You expect to be in business and hopefully make a profit as soon as possible, so you cannot reasonably project that you will have no revenue in the first year (unless you are pretty sure this will be the case).

IDEA 104: Reduce Unemployment Insurance Costs

Employers are required to pay for unemployment insurance, usually accomplished by use of a payroll tax computed on employees' wages. Employers are prohibited from deducting any portion of the tax from an employee's compensation (and can be penalized or subject to criminal prosecution for doing so). State unemployment insurance is based on the number of claims that are submitted against your company (your company's insurance payout experience). The state calculates this number and assigns the business a rating that is used to figure unemployment insurance costs. This rate is then applied to actual payroll (with a dollar cap on the wages paid to each employee). For example, in New York, the unemployment insurance tax (the employer's premiums for employee coverage is a payroll tax) is figured on the first $7,000 of wages. Assume that the assigned rate is 2.6%. Therefore, if an employee's wages are $15,000 per year, the payroll tax to cover unemployment insurance for this employee's wages is $182 ($7,000 × 2.6%).

Businesses with high turnover due to layoffs and other terminations pay higher premiums than businesses with low turnover. In the first year, the state unemployment insurance department assigns the business a general rate. Thereafter, the rate is adjusted for actual experience.

There is a two-prong approach to keeping unemployment insurance costs low:

- *Review hiring and firing policies to avoid unnecessary claims.* Do not hire someone you know will only work for a short time and then make a claim. States have minimum work periods before claims can be made (for example, at least three days per week for a five-week period). Do not hire someone who you think will go through an initial period with your company but be unable to fill the job indefinitely to your satisfaction, resulting in your terminating his/her employment and collecting unemployment benefits.

- *Fight erroneous claims made by former employees.* If, for example, a worker quit because he/she did not like the work, a claim for unemployment insurance should be contested. Benefits should also be denied if termination was due to job-related misconduct.

Warning

Be sure to follow your state's procedures for contesting claims that you believe have no merit. For example, there may be a limited period (e.g., 30 days) in which to contest a former employee's claim to benefits.

IDEA 105: Avoid Underinsuring a Home Office

If you run your business from an office in your home, you may be under the assumption that your homeowner's insurance will cover your losses if a client, customer or supplier is injured during an appointment to your office or if your computer or other business equipment is damaged or stolen. Your assumption is probably incorrect, or if not incorrect, at least inadequate. Just because you are starting or running a business on limited funds does not mean that you can ignore possible casualties or thefts or liability claims. Be sure that the insurance you carry will protect you in case of loss.

Check the Extent of Your Homeowner's Coverage

Your homeowner's coverage may provide you with some protection (perhaps enough to get started), but the type or the amount of coverage may be inadequate. Ask yourself (and your homeowner's insurance agent) the following questions:

- Does my policy cover my equipment in case of a casualty loss or theft?

- If my policy does cover my equipment, is there a dollar limit on the amount covered? Most homeowner's policies limit coverage for a computer to $2,500, or $5,000.

- If my policy does cover my equipment, does protection apply to off-premises use (such as a laptop taken on client calls)? Some policies limit off-premises coverage to as little as $250!

- If my policy does cover my equipment, do I need to provide the insurance company with any records or receipts to protect coverage (do I need to submit receipts showing the type and cost of equipment)?

- Does my policy cover me in case a client or customer is injured on the premises and sues? Most homeowner's policies do not cover any liability for injury of a client, customer or supplier on your premises.

- If I have a personal umbrella policy that piggybacks on my homeowner's policy, does it cover me in case a client or customer is injured on the premises and sues?

Upgrade your homeowner's policy where necessary

It may be possible to merely supplement your existing policy with some additional coverage. For example, if you only have clients or customers to your home office on an occasional basis, you may only need to add an inexpensive rider or endorsement (from as low as $10 per year) to your existing homeowner's policy to cover liability in case of injury. Similarly, if your equipment is modest and already partially covered by your homeowner's policy, additional coverage can be added for a modest cost. For example, your homeowner's policy may cover the first $2,500 of equipment; a rider can cover the balance in case of a casualty or theft. A rider can even be bought to cover a minimal amount of inventory (say $2,500).

Obtain a Separate Policy to Cover Your Business

The mere fact that your home-based business is a full-time occupation does not automatically mean that you need a separate policy. If, for example, you write a newsletter from home and your equipment is valued at about $3,000, then a rider may be sufficient. However, where your homeowner's policy simply will not cover potential liabilities for the type of business you are running from your home, get a separate policy. A separate business policy is generally advisable if you answer yes to any of the following questions:

	Yes	No
Does the business gross more than $25,000* annually?	_____	_____
Does the business own expensive equipment?	_____	_____
Does the business involve the storage of hazardous or flammable material?	_____	_____
Is inventory regularly stored on the premises?	_____	_____

*Note: Some experts recommend a separate policy for businesses that gross more than $5,000; others suggest a $35,000 threshold.

The cost of a separate business policy to protect your equipment and inventory as well as exposure in case of personal injury may be surprisingly low (only a few hundred dollars per year). Of course, since the cost is so reasonable, agents may not even suggest it (after all, their commissions are low) or may be lukewarm about selling it. Be sure to be firm about your desire for separate coverage.

Separate policies versus package deals

You can buy the business coverage you need in one of two ways: (1) as several individual policies to cover property, general liability and even business income insurance, or (2) as a single business insurance package that covers both business equipment and liability. The choice between separate policies versus package deals depends upon cost. Choose the alternative with the lower premium.

Where to Buy Business Insurance for a Home-based Business

You can generally get a separate business policy from the same company that currently carries your homeowner's insurance. Having multiple policies with the same insurer may entitle you to a premium discount. In some cases, you may be required to buy business insurance only from the same company that carries your homeowner's insurance.

You might also be able to obtain inexpensive coverage through a trade group. For example, Independent Business Alliance ($49 annual membership) offers a separate business policy to those members with existing homeowner's insurance. The policy covers office contents up to $15,000, additional expenses of $7,500, liability up to $500,000 per occurrence and data reconstruction of $10,000. There is a $250 deductible. The annual cost: $275 (plus membership).

For more information, call the Independent Business Alliance at (800) 450-2422. Home-based businesses in New York can obtain a separate business policy, also reasonable in cost ($150 per year for $5,000 office contents and $300,000 liability) through the Home Business Institute at (914) 946-6600.

IDEA 106: Cut Health Insurance Costs

When you start up or run a business, do not ignore the need for personal health insurance coverage. With the high cost of medical treatment today, it is simply foolish to go without insurance if you can afford to pay medical premiums. However, the cost of coverage can be extremely high. There are several ways for a small business owner to reduce personal health insurance costs. Here are some strategies to consider:

Get Coverage Through a Spouse's Employer

If your spouse is employed and his/her employer offers health insurance coverage, odds are that the coverage can be extended to cover you—the spouse of an employee. Some large employers, including a number of municipalities, have even provided spousal coverage for domestic partners. The cost of adding a spouse (or domestic partner) may be minimal for the employee—well under $100 per month. The extent of the coverage is the same for both the employee and spouse (domestic partner).

Warning

While an employee is not taxed on health coverage provided to him/herself and a spouse, this exclusion does not apply to health coverage for a domestic partner. This is because a domestic partner is not recognized as a spouse under state law and the tax law limits the exclusion to "spouses." Thus, an employee is taxed on the cost of covering a domestic partner.

Continue Coverage Through Your Former Employer

If you left employment—voluntarily or involuntarily—you may still be entitled to continue health insurance coverage. If you worked for a company that regularly employed more than 20 workers each year, then it was required to offer you COBRA coverage. This is a federal law that makes it mandatory for employers to continue to include former employees (and their spouses and dependents) in the group plan for 18 months following termination of employment. The cost to the employee is the same cost that the employer bears, plus a nominal administrative charge. This coverage is probably less expensive than any coverage you can buy individually or through your new small business. Even if you do intend to have the company coverage, be sure to continue with COBRA until your new policy picks up. You want to avoid any gap in coverage so that pre-existing conditions are not excluded by the new policy.

Did You Know. . .

Under a new law, insurance companies cannot deny coverage to workers who go to work for a new employer or those who have pre-existing health conditions.

Buy Coverage Through a Trade Group or Professional Association

Small businesses lack clout to command discounts on health insurance premiums otherwise available to larger employers. However, cognizant of the growing number of small businesses, a number of trade groups and professional associations are offering health insurance plans to self-employed individuals and small businesses. Some of these include:

Group Health Insurance Plans for Self-Employed Individuals and Small Businesses

Group/Association	Telephone
American Association of Retired Persons (AARP) —for members age 50 and over	(800) 424-3410
Council of Smaller Enterprises (COSE) for those in northern Ohio	(216) 621-3300
Independent Business Alliance for members	(800) 450-2422
National Association for the Self-Employed for members	(800) 232-NASE
National Organization for Women for members	(202) 331-0066
Small Business Service Bureau	(800) 343-0939

Other purchasing pools can be found through Chambers of Commerce or state health departments.

Take the Deductible Best Suited to Your Needs

A high deductible is a way to keep insurance costs down. Young and healthy individuals may not need medical care. When they do, a high deductible means that they will have to pay more out-of-pocket before insurance coverage takes over. Still, they are betting that their medical costs will be less than the cost of higher premiums with a smaller deductible.

But if you know that you will be using medical services on a regular basis (for example, you have a history of a particular illness or condition), then a high deductible will cost you more money in the long run. If you are forced financially to take a policy with high deductibles, it is still better to do so than go without coverage. Not only do you face enormous risks by going bare, you also create a period of no coverage that allows future insurance carriers to exclude pre-existing conditions when you resume coverage.

Claim a Tax Deduction For Your Personal Medical Coverage

Corporations that provide medical insurance for employees can deduct costs if coverage is provided on a nondiscriminatory basis (for both owners as well as rank-and-file workers). However, self-employed individuals cannot deduct the full cost of health insurance paid by them. Similarly, partners, limited liability company members and S corporation shareholders owning more than 2% of corporate stock cannot deduct the full amount of health insurance paid by their business even though they are fully taxed on this fringe benefit. In 1996, they can, however, deduct 30% of coverage as an adjustment to gross income on page one of Form 1040 (they do not have to itemize deductions to write off 30% of health insurance costs). The percentage will increase to 40% in 1997; 45% in 1998; 50% in 2003; 60% in 2004; 70% in 2005; and 89% in 2006. However, certain rules apply in order to claim this deduction:

- If a self-employed person has employees, they must be covered on a nondiscriminatory basis.

- No deduction can be claimed in any month in which you are covered under an employer's plan or a spouse's employer's plan.

- The deduction for health insurance cannot exceed net earnings from the business. The excess, however, can be treated as a deductible itemized expense, deductible to the extent that health insurance costs exceed 7.5% of adjusted gross income.

IDEA 107: Get Disability Insurance

Disability insurance is, perhaps, the insurance policy that receives the least attention and the one that deserves the most. If you start or run a small business, your personal efforts are probably a key factor in the success of the company. Without you, there may be little or no income from the business to meet your personal financial obligations. Recognize that you are far more likely to become disabled than to die. Still, you probably have life insurance (or at least recognize the need for it). But what would happen if you became disabled? You need to protect your income if this event should befall you. This type of coverage is particularly critical for self-employed individuals who are not covered by workers' compensation or a company's disability policy (workers' compensation and disability only cover employees).

Understand What You are Buying

Obviously the better the policy, the more expensive the premiums. What is meant by a "better" policy? It primarily turns on the definition of "disability." Some policies pay only if the insured is totally unable to perform any type of work. The better policies define disability relative to the insured's current work. Thus, for example, if the insured is a brain surgeon and becomes disabled and cannot function as a brain surgeon, the policy would pay benefits. This is so even though the surgeon is not so disabled as to be prevented from doing other types of work.

Who Should Buy Disability Insurance?

While it is clear that most everyone should have disability insurance, the issue of who should pay the premiums is less certain. In some cases, businesses automatically provide this coverage. In other cases, you may simply have to buy it yourself.

In deciding who should bear the cost, understand that if the employer (the corporation if the business has incorporated) pays for coverage, the payments are not treated as a taxable benefit to you, but when benefits are paid they are fully taxable to you. The corporation can, however, deduct the cost of the premiums. On the other hand, if you buy your own disability insurance, you cannot deduct the premiums, but if you collect benefits they are tax free to you.

Did You Know. . .

There is a special problem for those with home-based businesses when it comes to disability insurance. Until recently, it was often difficult for those operating a home business to buy disability insurance. Carriers were reluctant to offer coverage because they thought they would have difficulty determining when someone who worked at home became disabled. However, with the growing home business market (and its increasing clout), a growing number of insurers now offer disability policies for those working out of a home office. If you are one of these individuals and were turned down for coverage in the past, now may be the time to re-explore disability coverage.

IDEA 108: Pay for an Owner's Interest with Insurance

If you are in business with one or more other owners, think about what would happen in the event that one or more of you dies. This may seem like a remote question, particularly for those just starting up a business and those who are young, but it would be foolish to ignore the question.

The estate of the deceased owner will want to receive payment of his/her interest in the business. The remaining owner (or owners) wants to meet this obligation without depleting the resources of the business or personal assets. Insurance can be an inexpensive way to meet this need.

Buy-sell Agreement

Whether the business is organized as a corporation, a partnership or a limited liability company, a buy-sell agreement can be used to settle the question of what happens in the event of an owner's death. The agreement specifies who has the option or obligation to buy the deceased owner's interest. The agreement also fixes the price of that interest (or establishes the mechanism for setting the price).

There are two main types of buy-sell agreements: a cross-purchase agreement and a stock redemption agreement. In a cross-purchase agreement, the remaining owner buys the interest of the deceased owner. In the stock redemption agreement (which can be used only by businesses that have incorporated), the corporation buys back its stock from the deceased owner. In a hybrid type of agreement, a corporation can be required to buy some of its shares, leaving the remaining owner obligated to buy the balance.

Funding buy-sell agreements

Typically, buy-sell agreements are funded by having adequate life insurance. Insurance provides a fixed sum at the precise moment it is needed—the death of the owner. The ownership of the life insurance depends on the type of buy-sell agreement involved.

> **Example:** *Cross-purchase agreement.* Each owner buys insurance on the life of the other owner. When one owner dies, the proceeds are used to meet the buy-out requirements under the buy-sell agreement. For instance, two partners, Amy and Bob, have a cross-purchase buy-sell agreement. Amy buys a life insurance policy on Bob; Bob takes out a policy on Amy. If Amy dies, then Bob collects on the policy and uses the proceeds to buy Amy's interest.
>
> *Stock redemption agreement.* The corporation buys life insurance on the lives of each owner. When one owner dies, the corporation uses the proceeds to buy back the deceased owner's shares. For instance, two shareholders, Carol and Dan, have a stock redemption agreement with their corporation, XYZ Co. XYZ buys a policy on the life of Carol and one on the life of Dan. If Dan dies, then XYZ collects the proceeds and uses them to buy back Dan's shares of the corporation.

There are advantages and disadvantages to the different types of agreements. Obviously, it is easier to work a stock redemption agreement since it is the business that is buying (and paying for) the insurance. Thus, even if the owners are different ages, are of different sex and have different health histories (all of which affect the cost of coverage), the cost is shared more equitably by the owners. Each shareholder, in effect, pays for the coverage in proportion to his/her ownership interest. But, as mentioned earlier, it can only be used by a corporation; partnerships and limited liability companies cannot use stock redemption agreements.

In a cross-purchase agreement, where the cost of life insurance coverage on different owners varies greatly, one owner is paying a greater price than the other for participating in the agreement. When there are more than two owners, the cross-purchase agreement becomes even more complex. Each owner must maintain coverage on all of the other owners, thereby involving numerous policies.

$$Extra Savings

The cost of life insurance can be reduced if a single "first-to-die" policy is used. This policy insures two lives but pays only on the death of the first insured to die. The cost of this policy should be less than the cost of two single life policies.

The tax cost of the different agreements should also be weighed. In a stock redemption agreement, the corporation can deduct the cost of insuring the owners. In a cross-purchase agreement, the owners cannot deduct their premiums as a business expense and must pay the premiums with after-tax dollars.

Other uses for buy-sell agreements

Buy-sell agreements are not only used to buy out a deceased owner's interest. They can also be used to settle the question of what happens when an owner retires or becomes disabled. Of course, in these instances, life insurance cannot be used to fund the buy-out. Other solutions must be found.

It may be possible, for example, to use a "disability buy-out policy" to fund an agreement in case of disability. This type of policy is not the same as a disability income policy (discussed earlier in this chapter). The income policy is used to provide income to a disabled owner; a buy-out policy provides a lump-sum amount to be used to buy the interest of the disabled owner. As in the case of the disability income policy, be sure to check the definition of "disability" under the disability buy-out policy to make sure that it is the same as under the buy-sell agreement. Also, make sure that the waiting period under both the policy and the agreement are the same (such as 90 days or six months).

CHAPTER 12

Saving on Miscellaneous Costs

There are many different ways to save on the costs of starting and running a business. The number of ways is only limited by your imagination. In this chapter, you will learn about ways to save a little or a lot of money in your daily operations. Some of these ideas are tax-based—by saving on taxes you save on your cash outlays—and some of the ideas affect your daily operations.

IDEA 109: Maximize Your Tax Deductions

Tax on business profits is a significant cash outlay for any company. The smaller you can make your taxable income (your profit after expenses), the more you save in taxes. There are several strategies you can follow to achieve this.

Keep Good Records and Receipts

All businesses are required to keep good books and records, but you also need certain documentary evidence to support other deductible expenditures. The key to claiming many business deductions is a good paper trail; you must have records and receipts to back up certain deductions (travel and entertainment expenses, charitable contributions). You also need sales slips, invoices, canceled checks, paid bills, timesheets for part-time help, duplicate deposit slips and other types of supporting evidence to back up book entries. Be sure to keep books and records in a safe place. Lost files can result not only in a denial of deductions, but also in penalties unless you can show that you tried to keep them safe.

Travel and entertainment expenses

Use daily log books or diaries to record all business and travel entertainment expenses. Note the date, the type of expense, the business you transacted (or hoped to transact) and the cost of the expense. You need this information even if you rely on IRS per diem rates for claiming travel and meal costs or a mileage rate for business use of your car. Make the notation in the diary or log book as close as possible to the event since the law requires contemporaneous records. Also keep receipts of these expenses. Receipts for meal and entertainment costs are necessary unless the cost is less than $75 or a receipt is not readily available. Receipts for lodging are required without regard to cost.

Charitable contributions

If the business donates cash or property to charity, be sure to meet the tax law's special substantiation requirements in order to claim a deduction. If the contribution is no more than $75, a canceled check will do for proof. If, however, the contribution is more than $75 but under $250, a canceled check must be accompanied by a disclosure statement from the charity stating that the business did not receive any goods or services in exchange for the contribution. If the contribution is $250 or more, a canceled check is not considered substantiation. A written receipt or acknowledgment from the charity must describe the contribution (e.g., cash; description of the property) as well as a statement that no goods or services were received in exchange. For property donations over $5,000, special appraisals are also required.

Using computers

With more and more businesses using computers (and business owners becoming more comfortable with the technology), recordkeeping is being shifted from manual book entries and diary notations to computer spreadsheets and other software prompted entries. Computer records will be recognized by the IRS as long as you show the applications being performed, the procedures used in each application, the controls used to ensure accurate and reliable processing and, most importantly, the controls used to prevent the unauthorized addition, alternation or deletion of computer records. Be sure to back up data and keep back-up disks or tapes in a safe place (e.g., fire-proof safe).

Plan, Plan, Plan

Some business owners may assume that whatever they do for their business, the cost will be deductible. In most cases this is probably true. But these owners may not be getting the most for their cost. They may be entitled to greater deductions if they plan well.

Planning for depreciation

Time business purchases to take full advantage of depreciation deductions. Piling up year-end purchases can mean less of a write-off than if purchases had been spread throughout the year. A special depreciation rule called the "mid quarter convention" limits depreciation deductions when more than 40% of all property placed in service during the year is placed in service in the last quarter of the year. The 40% is based on the cost of equipment bought and put into use.

> **Example:** Your business needs two machines this year: One costs $5,000; the other costs $10,000. If you buy and use the $5,000 machine in February and the $10,000 machine in November, the mid-quarter convention applies since more than 40% of the property ($10,000/ $5,000, or 66.67%) is placed in service in the last quarter of the year. But if you had planned ahead, you could have avoided the mid-quarter convention by buying the more expensive machine first, or by buying the more expensive machine in the third quarter of the year.

Another way to plan for depreciation is to increase the business use of "listed property" (cars, computers and cellular phones). These items, which are used both for business and personal purposes, must be used more than 50% for business in order to claim accelerated depreciation. Keep a record of total use of the item, breaking down use between business and personal use. For example, keep a record of the number of miles a car is driven for business and the number of miles a car is driven for pleasure (including commuting).

Year-end planning

Cash basis businesses can, to some extent, adjust their taxable income by controlling year-end income and expenses. They can, for example, delay year-end billing so that payment will be received in the following year. But do not use this practice if the business needs immediate cash or if there is concern that delay may jeopardize collection entirely.

Year-end buying can also provide ready deductions. Pay utility bills and other outstanding bills otherwise due after the first of the year before year-end. However, do not prepay expenses for items extending more than one year.

> **Warning**
>
> The IRS says that prepaid expenses, such as a three-year subscription to a business publication, must be deducted ratably over the period to which it relates (three years in the case of this subscription) and not all at one time in the year of payment.

If the business is on the accrual method of accounting, year-end bonuses to employees can be accrued as long as it is paid within $2^{1}/_{2}$ months after the close of the year. This can allow a cash-tight business to reward employees without coming up with the cash immediately and still nail down a deduction.

> ### Warning
>
> Payments to "related parties" (which includes business owners) cannot be deducted by an accrual business until actual payment. Thus, salary, interest or other expenses that the business owes to an owner are not deductible until the year in which they are paid.

Make Favorable Tax Elections

In a number of instances, the tax law permits you to elect special treatment. Understand which elections are available and make them if they provide a benefit to the business. Just because they allow a greater current deduction does not mean that the election is advisable. The business may not have sufficient income to offset the greater deduction. Here are some tax elections (several of which have been explained earlier in this book) to look out for as ways to boost your tax savings:

- *Organizational and incorporation expenditures.* These costs are generally not currently deductible. However, a special election allows these costs to be deducted ratably over a period of not less than 60 months.

- *First-year expensing.* Equipment is generally subject to a depreciation allowance—a write-off, essentially—over the life of the property. However, the entire cost of equipment may be currently deducted if first-year expensing is elected. The deduction is limited to either $17,500 annually or the extent of the taxable income of the business, whichever is less.

- *Disaster losses.* Uninsured casualty losses are a deductible business expense. There are no dollar or income limits as there are for personal casualty losses. If the business suffers an uninsured casualty loss (fire, hurricane, earthquake) to property in an area declared by the President to be eligible for federal disaster relief, then the loss can be claimed on the tax return for the year preceding the year of the disaster. This can give a business an immediate cash infusion (in the form of a tax refund). The uninsured loss can be the result of inadequate insurance or a large deductible.

Avoid Interest and Penalties

What good is it to follow all the tax rules and deductions only to be socked with interest and penalties? None. Therefore, file returns on time and file properly to avoid interest and penalties. Pay particular attention to filing the following types of returns that you or your business may be required to complete:

- Federal (and state) income tax returns
- Quarterly returns reporting payroll taxes for employees
- W-2 forms for employees
- State sales tax returns
- State unemployment insurance returns

IDEA 110: Use Tax Losses Wisely

Businesses, even those that prove to be successful, can experience losses, especially in the start up years. How you handle these losses can mean extra tax savings. Understanding the limits on losses and the steps you can take to avoid them will allow you to get the most mileage from these losses. There are also elections you can make to take greater advantage of them.

Choose the Form of Business That Allows You to Use Business Losses on Your Personal Return

There are many factors that go into choosing the form of business organization (see Chapter 3). One important factor is how losses are treated. If the business is a regular corporation (a C corporation), then losses belong to the business and can be used only to offset business income. If the business is organized in any other way (a sole proprietorship, a partnership, a limited liability company or an S corporation), then losses can be used to offset your personal income from other sources. For example, you are a 100% owner of an S corporation which has a loss of $5,000 for the year. The loss is passed from the corporation to you and can be used to offset your income from other sources (such as your spouse's salary if you file a joint return, or your dividends and interest income).

Avoid the Hobby Loss Limits

If your business continues to lose money year after year (and you still decide to press forward), you may run into opposition from the IRS when you try to deduct the losses. This is because of the hobby loss rule which limits business deductions to the extent of business income. In other words, if you make a profit from a hobby, you must report all of it, but if you have a loss (expenses exceed income), you cannot deduct it. You cannot even carry the unused portion of losses forward.

While the rule was originally designed to prevent individuals from offsetting their salary and investment income with losses from coin collecting, dog breeding and other personal activities, the rule can be applied to any type of activity. Any activity that you do mainly for recreation, sport or personal enjoyment is particularly suspect. But even if there is little or no element of enjoyment or pleasure, the IRS can still try to apply the hobby loss rules to limit your loss deductions.

To overcome attack with the hobby loss rule, you must be able to show that you conduct the activity with a reasonable expectation of making a profit. There is no quantitative way to prove a profit motive, but you bear the burden of proof. Here are some of the factors used in making a determination of whether there is a profit motive:

- *Whether you carry on the activity in a business-like manner.* Keep good books and records separate and apart from your personal records. Maintain a business bank account, telephone and other indices of a business.

- *Whether the time and effort you put into the activity shows that you intend to make a profit.* Spending only a small amount of time may show that there is no realistic way in which you can make a profit.

- *Whether you depend on the income from the activity for your livelihood.* If you do, then it very well may be reasonable for you expect to make a profit to live on. If you run the activity as a sideline business, earning your livelihood from another source, then this can show that there is no reasonable expectation of profit.

- *Whether you change methods of operation to improve profitability.* Get the advice of experts to improve profitability. Change your methods as needed.

- *Whether the activity is profitable in some years, and how much profit is realized in those years.* Certainly an activity may not always be profitable, but if there has already been a profit in some years and that profit is substantial, then it shows an expectation of continued profit.

- *Whether you, or your advisors, have the know-how needed to carry on your business at a profit.* If you undertake some activity that you enjoy but know nothing about, it may indicate a lack of profit motive (unless, of course, you use experts to help you).

- *Whether you can expect to see a profit from the appreciation of the assets used in the activity.* While the operations of the business may not turn a profit, it may still be reasonable to expect a profit from the assets.

Presumption of a profit motive

The tax law does give you a special presumption that you can rely on to show a profit motive (and delay an IRS inquiry into your activity). An activity is presumed to be engaged in for profit if you make a profit in at least three out of five years. (If the activity is breeding, training, showing or racing horses, then the presumption period is two out of seven years.) If you meet this presumption, then the hobby loss rule does not apply and your losses in the off years can be claimed in excess of your income from the activity. Look at the instructions to Form 5213, Election to Postpone Determination with Respect to the Presumption that an Activity is Engaged in For Profit.

The down side to filing this form to raise the presumption of profit is that it extends the statute of limitations (the period in which the IRS can question your return and assess additional taxes) to two years after the due date of the return for the last year of the presumption period. However, the statute of limitations is extended only for deductions from the activity and any related deductions. Other items on your return, your personal itemized deductions for example, are not affected by this extension of the statute of limitations. And, even if you do not wind up showing a profit in three of the five years, you may still be able to demonstrate a profit motive based on all the facts and circumstances of your situation.

Your choice of business organization affects application of the hobby loss rules

The hobby loss rules apply to individuals and S corporations. They do not apply to C corporations. For partnerships, LLCs and S corporations whose business losses pass to owners, the determination of whether there is a profit motive is made at the business level, rather than at the owner level. In other words, the business itself must have a reasonable expectation of making a profit. The fact that an individual owner has a profit motive does not transform a hobby loss into a deductible loss if the business does not reasonably have a profit motive.

Avoid the Passive Activity Loss (PAL) Rules

If you work for your business full-time, you need not be concerned with the passive activity loss rules. But if you do not work in the day-to-day operations or management of the business, losses may not be currently deductible against non-passive activity income. Thus, silent partners who invest in partnerships, limited liability companies or S corporations may not be able to claim a current loss deduction if they fall victim to the PAL rules.

A passive activity is any activity involving the active conduct of a trade or business in which you do not "materially participate" and all rental activities (unless you qualify as a "real estate professional").

The tax law contains seven alternative tests for proving material participation:

1. You participate in the activity for more than 500 hours (for example, you participate for 10 hours a week for 50 weeks in the year).

2. Your participation is substantially all of the participation in the activity of all individuals for the year, including the participation of individuals who did not own any interest in the activity. This means that if you are a sole proprietor and do not hire someone else to run the business, you automatically meet this participation test, even if you only work five hours each week.

3. You participated in the activity for more than 100 hours during the tax year, and you participated at least as much as any other individual (including individuals who did not own any interest in the activity) for the year.

4. The activity is a "significant participation activity," and you participated in all significant participation activities for more than 500 hours. A significant participation activity is any business in which you participated for more than 100 hours during the year and in which you did not materially participate under any of the other material participation tests.

5. You materially participated in the activity for any five (whether or not consecutive) of the 10 preceding tax years.

6. The activity is a personal service activity in which you materially participated for any three (whether or not consecutive) preceding tax years.

7. You materially participated in the activity for more than 100 hours and, based on all the facts and circumstances, your participation was regular, continuous, and substantial. Managing the activity is not treated as participation if any person other than you received compensation for managing the activity or any individual spent more hours during the year managing the activity than you (regardless of whether such individual was compensated).

Warning

If your level of participation in an activity is questionable, be sure to keep the seven tests in mind. Try to eke out some additional participation to nail down your loss deduction. Keep a daily or log book to back up your claim of material participation.

Those who qualify as real estate professionals can escape the passive activity loss limitations altogether for purposes of deducting losses from their rental real estate activities. Individuals can be considered real estate professionals if they meet certain tests regarding their participation in real estate activities in general and rental real estate activity specifically.

How the passive activity loss rules limit deductions for expenses

If the rules apply, then your losses from passive activities that exceed income from all other passive activities cannot be deducted in the current year. You can carry over your unused deductions to future years. These are called "suspended losses." There is no limit on the carryover period for suspended losses. The passive activity loss limitation is figured on Form 8582, Passive Activity

Loss Limitations. Similar rules apply to credits from passive activities. The limitation on credits from passive activities is figured on Form 8583, Passive Activity Credit Limitations.

You can claim all carryover deductions from an activity in the year in which you dispose of your entire interest in the activity. Simply giving away your interest does not amount to a disposition allowing you to deduct your suspended losses.

Understand the At Risk Rules

Like the PAL rules, the at risk rules essentially limit loss deductions to the amount of your economic investment in the activity. If you have nothing at stake, the tax law prevents you from claiming losses. Both the PAL and at risk rules can apply to the same venture. The at risk rules are applied first. Any amounts that are deductible after applying your at risk loss limitation are then subjected to the passive activity loss rules. Complete Form 6198 for the at risk rules first; then complete Form 8582 for the PAL rules.

Use Net Operating Losses Most Effectively

If deductions and losses from your business exceed your income (and you are not subject to the hobby loss rules, the PAL rules or the at risk rules), you may be able to use the losses to offset income in other years. Net losses from the conduct of your business are called net operating losses (NOLs).

Net operating losses are not an additional loss deduction. Rather, they are the result of your deductions exceeding the income from the business. The excess deductions are not lost; they are simply used in certain other years.

Only individuals and C corporations can claim NOLs. Partnerships, limited liability companies and S corporations cannot have NOLs since their income and losses pass to owners, but partners, members in LLCs and S corporation shareholders can have NOLs on their individual returns. These NOLs are created by their share of the business's operating losses.

Carrybacks and Carryovers

In general, NOLs are carried back for three years and then carried forward for 15 years. You first carry the loss back to a year that is three years before the year in which the NOL arose (the NOL year). If it is not used up in this year, then you carry it back to a year that is two years earlier. If it is not used up in this year, then carry it to the year before the NOL year. If it is still not used up, then you can begin to carry it forward (with modifications explained below). However, if it is not used up after carrying it forward for 15 years, it is lost forever.

If your business is struggling, you can use an NOL carryback to generate quick cash flow. The carryback will offset income in the carryback years and you will receive a refund of taxes paid in those years.

Individuals can obtain a quick refund by filing IRS Form 1045, Application by Taxpayers Other than Corporations for Tentative Refund. The IRS will generally act on the refund within 90 days of the filing of the form.

$$Extra Savings

When you carryback an NOL, you may have to refigure certain deductions based on adjusted gross income in the carryback years. Remember that the NOL will lower your adjusted gross income in the carryback years and, therefore, allow for greater itemized deductions which have an adjusted gross-income floor. You may also have to refigure alternative minimum tax.

C Corporations can expedite a refund from an NOL carryback by using a special form, Form 1139, Corporation Application for Tentative Refund from Carryback of Net Operating Losses and Unused Investment Credit, to obtain a quick refund.

Warning

Form 1139 cannot be filed before the income tax return for the NOL year is filed. It must be filed no later than one year after the NOL year. What is more, if a corporation expects to have an NOL in the current year, it can delay filing the income tax return for the prior year with the knowledge that the tax on the prior year's return will be fully or partially offset by the NOL.

An NOL can also be claimed on an amended return, Form 1040X or Form 1120X. Individuals who carryback NOLs cannot refigure self-employment tax and get a refund of this tax. The NOL applies only for income tax purposes.

Election to forego carryback

Instead of carrying the loss back and then forward, you can elect to forego the carryback and just carry forward the loss for 15 years. You make this election in the NOL year by attaching a statement to your return if you are an individually owned business, or by checking the appropriate box on the corporate return for C corporations. Once the election is made, it cannot be changed. If you incur another NOL in a subsequent year, you must make a separate election if you want to also forego the carryback.

Some taxpayers prefer to forego the carryback because they are afraid of calling attention to prior tax years and risking an audit. While this is certainly a possibility, it is not necessarily true that claiming a carryback will result in an audit of a prior year.

IDEA 111: Plan Tax Strategies for Multi-State Businesses

You do not have to be a large corporation to do business in more than one state. Each state has its own tax rules (even different counties within each state can have special tax rules). A business that finds itself spilling across a border should explore some strategies for minimizing state taxes. For example, say a catering business with a kitchen in Ft. Lee, New Jersey services parties in New York City. To which jurisdiction is tax on business income owed? When doing business in more than one state, income must be allocated according to complex formulas. This allocation process has serious tax consequences since the tax rate is quite different between New Jersey and New York (with additional tax in New York City!).

> **Warning**
>
> Since the allocation rules are complex, it is advisable for businesses having operations in more than one state to discuss state tax issues with an accountant.

Physical location (an office, a factory, a warehouse) is an important factor in the allocation process. A review of a business's physical location can, therefore, lead to a profitable alteration of an allocation.

Example: An export business in New York City stores its goods in a warehouse located just over the border in Connecticut. The business does not own nor rent the warehouse, but merely pays for storage. By renting its own space—using virtually the same dollars it had paid for the usage of someone else's space—the business can allocate a portion of its income to Connecticut, thereby substantially slashing its total state (and New York City) tax bill.

IDEA 112: Save on Supplies and Postage

All businesses use supplies of one type or another. Depending on the nature of your business, supplies can be a big outlay each month. For example, the cost of office paper is surprisingly high because of the amount of paper used and the high cost of paper. To the extent you can reduce the use of supplies, you can save money for your business. Here are some strategies for saving on supplies:

- *Create your own stationery and business cards.* Instead of having them made at a printer, make your own on your computer. Today, with a laser printer and some special supplies, you can create professional looking stationery and business cards without the help of a printing service. You will save on printing costs and you will gain the flexibility of changing your stationery or business cards when needed (e.g., as you add another phone line or move to a new location).

- *Fax from the computer.* Instead of printing out hard copy to be faxed, get a software program that allows you to fax directly from your computer. Over the long term, you will save considerably on paper costs.

- *Save on postage.* Not only is paper a considerable expenditure, postage can also run high. Try to save on postage costs in various ways. Weigh mail (or use metered mail) for letters. This will save money on oversize letters for which you might otherwise attach too much postage, just to be sure. Using exact postage may seem like a small savings but it adds up. Use postal bar codes which allow you to use discounted postal rates. Use the right class of mail and pre-sort mail to save on postage costs. There are now three classes of business mail: first class, periodical (which had been second class) and standard (which had been both third and fourth class). Fax letters instead of mailing them where the cost of the fax is less than the postage. Unless the letters are lengthy (and your fax machine is slow), faxing local correspondence will save money. Use postcards instead of letters for promotions to save 12¢ per piece (letters cost 32¢ versus 20¢ for postcards). Some other ideas for saving on postage costs can be found in Chapter 9.

- *Recycle supplies.* Re-use computer disks, office paper and other materials. For example, shredded office paper (discarded paper from drafts of memos, contracts, etc.) can be used as packing material.

IDEA 113: Get Discounts and Rebates for Purchases and Services You Use

There are a number of places you can find discounts and rebates to reduce your costs. Sometimes discounts and rebates are automatic; if you make the purchase, you qualify. Sometimes you have to ask for them. Here is a listing of some of the places you may look for savings.

- *Long-distance carriers.* They are continually offering special deals to attract your business. Evaluate the deals as presented and switch carriers when better deals come along. Savings on long distance carriers is discussed in greater detail later in this chapter.

- *Hotels.* Business travelers may be eligible for room discounts, but you have to ask for the lower rates. Ask for "corporate rates" even if you are not a corporation but merely a business traveler. It will save you as much as 10% off the regular room rate.

- *Car rentals.* National car rental companies also offer discounts to members of various organizations (professional organizations, trade associations, AARP members).

- *Frequent flyer miles for air travel.* These miles can add up and be used to get free tickets or travel upgrades. Today, with competition among carriers fierce, frequent flyer programs offer mileage credit for more than just air travel. For example, American Airlines' frequent flyer program gives free miles to those who use MCI for long distance calls (provided you enroll in MCI's program, there is no additional cost).

- *Supplies.* Staples Office Supply runs purchase programs that give discounts against future purchases if you buy a certain amount of supplies during the quarter. You must sign up to be eligible for the discount program but there is no additional cost for joining. Check for other discount opportunities. Some businesses may, for example, offer discounts for volume purchases.

- *Subscriptions.* Most magazines offer subscription discounts to certain customers. For example, professionals can usually receive substantial discounts (as much as 50% off), just by asking. Call Below Wholesale Magazines (800) 800-0062, or the subscription departments of the magazines in which you are interested. You can also receive discounts for multi-year subscriptions. But it may not pay to sign on for more than a year as you may not know whether you will want to keep the subscription going (whether you get any use out of the magazine). Also, if you are tight for cash, you may not want to pay in advance for the extra year or two.

Cash-back Credit Cards

An increasing number of credit cards give cash back based on annual purchases. These cards may be specialized (for example, Shell MasterCard gives cash back only on gasoline purchases) or general (for example, Discover and credit cards from Chase Manhattan and General Electric).

Warning

These cards should only be used if you plan to pay the balance in full. They generally carry a higher interest rate than non-cash-back credit cards.

IDEA 114: Save on Telephone Costs

Today, a phone is the lifeline of just about any business. Use it wisely and save some money. These savings add up during the course of a year.

Comparison Shop

First, use the long distance carrier that offers you the best prices. Get quotes from AT&T (800-222-0400), MCI (800-888-0800), Sprint (800-877-4646) and others before taking one on. Change carriers as better deals come along.

If you plan to offer 800 toll-free service (or 888 numbers where you pay for in-coming calls), comparison shopping is essential. Charges and rates vary. Here is a sample of 800 number charges from the major carriers:

	AT&T	MCI	Sprint
Installation	No charge	$10	No charge
Monthly fee	$5	$10	$5
Per call per minute	26¢ in-state charge	28-30¢ peak 28¢ out-of-state	19¢ 23¢ off peak

Major providers of 800 (or 888) number services include: Allnet (800) 783-2020; AT&T (800) 222-0400; Cable & Wireless (800) 486-8686; LDDS (800) 737-8423; MCI (800) 444-2222; and Sprint (800) 877-2000.

Warning

Long-distance carriers are highly competitive. New programs are constantly being offered. Check the latest offers. Be sure to re-check the available programs on a regular basis.

Use a Phone Wisely

Try to make maximum use of the phone during reduced rate hours. For example, if you need to fax material to clients or customers, do so before 8:00AM when lower telephone rates are in effect or make calls after 5:00PM for discounts of up to 30% less than calls made during normal business hours. Calling after business hours is especially helpful to businesses on the East Coast trying to reach contacts on the West Coast since the cost of the call is determined by the time in which it is placed (not where it is received). Those on the West Coast can call to the East Coast before normal business hours for savings.

Eliminate excess telephones and telephone lines

Do you really need a car phone? Today many business owners believe that if they can't be reached immediately in an emergency, the business will fall apart. This may or may not be true, but a telephone is not the only way to get through to a business owner. A more cost effective solution is to use a pager. The monthly charges for a pager (and phone-in calls in response to pages) are considerably less than monthly charges for a car phone.

Do you run not only a phone but also a fax and a modem? Do you need a second phone line dedicated to this electronic technology? Not necessarily. Depending on the nature of your business and the volume with which you use a fax/modem, you may be able to get by with one phone line. There are even special devices (available at office supply and equipment stores) that direct incoming communications to a particular electronic device (phone, fax, etc.).

Fax smartly

Review your fax cover sheet to eliminate excess print; the extra phone charges from this excess print that will mount up over the course of a year. For example, if you have put lines in the message area, eliminate the lines and write your message on blank space to save phone time. Or better yet, eliminate the cover sheet altogether and just use the Paste-It fax notes. Also, send faxes before or after normal business hours to save on phone charges.

Use 800 (or new 888) telephone numbers

Whenever possible use 800 (and 888) numbers to shift the cost of calling to your contact. Get an 800/888 directory or check with directory assistance (800-555-1212) to find 800/888 numbers of suppliers, customers and others you need to call.

Save on directory assistance

Charges for directory assistance are surprisingly steep (75¢ a request) and can quickly mount up. Order phone directories for areas you know you will be calling frequently and look up the numbers yourself (the books are free!). Or use AT&T's special information service for long-distance numbers (900-555-1212). The cost is 75¢ for two numbers, or half the usual directory assistance charge. Or, if you are a CompuServe subscriber, use your computer to find telephone numbers. The cost of an on-line search for a telephone number is 10¢ per request. There is also a special computer program (PC411) that you can use to access a directory database at a cost of 50¢ per request. The following is a listing of on-line sites for finding telephone numbers (and e-mail addresses).

Guides/Directories	Web Site
Bell Atlantic Yellow Pages	http://yellowpages.badg.com
Director of Yellow Pages sites	http://www.wahlstrom.com/ypsites.html
411	http://www.four11.com
Switchboard	http://www.switchboard.com
Yahoo's telephone directory	http://www.yahoo.com/reference/phone_numbers

Phones For Home Offices

For those who run a business from a home office, decide how you want to set up your phone lines. Depending on the type of your business, you may be able to avoid the cost of a second phone line and continue to use your residential line for business. On the positive side, you will save by not paying for a second line. However, you cannot get a listing in your local Yellow Pages which is available only to business customers (who pay an additional amount for each business call!). But if the business is in your name, then clients, customers and suppliers can find you through the White Pages.

Warning

There is another downside to having only one line related to taxes: you cannot deduct the basic charges of the first phone line to your home while the full cost of a second line is deductible.

Use Your Computer Instead of Your Phone

Contact clients, customers or suppliers via your computer modem. E-mail can connect you to these contacts for a fraction of the cost of a telephone contact because modem transmission is faster (therefore less phone time). However, in comparing costs, do not forget to take into account the cost of your e-mail provider (e.g., America Online, CompuServe or a local carrier). Time may, or may not, be a factor depending on your provider.

IDEA 115: Save On Overnight Delivery

If you regularly use overnight delivery services, shop around for the best price. The difference between one carrier and another may be surprisingly significant (as much as $7.50 for a one-pound package!). Compare Federal Express with, for example, DHL, UPS and even the U.S. Postal Service. Also consider foregoing a demand for delivery before 10:00AM; afternoon delivery can save additional dollars. Further, ask whether the carrier will pick up packages from your location (instead of having to drop off your packages at the carrier's location (office or drop box). Use the following chart to help you compare costs of overnight carriers:

	U.S.P.S.	*FedEx****	*DHL*	*UPS*	*Airborne****
Cost of 8oz. package	$10.75	$10.00**	$15.50	$10.00**	$14.00
Cost of 1lb. Package (morning delivery)*	$15.00	$20.00	$22.50	$18.00/up	$25.00
Cost of 1lb. Package (afternoon delivery)	$15.00	$14.00	$22.50	$18.00/up	$ 8.00
Cost of 2lb. package	$17.50	$21.75	$24.50	$20.75/up	$25.00
Pickup?	No	Extra	Free	$3 extra	Free
Saturday delivery	Yes	$10 extra	No	$10 extra	$10 extra

*Delivery before noon (or by 3:00PM) depends on time of drop off and zip code of delivery area; may be next day to Hawaii, parts of Alaska and less populated areas in continental U.S.

**Letter size of any weight that is placed in drop box.

***Discounts for volume deliveries.

Is Overnight Delivery Necessary?

The biggest cost saver is to not use overnight delivery. Many business owners, particularly those who came from large corporations, are accustomed to using overnight delivery. But small business owners need to watch these expenditures. Ask yourself whether overnight delivery is really necessary. Can you get away with second day delivery? Will first class mail do? Can letters simply be faxed?

IDEA 116: Reduce Bank Charges

Small businesses may pay surprisingly high bank fees for maintaining commercial accounts. Some of these fees are unavoidable; others can be reduced or eliminated.

First, shop around between banks. Some banks are more interested in attracting small business than others. Ask for a list of charges (for deposits, checks, monthly service charges, etc.) from different banks. Then compare.

Ask the bank about ways that you can reduce costs. In figuring its monthly service charge, will the bank take into account other accounts you may have in the same branch? For example, if you maintain your personal checking account and a savings account at the bank where you open a business checking account, ask if the bank will lump all your balances together (which can reduce your monthly service charge on the business checking account. Ask which checks are the least expensive. Banks generally offer a variety of business checks. You may be able to use personal-type checks (the least expensive) for your business account.

Bank where you borrow; borrow where you bank. If you have an existing business loan with a particular bank, ask whether you are entitled to any special account rates if you open a business account with the branch. By the same token, if you already have an existing business bank account, look at the same bank first for a needed business loan. As an existing customer, you may be entitled to a lower interest rate. You may also be able to reduce the interest rate (perhaps by one percentage point) if payments are automatically debited from the account (rather than writing a separate check for payment).

IDEA 117: Reduce Utility Charges

Utilities to power your equipment, heat or cool your office and run your factory can be a significant monthly cost to the business. Finding ways to save on utility costs, whether big or small, can add up to important savings over time. Here are some ideas to consider:

- *Use energy efficient fixtures.* Use fluorescent rather than incandescent fixtures. Also, the life of fluorescent bulbs may mean that they require less frequent changing—another labor saver.

- *Turn down the thermostat.* This will reduce heating and air conditioning costs.

- *Co-op for oil savings.* If your office is heated with oil, see whether there is an oil co-op in your area. A co-op can provide lower-cost heating oil (typically 10¢ to 20¢ per gallon) without causing any reduction in service. There may be a modest annual membership fee, but the amount will be more than offset by the savings on heating oil.

$$Extra Savings

Your local electric company may provide free "energy audits" of your facilities. It will then make recommendations on how you can become more cost-efficient. The utility company may even provide low-cost loans for the purpose of making energy-saving improvements.

Resources Phone Directory

Resource	Information	Phone Number
Aaron Rents & Sells	second-hand office equipment/furniture	(703) 750-0787
Accommodations Express	hotel room reselling consolidator	(800) 307-8680
America Online	on-line service provider	(800) 827-3338
American Assn of Franchisees and Dealers	Franchises	(800) 733-9858
American Assn of Home Based Business	fringe benefits, info, lobbying for home businesses	(800) 447-9710
American Assn of Retired Persons (AARP)	health insurance for members age 50+	(800) 424-3410
American Franchisee Association	Franchises	(800) 334-4232
AT&T	long-distance carrier (including 800 service)	(800) 222-0400
	special information service for long-distance numbers	(900) 555-1212

Below Wholesale	magazine subscriptions	(800) 800-0062
Business Information Centers (BICs)	Atlanta District Office 1720 Peachtree Road, NW, 6th fl. Atlanta, GA 30309	(404) 347-4749 (404) 347-2355 (fax)
	SBA/NationsBank/ MBDA Bell Atlantic 3 West Baltimore Street Baltimore, MD 21201	(410) 605-0990
	Boise District Office 1020 Main Street Boise, ID 83702-5745	(208) 334-9077 (208) 334-9353 (fax)
	Boston District Office 10 Causeway Street, Room 265 Boston, MA 02222-1093	(617) 565-5615 (617) 565-5598 (fax)
	SBA/NationsBank/MBDA/ Bell South/College of Charleston Small Business Resource Center 284 King Street Charleston, SC 29401	(803) 853-3900 (803) 853-2529 (fax)
	Chicago District Office 500 Madison Street, Suite 1250 Chicago, IL 60661-2511	(312) 353-1825 (312) 866-5688 (fax)
	SBA/Greater El Paso Chamber of Commerce Ten Civic Center Plaza El Paso, TX 79901	(915) 534-0531 (915) 534-0513 (fax)
	SBA/WVHTC Foundation Business Information Center 200 Fairmont Avenue, Suite 100 Fairmont, WV 26554	(304) 366-2577 (304) 366-2677 (fax)
	Fort Worth Business Assistance Center 100 East 15th Street, Suite 400 Fort Worth, TX 76102	(817) 871-6000 (817) 871-6031
	Houston District Office 9301 Southwest Freeway Suite 550 Houston, TX 77074-1591	(713) 773-6545 (713) 773-6550 (fax)

	Kansas City District Office 323 West 8th Street, Suite 104 Kansas City, MO 64105	(816) 374-6675 (816) 374-6759 (fax)
	Business Administration Center 3600 Wilshire Blvd., Suite L100 Los Angeles, CA 90010	(213) 251-7253 (213) 251-7255 (fax)
	SBA/NationsBank/MBDA Small Business Resource Center 3401 West End Avenue Nashville, TN 37203	(615) 749-4000 (615) 749-3685 (fax)
	San Diego District Office 550 West C Street, Suite 550 San Diego, CA 92101	(619) 557-7252 (619) 557-5894 (fax)
	Seattle District Office 1200 Sixth Avenue, Suite 1700 Seattle, WA 98101-1128	(206) 553-7310 (206) 553-7099 (fax)
	SBA/Spokane Chamber of Commerce 1020 W. Riverside Spokance, WA 99201	(509) 535-2800
	Business Information Center 121 S. Meramec Avenue Lobby Level St. Louis, MO 63105	(314) 854-6861 (314) 854-7687 (fax)
	SBA/Bell Atlantic Business Information Center Washington District Office 1110 Vermont Avenue N.W., Suite 900 Washington, DC 20043-4500	(202) 606-4000 (202) 606-4225 (fax)
Cable & Wireless	800 number phone service	(800) 486-8686
Card Establishment Services, Inc.	merchant authorization for credit cards (home-based businesses)	(212) 262-5299
Central Reservations Service	hotel room reselling consolidator	(800) 950-0232
Chicago Computer Exchange	second-hand computers	(312) 667-5221
CompuServe	on-line service provider	(800) 848-8990

Computer Renaissance— main office	second-hand computers	(612) 520-8500
Copyright Office, Register of Copyrights, Library of Congress	copyright protection	(202) 707-3000
Council of Smaller Enterprises	health insurance for members —northern Ohio	(216) 621-3300
Dun & Bradstreet	credit information services	(800) 234-3867
Economic Bulletin Board U.S. Commerce Dept.	electronic bulletin board with info on trade, statistics	(202) 482-1986
Economic Development Office	Alabama	(205) 263-0048
	Alaska	(907) 454-2018
	Arizona	(602) 255-5374
	Arkansas	(501) 682-7500
	California	(916) 445-6545
	Colorado	(303) 892-3840
	Connecticut	(203) 566-4051
	Delaware	(302) 736-4271
	District of Columbia	(202) 727-6600
	Florida	(904) 488-9357
	Georgia	(404) 656-6200
	Hawaii	(808) 548-7645
	Idaho	(208) 344-2470
	Illinois	(312) 917-7179
	Indiana	(317) 634-1690
	Iowa	(515) 281-3251
	Kansas	(913) 296-3483
	Kentucky	(502) 564-4252
	Louisiana	(504) 342-5359
	Maine	(800) 872-3838
	Maryland	(301) 333-6975
	Massachusetts	(617) 727-3221
	Michigan	(517) 373-6241

	Minnesota	(612) 296-3871
	Mississippi	(601) 359-3449
	Missouri	(800) 523-1434
	Montana	(406) 444-3923
	Nebraska	(402) 471-3782
	Nevada	(702) 855-4325
	New Hampshire	(603) 623-5500
	New Jersey	(609) 984-4442
	New Mexico	(505) 827-0300
	New York	(800) 782-8369
	North Carolina	(919) 733-4151
	North Dakota	(701) 777-3132
	Ohio	(614) 644-8748
	Oklahoma	(405) 843-9770
	Oregon	(503) 373-1225
	Pennsylvania	(717) 783-5700
	Rhode Island	(401) 277-2601
	South Carolina	(803) 737-0400
	South Dakota	(605) 394-5725
	Tennessee	(615) 741-1888
	Texas	(512) 472-5059
	Utah	(801) 581-7905
	Vermont	(802) 828-3221
	Virginia	(804) 786-3791
	Washington	(206) 753-5630
	West Virginia	(304) 348-2960
	Wisconsin	(608) 266-1018
	Wyoming	(307) 325-4827
EG&G Dynatrend, PAL Customers Service Support	forfeited property (used) seized by U.S. Customs Service	(703) 351-7887
Environmental Protection Agency	Small Business Ombudsmen	(800) 368-5888

General Services Administration	government surplus	(800) 472-1313
Home Business Institute	trade group offering home office insurance	(914) 946-6600
Home Office Assn of America (HOAA)	fringe benefits, info, lobbying for home businesses	(800) 809-4622
Hotel Reservations Network	hotel room reselling consolidator	(800) 964-6835
Independent Business Alliance	trade group offering home office insurance	(800) 450-2422
Insurance—state departments	Alabama	(205) 269-3591
	Alaska	(907) 349-1230
	Arizona	(602) 912-8400
	Arkansas	(501) 686-2945
	California	(800) 927-4357
	Colorado	(303) 894-7499
	Connecticut	(203) 297-3800
	Delaware	(800) 282-8611
	Distrist of Columbia	(202) 724-7424
	Florida	(800) 342-2762
	Georgia	(404) 656-2070
	Hawaii	(800) 468-4644
	Idaho	(208) 334-2560
	Illinois	(217) 782-4515
	Indiana	(317) 232-2395
	Iowa	(515) 281-5705
	Kansas	(800) 423-2484
	Kentucky	(502) 564-3630
	Louisana	(504) 342-5300
	Maine	(207) 582-8707
	Maryland	(800) 492-6116
	Massachusetts	(617) 727-3357
	Michigan	(517) 373-9273

	Minnesota	(612) 296-6848
	Mississippi	(601) 359-3569
	Missouri	(800) 332-6148
	Montana	(404) 444-2040
	Nebraska	(402) 471-2201
	Nevada	(800) 992-0900
	New Hampshire	(800) 852-3416
	New Jersey	(609) 292-5317
	New Mexico	(505) 827-4500
	New York	(212) 602-0387
	North Carolina	(800) 662-7777
	North Dakota	(800) 247-0560
	Ohio	(800) 686-1526
	Oklahoma	(800) 522-0071
	Oregon	(503) 378-4271
	Pennsylvania	(717) 787-5173
	Rhode Island	(401) 277-2223
	South Carolina	(800) 768-3467
	South Dakota	(605) 773-3563
	Tennesseee	(800) 342-4029
	Texas	(512) 322-2266
	Utah	(801) 538-3800
	Vermont	(802) 828-3301
	Virginia	(800) 522-7945
	Washington	(800) 562-6900
	West Virginia	(800) 642-9004
	Wisconsin	(608) 266-3585
	Wyoming	(307) 777-7401
Internal Revenue Service (IRS)	Tax forms, publications, help	(800) 829-1040
International Franchise Association	Franchises	(202) 628-8000
Kinkos	videoconferencing	(800) 78-KINKOS

Mail Boxes Inc.	commercial mail boxes; shipping; office "front"	(800) 789-4MBE
MCI	long distance carrier	(800) 888-0800
	800 number phone service	(800) 444-2222
Minority Business Development Centers	Atlanta (GA)	(404) 730-3300
	Boston (MA)	(617) 565-6850
	Chicago (IL)	(312) 353-0182
	Dallas (TX)	(214) 767-8001
	Los Angeles (CA)	(213) 613-1300
	Miami (FL)	(305) 536-5054
	New York (NY)	(212) 264-3262
	Philadelphia (PA)	(215) 597-9236
	San Francisco (CA)	(415) 744-3001
NASA	Technical Outreach Office for engineering assistance	(407) 867-1356
National Assn of Development Companies	504 loan programs	(800) 972-2504
National Assn of Investment Companies	loan programs for SSBICs	(202) 289-4336
National Assn of Small Business Investment Companies	loan programs for SBICs	(703) 683-1601
National Assn of Temporary and Staffing Services	locate staffing/leasing companies	(703) 549-6287
National Assn of the Self-Employed	fringe benefits, info, lobbying for self-employed	(800) 232-NASE
National Assn of Women Business Owners	loan programs for women-owned businesses	(212) 916-1473
National Business Incubation Assn	"incubator" (space for start-ups)	(614) 593-4331
National Venture Capital Assn	venture capital	(703) 528-4370
Prodigy	on-line service provider	(800) 776-3449
Quickbook	hotel room reselling consolidator	(800) 789-9887
RCM Travel Center	hotel room reselling consolidator	(800) 245-5738

Room Exchange	hotel room reselling consolidator	(800) 846-7000
Second-Life Exhibits Inc.	used displays for trade show exhibits (tabletops, portables)	(617) 884-7455
Small Business Administration	Answer Desk	(800) 827-5722
	Development Centers; loan programs	(202) 205-7701
	Referrals for hearing impaired	(202) 205-7333
	Women-owned businesses	(202) 482-2000
Small Business Service Bureau	health insurance for members	(800) 343-0939
Sprint	long distance carrier	(800) 877-4646
	800 number phone service	(800) 877-2000
Unemployment insurance	Albama	(205) 242-8371
	Alaska	(907) 465-2757
	Arizona	(602) 255-4755
	Arkansas	(501) 682-3253
	California	(916) 653-1528
	Colorado	(303) 839-4959
	Connecitcut	(203) 566-2128
	Delaware	(302) 368-6635
	District of Columbia	(202) 724-7462
	Florida	(904) 921-3100
	Georgia	(404) 656-6225
	Hawaii	(808) 586-8927
	Idaho	(208) 334-6240
	Illinois	(312) 793-1916
	Indiana	(317) 232-7682
	Iowa	(515) 281-8200
	Kansas	(913) 296-5026
	Kentucky	(502) 564-6838
	Louisiana	(504) 342-2992
	Maine	(207) 287-1239
	Maryland	(410) 333-5782

(continued)	Massachusetts	(617) 727-5054
	Michigan	(313) 876-5131
	Minnesota	(612) 296-3736
	Mississippi	(601) 961-7755
	Missouri	(413) 751-3328
	Montana	(406) 444-3686
	Nebraska	(402) 471-9839
	Nevada	(702) 687-4599
	New Hampshire	(603) 224-3311
	New Jersey	(609) 292-2810
	New York	(518) 457-4120
	North Carolina	(919) 733-7395
	North Dakota	(701) 328-2814
	Ohio	(614) 466-2578
	Oklahoma	(405) 557-7135
	Oregon	(503) 378-3257
	Pennsylvania	(717) 787-2097
	Rhode Island	(401) 277-3688
	South Carolina	(803) 737-3070
	South Dakota	(605) 626-2312
	Tennessee	(615) 741-2346
	Texas	(512) 463-2712
	Utah	(801) 536-7755
	Vermont	(802) 828-4242
	Virginia	(804) 786-1256
	Washington	(206) 753-3822
	West Virginia	(304) 588-1324
	Wisconsin	(608) 266-3177
	Wyoming	(307) 235-3201

Uniform Product Code Council	UPI codes	(513) 435-3870
U.S. Postal Service Business Center	post office supplies	(800) 374-8777
Venture Capital Network	venture capital	(617) 253-7163
Western Assn of Venture Capitalists	venture capital	(415) 845-1322

APPENDIX B

Resources
Web Sites

Resource	Information	Web Site
American Express Small Business Exchange	general info of interest to small business	http://www.americanexpress.com/smallbusiness
Bell Atlantic Yellow Pages	telephone number directory	http://yellowpages.badg.com
Business News	articles on recent business developments	http://www.yahoo.com/headlines/current/business
Business Resource Center	general info for business	http://www.kcilink.com/brc/
The Company Corporation	incorporate on-line for $45 plus state filing fees	http://www.service.com/tcc/home.html
Directory of Yellow Pages	telephone number directory	http://www.wahlstrom.com/ypsites.html
Economic Bulletin Board —Commerce Dept	trade leads, current econ-omic statistics, analysis of foreign markets	http://www.stat_usa.gov
Entrepreneur Xchange	share info with others	prodigy jump:entrepreneur xchange

Entrepreneur Zone	general info of interest to small business	aol key word: ezone
Foundation Center	grant money	http://fdncenter.org
411	telephone number directory	http://www.four11.com
The Idea Cafe	resources, info, expert advice for small business owners	http://www.ideacafe.com
Income Tax Information in Internet	federal/state forms and instructions/tax articles and more	http://www.best.com/ ~ftmexpat/htm;/taxsites .html
Internal Revenue Service	tax forms and instructions	http://www.irs.ustreas. gov/prod/
NASA	Technical Outreach Office for engineering assistance	http://technology.ksc. nasa.gov
National Business Incubation Assn	"incubator" space for start-ups	http://www.nbia.org
Small Business Administration	general information shareware programs	http://www.sbaonline. sba.gov http://www.sbaonline.sba. gov/shareware/starfile.html
Small Business Investment Companies (SBICs)	small business investment companies	http://www.sbaonline.sba.gov/ business_finances/sbic.html
Switchboard	telephone number directory	http://www.switchboard.com
U.S. Patent & Trademark Office	U.S. patents and trademarks	http://www.uspto.gov
U.S. Tax Code On-Line	Internal Revenue Code	http://fourmilab.ch/ ustax.html
Working from Home Forum	Tips, downloadable software from home business experts	compuserve go: work

| Yahoo's Small Business Information | general info for small business | http://www.yahoo.com/business/small_business_information |
| telephone directory | telephone number directory | http://www.yahoo.com/reference/phone_numbers |

Index